Selbst und Andere/s

Beiträge zur Kanadistik

Band 7

Schriftenreihe der Gesellschaft
für Kanada-Studien

Herausgegeben von
Wolfgang Klooss (Vorsitzender),
Annegret Bollee, Udo Sautter

Die Deutsche Bibliothek – CIP-Einheitsaufnahme

Selbst und Andere-s : von Begegnungen und Grenzziehungen ; feministische Arbeiten im Rahmen der Kanada-Studien / Christina Strobel und Doris Eibl (Hrsg.). – Augsburg : Wißner, 1998
   (Beiträge zur Kanadistik ; Bd. 7)
   ISBN 3-89639-124-0

© 1998 by Dr. Bernd Wißner, Augsburg
Das Werk und seine Teile sind urheberrechtlich geschützt.
Jede Verwertung in anderen als den gesetzlich zugelassenen Fällen
bedarf deshalb der vorherigen schriftlichen Einwilligung des Verlages.

Selbst und Andere/s
Von Begegnungen und Grenzziehungen

Feministische Arbeiten im Rahmen der Kanada-Studien
Feminist Research in Canadian Studies
Recherches Féministes dans les Études Canadiennes

Christina Strobel und Doris Eibl (Hrsg.)

Wir danken der Gründerin
der Sektion Frauenstudien

Dr. Katrina Bachinger

für ihren bewundernswerten Einsatz für die Sektion
und für die tatkräftige Förderung
der Mitglieder dieser Sektion.

Dieser Band ist ihr gewidmet,
als Zeichen unserer Anerkennung.

Vorwort

Mit der vorliegenden Publikation der Sektion Frauenstudien wird die Schriftenreihe der Gesellschaft für Kanada-Studien um einen Band erweitert, der erstmals umfassenden Einblick in die Tätigkeit einer der acht in der Gesellschaft angesiedelten Disziplinen gewährt. (Neben den Frauenstudien markieren die Sektionen Englisch-Kanadische Sprache und Literatur, Französisch-Kanadische Sprache und Literatur, Geschichte, Geographie, Politikwissenschaft, Wirtschaftswissenschaften sowie die Sektion Andere Disziplinen das Fächerspektrum der Kanadistik in den deutschsprachigen Ländern.) Die insgesamt zwölf, zum Teil in Kooperation abgefaßten Aufsätze stammen durchweg aus der Feder jüngerer Kanadistinnen. Sie belegen nachhaltig, welche Bedeutung die Sektion Frauenstudien der Nachwuchsarbeit beimißt und welche Impulse die Frauenstudien der Kanadistik in Deutschland, Österreich und der Schweiz im letzten Jahrzehnt vermittelt haben.

Erst 1989 gegründet, haben sich die Frauenstudien dank einer sehr engagierten Mitgliederarbeit sehr schnell als eigenständiger Forschungsbereich in der Gesellschaft für Kanada-Studien etabliert. Hiervon zeugt u. a. die Ausrichtung der Jahrestagung 1992, die dem Generalthema "Geschlechterrollen und Institutionen in Kanada" gewidmet war. Gemäß des von der Gesellschaft verfolgten Rotationsprinzips werden die Frauenstudien auch 1999 wieder den inhaltlichen Rahmen dieser für die deutschsprachige Kanadistik so zentralen Veranstaltung vorgeben und als verantwortliche Sektion maßgeblich an der Durchführung der nächsten Jahrestagung beteiligt sein.

Der Dank gilt den Beiträgerinnen, allen voran den beiden Herausgeberinnen Christina Strobel und Doris Eibl, die mit diesem Band eindrucksvoll das thematisch weitgefaßte Spektrum und die methodische Vielfalt unter Beweis stellen, die die kanadistische Frauenforschung innerhalb der Gesellschaft für Kanada-Studien auszeichnen.

Trier, im Juli 1998   *Wolfgang Klooß*

Inhalt

Einleitung: Selbst und Andere/s –
Von Begegnungen und Grenzziehungen 1

The Gaze of/at *the other*. The New Looks of Lesbian Love in
Patricia Rozema's *When Night Is Falling* (Can. 1993). 8
    Andrea B. Braidt

Femmes autochtones, médiatrices de changement:
la prise de parole d'An Antane Kapesh 26
    Hélène Destrempes

"We Appear Silent To People Who Are Deaf To What We Say":
Women of Colour Speak Out 41
    Pamela Z. Dube

Über die Langsamkeit des Blicks in Suzanne Jacobs *Maude* 54
    Doris Eibl

'When you are a new immigrant you are just half and half:'
The process of becoming Canadian
among post-World-War-Two German Immigrants 66
    Christiane Harzig

Vision und Transgression – "La femme au volant"
in Monique Proulx' *Le sexe des étoiles* 80
    Ulrike C. Lange / Marion Schomakers

Die Rolle des Monologs für "Spectacles de femmes" und
"Théâtre de femmes" in Québec oder
Von Hexen, Feen und anderen Unheimlichkeiten 95
    Birgit Mertz-Baumgartner

The Split Self in Margaret Atwood's Female Dystopia
The Handmaid's Tale 110
    Dunja M. Mohr

Bodyscape/s: Access, Colonization and Exclusion:
An Emancipation of Literary Landscapes 124
    Katja-Elisabeth Pfrommer / Tamara Pianos

Re-membering Self and (M)other in Daphne Marlatt's *Ana Historic*   135
   Caroline Rosenthal

Women Writers as Historical (Re)Source: Leading a Double Existence   151
   Colleen M. Ross

The Ethics of Difference in Jane Rule's Work   161
   Christina Strobel

Angaben zu den Autorinnen   183

Einleitung: Selbst und Andere/s – Von Begegnungen und Grenzziehungen

Kategorisierungen sowie der Umgang mit diesen Ordnungen sind ein klassischer Gegenstand wissenschaftlicher Untersuchungen. Mit Nachdruck gehen spätestens seit Beginn der 1980er Jahre nordamerikanische Studien der Frage nach, inwieweit Ordnungen, durch die Menschen sich die Welt und ihr Dasein darin erklären, immer Vorstellungen sind, die von Menschen zu einem bestimmten Zweck geschaffen werden. Daß Ordnungen in einer sogenannten "Natur der Dinge" liegen sollen, wurde u. a. von Michel Foucault aus philosophischer und wissenschaftshistorischer oder von Mary Douglas aus kulturanthropologischer Perspektive überzeugend widerlegt.

In verschiedener Hinsicht wurden durch diese Forschungen "existentielle" Wahrheiten relativiert. So fiel der Blick darauf, daß das Bedürfnis, ein Selbst vom Anderen zu unterscheiden, in kulturell unterschiedlichen Ausprägungen erfahren wird: Das Individuum, so lehrte ein Blick in die Geschichte, ist ein Produkt bürgerlicher westlicher kapitalistischer Gesellschaften; der Begriff 'indidvidual' - "Individuum" – im heutigen Sinne kam erst im 18. Jahrhundert auf (Williams, 1983, S. 162f.).

Dieses Individuum schuf sich als Gegenüber, vom dem es sich abzugrenzen und über das es sich zu erheben galt, Wesen, deren "Natur" "anders" war, und zwar von einer grundsätzlich unterschiedlichen Andersartigkeit, sei diese durch ein nicht-männliches Geschlecht oder eine nicht-weiße Rasse bestimmt. Die Arbeiten von Thomas Laqueur (z. B. 1990) zeigen, wie ein Wechsel von einem homologen Körpermodell, in dem Männer und Frauen als verschiedene Ausprägungen eines Geschlechtes galten, im Zuge des 18. Jahrhunderts einem heterologen Modell wich, das einen grundlegenden Unterschied zwischen Männern und Frauen postulierte. Dieser Unterschied zog sich von einer nunmehr oppositionellen biologischen bis zur daraus folgenden psychischen Strukturierung bruchlos hindurch. George Mosse (z. B. 1987), Sander L. Gilman (z. B. 1985; 1992), Christina von Braun (1995) gehören zu den Wissenschaftlern und Wissenschaftlerinnen, die in ihren Forschungsbeiträgen die Verschränkung der Diskurse zu Nationalität, Rasse, Geschlecht und Sexualität verfolgt haben.

Zunehmend gerieten schließlich die Körper, mit denen und durch die diese verschiedenen Ordnungen erfahren und zum Ausdruck gebracht werden, in den Mittelpunkt des wissenschaftlichen Interesses. Inwieweit diese diskursiv hergestellt oder "nur" geformt werden, wurde ein zentraler wissenschaftlicher Streit der 1990er Jahre. Die theoretischen Klärungsversuche der Philosophin Judith Butler, der Filmwissenschaftlerin und Semiotikerin Teresa de Lauretis, zunehmend auch der Biologin und Wissenschaftshistorikerin Donna Haraway, sowie der Biologinnen Evelyn Fox Keller, Ruth Hubbard und Ruth Bleier, um nur einige der herausragenden Forscherinnen zu nennen, formten diese Diskussionen entscheidend. Im Zuge dieser Auseinandersetzungen – oder vielmehr – Lernprozesse wurde für die meisten WissenschaftlerInnen, die diese Fragestellungen verfolgten, "gender" zur Kategorie, die "sex" erst herstellt. Jede Frage nach dem biologischen Geschlecht hat schließlich bereits den Unterschied im Blick – und kann somit nicht umhin, ihn erneut herzustellen. Suzanne Kessler und Wendy McKenna verwenden in ihrer bahnbrechenden Untersuchung *Gender: An Ethnomethodological Approach* (1978) ausschließlich die Bezeichnung *gender*, um jeglicher Verankerung der Kategorie Geschlecht in Biologie Widerstand zu leisten.

Die deutsche Philosophin Andrea Maihofer faßt Geschlecht als "hegemonialen Diskurs". Unter Diskurs versteht sie dabei im Anschluß an Foucault "eine jeweils komplexe Verbindung einer Vielzahl spezifischer Denk-, Gefühls- und Handlungsweisen, Körperpraxen, Wissen(schafts)formen, aber auch staatlicher und gesellschaftlich-kultureller Institutionen sowie Gesellschafts- und Herrschaftsverhältnisse" (1994, S. 256). Hegemonial ist für Maihofer ein Diskurs, "insofern er die herrschenden Normen, Werte und Verhaltensstandards einer Gesellschaft formuliert. Hegemonial ist ein Diskurs aber auch deshalb, weil in ihm das Denken, Fühlen und Handeln der Menschen sowohl normiert, zensiert und diszipliniert als auch konstituiert wird" (ibid.). Indem sie auf die repressive wie zugleich produktive Wirkungsweise des Diskurses verweist, begreift sie Geschlecht als eine historisch spezifische Existenzweise, die sowohl psychisch und kulturell als auch materiell körperlich verankert ist (siehe auch Maihofer, 1995). Dieser Weg ist charakteristisch für neuere Forschung, die eine Balance zu finden sucht zwischen der Betonung von Materialität des Körpers und seiner kulturell spezifischen Erzeugung (vgl. u. a. Butler 1993; 1995 oder als frühes Beispiel Jaggar, 1983).

Vor dem Hintergrund dieser wissenschaftlichen Diskussionen umreißt der Titel unseres Bandes seinen Untersuchungsgegenstand mit "Selbst und Andere/s: Von Begegnungen und Grenzziehungen". Viele Fragen sind damit zugleich gestellt: Wie werden jeweils die Grenzen des Selbst zum Anderen gezogen, was ist "drinnen", was "draußen"? Mit welchen Begriffen wird unterschieden – wie z. B. Identität, Differenz, Alterität, Marginalität, Opposition – und was bedeuten die Begriffe jeweils? Welche (rechtlichen, sozialen, politischen, ästhetischen) Konsequenzen sind mit diesen Grenzziehungen verbunden? Wie verhalten wir uns zu bestimmten Ordnungen und zu ihren Folgen? Wie verhandeln wir Neubestimmungen von Grenzziehungen, oder wie ist handelnder Widerstand möglich?

Gerade für Kanadistinnen schienen uns diese Fragestellungen Grundlage einer fruchtbaren multidisziplinären Auseinandersetzung zu sein. Kanada ist in seiner Geschichte wiederholt von seinem geographischen Nachbarland als das Andere betrachtet worden, das zum Eigenen zu machen sei; der kanadische Staat lebt auch mit und durch die Auseinandersetzungen mit Vorstellungen von "twin solitudes" und "other solitudes", die kulturelle und ethnische Ausprägungen von Differenz aufgreifen. Im Bild des auf dem Erhalt von Differenzen beruhenden "Canadian mosaic" setzt sich Kanada ein anderes Ideal des Umgangs mit dem Anderen als eine Metapher vom assimilierenden "melting pot" nahelegt. Auch für den Umgang mit Geschlecht liefert die neueste kanadische Geschichte ein die engagierte Kultur ihres Landes prägendes Beispiel: Am 6. November 1989 stürmte ein junger Mann in die Ecole Polytechnique in Montréal, um sich an "den Feministinnen" zu rächen. Er sortierte die Frauen von den Männern, um wahllos vierzehn Frauen (Studentinnen wie Universitätsangestellte) zu erschießen (vgl. den Band von Malette/Chalouh, 1991). Selten haben Frauen in Kanada so krass im Schrecken des eigenen Leibes erfahren, was es bedeuten kann, eine Frau zu sein: Soziale Kategorisierungen können über Leben und Tod entscheiden, eine Erfahrung, die in der Entwicklung medizinischer Forschung oder in individuellen Beziehungsabhängigkeiten weniger offensichtlich ins Bewußtsein gerät. Weniger bekannt als die Geschichte dieser Morde ist, wie eine junge Frau dem Tod entkam, weil der Täter sie für einen Jungen hielt und zu den Männern an die Wand stellte (vgl. Minnie Bruce Pratt, 1995, S. 186f.). Was mag sie gefühlt haben, als die Frauen erschossen wurden? Was empfanden die Männer?

Zum Glück sind die Folgen von Kategorisierungen nicht immer eine Frage von Leben und Tod, auch wenn sie dies für Personen, die um politisches Asyl ansuchen, oder für Ausländer in der Berliner U-Bahn, oder für schwule Opfer von "gay-bashing" immer wieder bedeuten. Wie aus diesen Überlegungen anklingt, ist der Umgang mit Kategorisierungen für uns eine ethische Frage. Feministische Wissenschaft ist nicht in der Vorstellung einer objektiven Wahrheit verhaftet; das hat sie mit vielen anderen heutigen Forschungsansätzen gemeinsam. Vielmehr entspringt sie politisch begründeten Interessen, die praktische Veränderungen für ein gerechteres Leben fordern. Feministische Wissenschaft, wie wir sie in diesem Band verstehen, fragt danach, was Ordnungen wie "Weiblichkeit" und "Männlichkeit", "Frauen" und "Männer" und deren Überschneidungen mit anderen Ordnungskategorien wie sexuelle Orientierung, ethnische Herkunft oder soziale Schicht für jeweils einzelne sowie für Gruppen bedeuten – und bewertet dies anhand verschiedener Modelle.

Wie dieses Verhältnis von Selbst und Anderem/n aussehen kann oder soll, dazu sind von feministischen WissenschaftlerInnen verschiedene Konzepte entwickelt oder übernommen worden. In unserem "Call for Papers" nannten wir Martin Bubers Dialogphilosophie, die das Ich nicht absolut, sondern immer im Kontext sieht; Julia Kristevas Vorstellung von einer "inneren Differenz", die uns erlaube, "das Andersartige am Anderen zu tolerieren"; Audre Lordes Kritik an Toleranz und ihre Forderung, daß Frauen die Differenzen untereinander als notwendige dialektische Pole verstehen mögen, zwischen denen Kreativität entstehen kann; Untersuchungen der Aneignung bzw. Vernichtung des Fremden (z. B. die Tzvetan Todorovs) oder das ethische Postulat zu einem Umgang mit dem Fremden, der die Erfahrung des Fremden in seiner Fremdheit sucht und erlaubt, den Selben durch den Anderen infragezustellen (Emmanuel Lévinas); Jessica Benjamins Konzept einer zu erhaltenden Spannung zwischen Selbstbehauptung und gegenseitiger Anerkennung, das eine Begegnung von Selbst und Anderer als Gleichwertige erlaubt; oder schließlich Donna Haraways *cyborg*-Figur, die das Aufbrechen von Grenzen (auch gattungsüberschreitend) konstatiert und einklagt. Diesen und anderen in feministischen Überlegungen vorgebrachten Konzeptualisierungen von Selbst und Andere/s sind gemeinsam der ethische Anspruch, den Umgang mit dem Anderen nicht in Herrschaftsverhältnissen (Herr und Knecht) zu denken sowie das Wissen darum, daß ein Bewegen innerhalb von Machtverhältnissen immer erfordert, daß wir im Wissen um unser Tun Verantwortung für das eigene Handeln übernehmen müssen.

Selbstreflexivität und verantwortliche Positionierung sind Postulate jeder emanzipatorischen Theorie; sie sind leichter gefordert als beständig umgesetzt. Gerade weil wir uns innerhalb der Machtverhältnisse bewegen, die wir verändern wollen, haben wir an ihnen oft in einer Weise teil, in der wir sie eher bestätigen denn subversiv unterwandern. Gerade oppositioneller Widerstand verwickelt oft in Mit-Täterschaft (Thürmer-Rohr), und jeglicher Widerstand erfolgt in einem ständigen Prozeß des Lernens um die eigenen Verstrickungen und Ausgrenzungen. "Männer", "das Patriarchat" und "Heterosexualität", die als die Feindbilder der ersten Stunde herhalten konnten und mußten, sind abgelöst durch die – idealerweise – verhandelnde Auseinandersetzung mit der eigenen wie anderen Teilhabe und Widerständigkeit. Bekannte Beispiele dieser Diskussionen sind die um die Ausgrenzungen farbiger Frauen durch weiße Mittelschichtfrauen, oder die um die Annahme, eine marginalisierte Position verleihe einen privilegierten Erkenntnisstandpunkt.

Die Herausgeberinnen verstehen diesen Band als Beitrag zu einer feministischen Wissenschaft, die sich ihrer politischen Verantwortung bewußt ist und innerhalb einer Disziplin oder in der Begegnung mit verschiedenen Disziplinen spezifische Kategorisierungen und ihre Wirksamkeit, ihre Ausschlüsse und ihre Durchlässigkeit, und nicht zuletzt deren Zweckmäßigkeit untersucht – und dabei nicht vergißt, diese Überlegungen auch auf ihr eigenes

Vorgehen anzuwenden. In diesem Sinne sehen wir diesen Band als Beitrag zur Kanadistik, und insbesondere als Beitrag der Sektion Frauenstudien zur kanadistischen Forschung innerhalb der Gesellschaft für Kanadastudien. Alle Autorinnen sind Mitglied der Sektion Frauenstudien, alle sind auch in anderen Sektionen der Gesellschaft zu Hause. Dieser Tatsache ist die erfreuliche Ergänzung des Schwerpunkts Literaturwissenschaft durch Artikel aus der Filmwissenschaft und der Geschichte zu danken. Was den Band kennzeichnet, ist eine bestimmte Perspektive auf den Untersuchungsgegenstand, die sich für die meisten aus der Kategorie "Geschlecht" ergibt. In sich und zueinander sind die vertretenen Positionen oft widersprüchlich – die Herausgeberinnen haben nicht auf einer "einheitlichen feministischen Linie" (so es die gäbe) bestanden. Manche Beiträge nehmen Kategorien wie "Mann" und "Frau" als Ausgangspunkt ihrer Untersuchung und fragen, wie diese neu zu füllen seien, andere zielen auf ein grundsätzliches Aufbrechen der Kategorie Geschlecht. In diesem Spannungsfeld bewegen sich grundsätzlich alle feministischen Ansätze, die 'Geschlecht' oder 'Heterosexualität' zugleich als soziales und fiktionales Faktum an/erkennen müssen.

In allen Beiträgen scheint klar der Anspruch auf, den Stand der feministischen Forschung zur Kenntnis zu nehmen und an aktuellen Diskussionen formend teilzuhaben. Für viele feministisch engagierte Kanadistinnen ist dies, zumindest im deutschsprachigen Raum, immer noch ein persönlich zu investierender Zusatzaufwand außerhalb eines institutionellen Rahmens, der oft ohne die notwendigen fruchtbaren Diskussionszusammenhänge geleistet werden muß. Wir hoffen, mit diesem Band auch ein Signal zu setzen, daß innerhalb der Gesellschaft für Kanada-Studien nicht nur Raum ist für solche Diskussionen, sondern daß wir Aktivitäten und Diskussionen begrüßen, die Theorien und Texte, politische, wirtschaftliche und soziale Entwicklungen, sei es Stadtplanung oder die Gründung von Nunavut, in ihren – sei es unterschiedlichen oder auch gleichen – Auswirkungen auf Menschen in verschiedenen Positionierungen untersuchen.

Die Sektion Frauenstudien ist die "jüngste" Sektion der GKS. Sie wurde 1989 gegründet und ist relativ rasch gewachsen. Die Frauenstudien sind auch die jüngste Sektion in dem Sinne, daß wohl keine andere Sektion so wenig Professoren bzw. Professorinnen zu ihren Mitgliedern zählt, so viele aktive Studentinnen aufweist, und prozentual so viele Mitglieder promovieren. Wir sind sehr stolz, daß wir aus diesem Potential einen Band zusammenstellen konnten, der einen Eindruck von der Interessenvielfalt der Sektionsmitglieder gibt.

Die Beiträge befassen sich mit verschiedenen Gattungen, von Lyrik (Dube) über Drama (Mertz-Baumgartner), Erzählprosa in verschiedenen Ausprägungen (ein Schwerpunkt der Mehrheit der Beiträge), historische Tonbandaufzeichnungen (Harzig) und Film (Braidt). Sie unterscheiden sich in ihrem Fokus auf bestimmte Schnittstellen weiblicher Marginalisierung oder ihrer Ermächtigung: weiße lesbische Identität (Braidt, Rosenthal, Strobel), autochtone Frauen (Destrempes), *women of color* (Dube), deutsche Einwanderinnen (Harzig), frankokanadische Geschlechterverwirrung (Lange/Schomakers). Sie unterscheiden sich in der Hinwendung zur Vergangenheit – wie in Christiane Harzigs Untersuchung deutscher Einwanderer nach dem Zweiten Weltkrieg – oder in der Beschäftigung mit einem Zukunftsentwurf, wie in Dunja Mohrs Lektüre von Margaret Atwood's *The Handmaid's Tale*. Die Mehrheit lotet bestimmte Fragestellungen anhand *eines* literarischen Textes aus, einige verfolgen ihr Thema am Beispiel einer Reihe von Texten, wie Katja-Elisabeth Pfrommer und Tamara Pianos in ihrer Darstellung literarischer Landschaftskörper in Texten von Autoren und Autorinnen, oder wie Colleen Ross, die dem Umgang von Autorinnen mit der historischen und geschlechtsspezifischen Bedingtheit von Diskursen nachgeht.

Immer wieder begegnen sich die Beiträge in ihren Themen und Ansätzen. Wenn Christiane Harzig das Verhältnis der Forscherin zu ihrem Gegenstand reflektiert, oder Birgit Mertz-Baumgartner den notwendigen Bezug eines "moi" zu einem "autre" konstatiert, oder Dunja Mohr das Andere als nicht allein äußerliche Kategorie des Selbst bezeichnet, oder wenn Doris Eibl in Anlehnung an Lévinas die notwendige Infragestellung des Selben nur durch den Anderen beschreibt, scheint in allen ein Anliegen auf, das Verbindung, Zusammenhang und Verhandlung anstelle von säuberlicher oppositioneller Trennung postuliert.

Fast allen Beiträgen ist gemeinsam die Suche nach einem Weg, der aus der gegenwärtigen dichotomen Geschlechterkonstruktion herausführt. Ulrike Lange und Marion Schomakers verfolgen das Überschreiten und Aufbrechen von Geschlecht in Monique Proulx' *Le sexe des étoiles* als produktiven Verstoß gegen Normen, Andrea Braidt und Caroline Rosenthal zeigen, wie "Frau" außerhalb einer heterosexuellen Ökonomie neu konstituiert werden kann, und wie dies durch das Nutzen der Konventionen des Films oder das Ausloten von Sprache innerhalb bestehender Ordnungen erfolgen kann. Hélène Destrempes und Pamela Dube betonen und zeigen, wie Geschlecht niemals unabhängig von anderen Kategorien wie z. B. Ethnie betrachtet werden kann; eine Forderung, die auch in anderen Beiträgen erhoben wird.

Bemerkenswert ist schließlich, wieviel – sichtbare und unsichtbare – Zusammenarbeit in diesen Band geflossen ist. So sei allen Beiträgerinnen an dieser Stelle herzlich für ihr Engagement gedankt. Aufrichtiger Dank geht von den Herausgeberinnen ebenso an die Gesellschaft für Kanada-Studien, die dieses Projekt in jeder Hinsicht – durch Motivation wie finanzielle Unterstützung – mitgetragen hat.

München, im Juli 1998   *Christina Strobel mit Doris Eibl*

Literatur

Butler, Judith, 1993, *Bodies That Matter: On the Discursive Limits of "Sex."* New York and London: Routledge.

——, 1995, Mit Isabell Lorey, Maria Mesner, Johanna Borek, Ingvild Birkhan, Edith Saurer, Birgit Wagner, und Herta Nagl-Docekal, "Diskussion mit Judith Butler", *L'Homme. Z.F.G*, 6:1, 82–97.

Douglas, Mary, 1986, *How Institutions Think*. London: Routledge & Kegan Paul.

Gilman, Sander L., 1985, "Black Bodies, White Bodies: Toward an Iconography of Female Sexuality in Late Nineteeth-Century Art, Medicine, and Literature", in: Henry Louis Gates, Jr. (Hrsg.), *Race, Writing, and Difference*. Chicago: University of Chicago Press, 1986, 223–261.

——. 1992. *Rasse, Sexualität und Seuche: Stereotype aus der Innenwelt der westlichen Kultur*. Reinbek: Rowohlt.

Jaggar, Alison. 1983. *Feminist Politics and Human Nature*. Totowa, NJ: Rowman & Allanheld.

Laqueur, Thomas, 1990, *Making Sex: Body and Gender from the Greeks to Freud*. Cambridge, MA: Harvard University Press.

Maihofer, Andrea, 1994, "Geschlecht als hegemonialer Diskurs: Ansätze zu einer kritischen Theorie des 'Geschlechts'", in: Theresa Wobbe und Gesa Lindemann (Hrsg.), *Denkachsen: Zur theoretischen und institutionellen Rede vom Geschlecht*. Frankfurt/Main: Suhrkamp, 236–263.

——, 1995, *Geschlecht als Existenzweise: Macht, Moral, Recht und Geschlechterdifferenz*. Frankfurt/Main: Ulrike Helmer Verlag.

Malette, Louise, und Marie Chalouh, (Hrsg.),.1991, *The Montreal Massacre*. Übers. Marlene Wildeman, Charlottetown, P.E.I.: gynergy books.

Mosse, George L., 1987, *Nationalismus und Sexualität: Bürgerliche Moral und sexuelle Normen*. Übers. Jörg Trobitius. Reinbek: Rowohlt.

Pratt, Minnie Bruce, 1995, *S/HE*. Ithaca, NY: Firebrand Books.

Thürmer-Rohr, Christina, 1987, *Vagabundinnen: Feministische Essays*. Berlin: Orlanda Frauenverlag.

Todorov, Tzvetan, 1985, (1982), *Die Eroberung Amerikas: Das Problem des Anderen*. Frankfurt: Suhrkamp.

von Braun, Christina, 1995, "'Frauenkrankheiten' als Spiegelbild der Geschichte", in: Farideh Akashe-Böhme (Hrsg.), *Von der Auffälligkeit des Leibes*. Frankfurt/Main: Suhrkamp, 98–129.

Williams, Raymond, ^{3}1983, *Keywords: A vocabulary of culture and society*. London: Fontana/HarperCollins.

The Gaze of/at *the other*: The New Looks of Lesbian Love in Patricia Rozema's *When Night Is Falling* (Can. 1993)

Andrea B. Braidt

> The satisfaction and reinforcement of the ego that represent the high point of film history hitherto must be attacked. Not in favor of a reconstructed new pleasure, which cannot exist in the abstract, nor of intellectualized unpleasure, but to make way for a *total negation* of the ease and plenitude of the narrative fiction film. The alternative is the thrill that comes from leaving the past behind without reflecting it, transcending outworn or oppressive forms, or daring to break with normal pleasurable expectations in order to conceive a *new language of desire*.
>
> (Laura Mulvey, 1975, italics A.B.)

Introduction

The mainstream narrative fiction film[1] is obsessed with heterosexual romance. "Since 1906, Hollywood has been the central agent of romance, what is known in the trades as the 'love interest'" (Mellencamp, 1995, p. 17). "The trick [of the romance-film, A.B.] is to make us believe women are significant while the only thing that matters is obsessive male desire" (Mellencamp, 1995, p. 15). Psychoanalytically speaking, the politics of romance is to represent woman as the male *other*, the simultaneously castrated and castrating male, the silent and passive visual spectacle. The narrative of men pursuing, getting and losing women is central to every film genre; the characters of the "lover" and the "beloved" are scripted into almost every movie. Laura Mulvey was the first to analyse the relationship of visual pleasure to heterosexual male desire when she pinned down scopophilia and narcissism as the constituting factors in the process of (male) spectatorship and hence of cinematic pleasure. With her "notorious" essay "Visual Pleasure and Narrative Cinema" Mulvey tried to destruct this pleasure with the aid of psychoanalysis. Her project was to do away with narrative pleasure and to find a new form for cinematic representation, a "new language of desire" (Mulvey, 1990, p. 30).

According to Mulvey only alternative, experimental cinema could provide a language that was beyond the objectifying and therefore oppressive nature of narrative cinema. Even now in the nineties the visual conventions of mainstream narrative cinema are fundamentally the same as in the forties and fifties (the period Mulvey talked about). The "language of desire" is unaltered. But what happens if the nature of the desire that is depicted by the narrative changes?

When Night Is Falling by the Canadian filmmaker Patricia Rozema is the latest prime example of the phenomenon of a mainstream narrative film depicting a desire other than heterosexual. Rozema's film, a major box-office success, is absolutely mainstream in its form but radically anti-Hollywood in its politics of romance as it employs lesbian desire as its narrative drive. In this article I wish to uphold this hypothesis by looking closely at the way sexual desire is represented in Rozema's film. I will take close account of the conventions of mainstream continuity narrative[2] and how Patricia Rozema conforms to these conventions in *When Night Is Falling*. Special emphasis will be put on the analysis of the end of the film within the theoretical framework given by Richard Neupert as the film's ending is of particular significance for the construction of female desire. Furthermore, I will work out two principles that constitute female desire in filmic terms: "woman in command of language" and "woman in possession of the gaze." By identifying these principles in Rozema's film it becomes clear that a romance narrative that is motivated by female desire certainly embraces politics which can subvert the "patriarchal affirmative" (woman as other) of (not only) Hollywood.

The "mainstream": conventions of continuity style

"The primary principle [of continuity style] is that the formal properties of film time and film space are subordinated to the narrative" (Mellencamp, 1995, p. 22).

Many critics have dealt with the definition of the "Hollywood film." Departing from the writings of David Bordwell and Kristin Thompson feminist film theorists from Annette Kuhn to Patricia Mellencamp have pointed out how the process of the production of meaning (the "cinematic discourse") is concealed in order to construct a tight continuity of coherent narrative time and space (cf. Kuhn, 1994, p. 41). The spectator conceives a "naturalistic" representation; what (s)he really sees is a strict set of rules and conventions which renders filmic cuts, special lighting, camera angles and so on invisible. This invisibility turns the cinematic image into naturalistic "meaning." The formalistic aspects are closely tied to certain narrative principles which then inform the politics of the filmic text: Male desire serves as the trajectory of the plot, which is established via a cinematic apparatus that privileges the male gaze, the male narrative voice and male subjectivity by constructing the female as spectacle for the gaze, as obstacle to the narrative and as essentially "other" to the male subject. The concealment of the cinematic apparatus gives way to the notion that the meaning of the story is 'already there' and not the outcome of a specific process (cf. Kuhn, 1994, p. 36). Kuhn singles out cinematography, mise-en-scène and continuity editing as the three main components of this process. The relation of close-ups to medium-shot and long-shot determine characterization and detail in information. Mise-en-scène draws upon graphic codes to establish atmosphere and the value system. Continuity editing as the most important device in terms of narrative convention is responsible for the illusion of coherence (Kuhn, 1994, p. 36 f).

Patricia Mellencamp describes in detail the practice of continuity editing or the "continuity system." Numerous cinematic principles govern the classical narrative and construct what is so often referred to as the "mainstream." First of all, the filmic story has to be told and shown in more than 80 but less than 180 minutes (Mellencamp, 1995, p. 22). It may sound obvious to state that most mainstream films are between 90 and 100 minutes long but this convention is a powerful factor in the reception process. As the spectators are used to this time pattern they know exactly *when* to expect *what*. The resolution of the film (the "end") will not happen before the usual amount of time has elapsed; the couple will not fade into the happy end before the 90th minute and the obstacles will only then be solved. A perfect example of the irritation that happens when this time convention is broken is Hitchcock's *Psycho* (Paramount, 1960) when the established protagonist (Janet Leigh) "ends" (is killed) after only twenty minutes. The experience of the unexpected construes the horror of the audience. Usually a protagonist, the star, "lasts" for 90 minutes and not for only twenty minutes. A feature film is not only limited in minutes but also in characters: it is more than common that only the central couple matters to the narrative (and to the audience). It is this convention that establishes the star system which makes the audience perceive "stars as more powerful, beautiful, and attractive" (Mellenkamp, 1995, p. 22).

Another extremely important trait of the feature (film) is the cause-effect logic: Scene A establishes a cause which motivates scene B which shows the effect that produces the cause for scene C, and so on. The repetition of elements and their symmetrical order affirms the cause-effect logic. Mainstream films are further characterized by their neatly tied-up endings: every item of the film is used up; nothing is left unexplained; "there are no loose ends" (Mellencamp, 1995, p. 23). Strong ends suggest the connection between actions; the filmic text makes the connection for the audience. Characters get fully explained; every plot line "makes sense" in context with the other plot lines. Center framing makes sure that the center of the filmic frame is occupied by a human character or an object which has an important function for the narrative. Thus the margins and the background of the frame never distract from the narrative. Graphic continuity and design display the setting and mise-en-scène as signifiers.

All these conventions do not exist in a signifying vacuum but are constitutive for a "double standard of gender, race, and age, with different conventions of lighting, make-up, speech, and even action for men and women" (Mellencamp, 1995, p. 24). And this double standard which is created along the lines of gender difference is developed in the ever-present subplot of (heterosexual) romance, which cuts across all movie genres and never ceases to represent women in relation to men. "The one hundred years dominance of this story of the couple coupling has had cumulative significance, and, I would argue, major cultural impact. For Hollywood has created the story many little girls and women believe they must make of their lives" (ibid.).

Used to these and other countless conventions, the audience perceives every deviance as "error." It is the expertise in these filmic conventions that determines whether a director will get her film produced or not. Artistic sophistication may serve as a "side dish" but the mainstream pleasure that a mainstream narrative film offers comes from the often seen and internalised patterns of filmic "story-telling."

Patricia Rozema's "mainstream": the conventions of *When Night Is Falling*

In an interview Patricia Rozema makes it clear that it is exactly the "visual pleasure" that Mulvey wanted to destruct that she is interested in: "The career goal for me is not to succeed in any money-making way or any career way, but to keep the pleasure there. Stories are very like sexuality, you know – introduction, action, culmination, climax. [...] That's why we need to hear stories over and over again" (Smith, p. 55). After her independent debut *I've Heard the Mermaids Singing* (1987) and her flopped second feature *White Rooms* (1990), *When Night Is Falling* marks Rozema's entry into the "big business." This latest work is the most "mainstream" in terms of cinematic principles. In the center of the story are Camille and Petra, the two main protagonists with star qualities: depicted by extensive use of close-ups of their faces and central framing they are the sole motivators for the narrative. At the very beginning of the film, in the title sequence, Camille and Petra are shown under water, naked, touching, and kissing each other. When the story starts with the characterization of Camille (Camille in bed waking up, going to work, teaching in the classroom), the mainstream-trained audience is certain who the "central couple" is that will get together in the next 90 minutes. The cause-effect logic of continuity editing dominates the filmic narrative: the sudden death of Camille's beloved dog irritates her so much that she does what most people would do in a state of shock: hold on to the familiar routines of life. The sequence of Camille "burying" the dog in her refrigerator leads to the sequence where she sits in the laundrette washing her clothes. The comfort of the familiar (watching the tumble-dryer) leads to the realization of the traumatic experience and allows her the first tears of grief. Her crying motivates the woman who sits next to her in the laundrette to talk to her, be attracted by her, and make a switch-rule with the washing load so they will have to meet again in order to get the right clothes. The next scene depicts Camille at home, discovering that she has taken the wrong clothes with her. She tries on one particularly daring item: a tight blouse with a zip across the front. As this piece of clothing marks an opposition to her "well-behaved" character, her determination to wear it for an interview with the reverend provokes a feeling of alienation in her boyfriend. This sense of alienation (and the need to get her own clothes back) makes her look for the woman from the laundrette whom she finds in the circus.

In terms of graphics and mise-en-scène *When Night Is Falling* is a very rich film. The cinematographic language makes much use of color metaphor, of shapes as signifiers, of warm and cold compositions of the frame. The organizing principle for these devices is dichotomy, which establishes the two women protagonists as fundamentally different. Mellencamp's "double standard" works in our case for lesbian/heterosexual, exotic/conventional, erotic/prudish, black/white, single/engaged, physically trained/rationally educated, geographically flexible/ geographically fixed. The male/female dichotomy – prominent in most Hollywood films – is therefore translated into a system of dichotomy which is not gender-based[3] . Rozema establishes two worlds which meet in the "love" between Petra and Camille. Two different spheres are developed on two levels. The first level depicts strong oppositions in the character or in the living practice of the two protagonists whereas the second level brings about a confrontation of two sets of cinematographic realms: the realm occupied by Camille and the one occupied by Petra. Camille's "world" is shown in bright colors, strong contours, sharp edges, orderly shapes ("square"[4]). Petra's context, the circus, is full of strong dark colors and shades, soft contours, no edges, and confusing shapes. Whereas Camille's apartment is full of strong corners, square cupbords, a geometrical bed, Petra's "housing" is a caravan, equipped with anti-geometrical props (a whisky-glass that "rolls" rather than "stands" on the table) and a bed which is hidden by a mass of cushions. The metaphor which depicts Petra's sphere best is probably the pitch-black outside of her caravan which is painted with tiny phosphorizing dots. At night the shape of her caravan cannot be distinguished from the starlight night in the background. Petra's sphere is only reachable when one opens an invisible door in the "heaven" among stars. Graphic continuity and consistent mise-en-scène constitute the easy flow of the narrative and hide the cinematic apparatus. The two opposite spheres, which are primarily important for the construction of the romance, are introduced almost subconsciously on a graphic level which reinforces the level of obvious narration. The constructedness of the opposite characters is hidden by the associative way in which the audience is drawn into the opposite spheres.

"The *happy-ending* is a micro-structure of the narrative, and as such, hypercodified – but it is *also* the necessary form for an ideology of reconciliation" (Jacques Aumont in Neupert, 1995, p. 40). An examination of the ending strategies of a narrative will reveal its whole narrative construct and the introduction of a specific terminology provides the neccessary tools for such an examination. What Neupert calls a "Closed Text" refers to a text which closes off neatly the two narrative levels: the represented and the representational level; "Open Story Narrative" closes the representational level but leaves the represented level (the story) open; an "Open Discourse Narrative" works the other way round (closing the story but leaving the narrative discourse – the representational level – open), and an "Open Text Narrative" closes neither level. By determining whether a film belongs to the category of "Closed Text" or to either of the other three categories we can determine its narrative politics: "The latter three categories [...] challenge classical notions of resolution, completeness, or even unity in ever more dramatic and radical ways" (Neupert, 1995, p. 33). The above quoted "ideology of reconciliation" obviously prevails in Closed Text Narratives, which are thus unable to challenge notions of resolution and completeness. We will further see how this ideology of reconciliation in the form of a happy-ending is linked to the idea of marriage and how gender politics are established. In the following I will take a closer look at Richard Neupert's work on closure in narrative films in order to analyse the end in *When Night Is Falling* and come to terms with the film's sexual politics.

Neupert offers a systematic approach to film endings and first of all distinguishes two levels which are responsible for making up the "narrative": the film's story or the "represented level," and the film's narrative discourse or the "representational level" (Neupert 1995, p. 15). Neupert describes narrative as a "dynamic relation between narrative discourse and story, so that we might understand narration, and more specifically endings, as the results of a productive process between these two signifying systems" (ibid.).

Neupert explains the represented level by using Barthes' concept of primary and secondary story components, the former entailing actions or characters of great consequentiality to the story, the latter category describing so-called indices with a more complementary function. The characters of Camille and Petra, for example, belong to the primary story components: their actions and characteristics are of great consequence to the progression of the narrative. The character of the reverend, on the other hand, serves primarily as an "index" for the atmosphere of the calvinist surroundings of Camille, which signifies the value system opposing homosexuality. Signs from both categories are interlinked with each other so they can produce several "sign systems" or story lines. These story lines, then, are brought together in the end; they are "closed-off" and completed and therefore add up to one rounded conglomerate of sign systems; in other words, they form the "narrative." A narrative is identifiable as a resolved or completed narrative by one important element: the achievement of a stasis point or equilibrium. Neupert quotes Tzvetan Todorov: "An 'ideal' narrative begins with a stable situation which is disturbed by some power or force. There results a state of disequilibrium; when a force is directed in the opposite direction, the equilibrium is re-established" (Todorov in Neupert, 1995, p. 17).

The representational level, which is called the film's narrative discourse, explains the "telling" dimension of the text, centering around questions of narrative voice, discursive style, and point of view (Neupert, 1995, p. 21). The end of a film (or any narrative) has to be examined for its story's degree of resolution and for the systems of closure of its narrative discourse. One such system would be the establishment of a narrative parallelism: two related stories are resolved at the same time. According to Neupert, this parallelism "helps bracket the text by maintaining constancy in the relations of the textual structures to the plotting of the story" (Neupert, 1995, p. 21). The resolution becomes stronger; a full closure is achieved. Camille's decision to stay with Petra is reinforced by her decision to leave the college and to change her profession. On the level of the represented, on the story level, this parallelism adds to the plausibility of the story: in order to live her lesbianism, Camille has to commit herself to a completely different lifestyle, which involves giving up her university carreer. On the level of the representational, two plot-systems are intertwined in the resolution: Camille's struggles with the morality codes of her environment and the romance plot between her and Petra. By resolving these two systems at the same point of time in one action – Camille and Petra finally getting together – the narrative structures of the text become all the more enclosed. Neupert holds parallelism responsible for the homogeneity of the narration: "The discursive strategy of parallelism works closely with the story progression to create a solidly homogeneous narrative" (Neupert, 1995, p. 22).

Neupert identifies "bracketing" as a second unifying strategy: the filmic text is bracketed by stylistic repetition of various forms, for example, music: the film's overture is repeated at the end in a reprise. Repeating the opening shot at the end of a film serves the same purpose (ibid.). *When Night Is Falling* uses both strategies but twists the latter slightly. Two components are repeated. First, the visual metaphor of two swimming women behind a wall of ice serves as background for the beginning titles and returns again at the end. The second element repeated, the appearance of Camille's dog, is twisted: the dog, shown at the beginning sleeping in Camille's bed and waking her up by licking her face, returns at the end. He is resurrected from the dead and jumps out of his icy grave under a heap of snow, running towards the caravan to join Petra and Camille on their journey into the happy fade-out. The image of the dog's resurrection is filmed in extreme slow motion and adds a certain comical effect to the ending. Bracketing serves not solely as reinforcement of the resolution in this example. The impossibility of the resurrection of a dog could be read as a comment on the actions and elements, which are its parallels: Camille's and Petra's happy end. If the end shot would consist of a close-up of the dog's grave and the camera would then pan to the caravan, bracketing and parallelism would be at work in their classical ways reinforcing the happy ending and adding a certain melodramatic qualitiy: suffering and loss is also part of the happy romance. The comical resurrection of the dog questions the realistic depiction of the romance: How trustworthy is the narrator of a story in which a dog is resurrected? How seriously can we take the classical "marriage-ending" which would quote the "ideology of reconciliation" and which would render the filmic criticism that the spectator could expect from a "feminist" movie with a somewhat emancipatory political agenda (after all, it is a lesbian marriage that is depicted) ineffective?

The narrative closure of a text and the ending of the female protagonist in marriage are observed as being interlinked by Annette Kuhn: Kuhn argues that woman often constitutes the motivation of a narrative, woman – "as structure, character, or both" (Kuhn, 1994, p. 34) – serves as the narrative obstacle and therefore has to be "finished off" in the end. Hollywood "recuperates" woman into the male/female bond. "In classic Hollywood cinema, this recuperation manifests itself thematically in a limited number of ways: a woman character may be restored to the family by falling in love, by 'getting her man', by getting married, or otherwise accepting a 'normative' female role. If not, she may be directly punished for her narrative and social transgression by exclusion, outlawing or even death" (ibid.). *When Night Is Falling* recuperates woman in a female/female bond and therefore subverts Hollywood standards. On the other hand, the closing of the narrative by coupling is used in such a classical way that the "lesbian" or "subversive" quality becomes almost invisible. This observation becomes all the more valid as the bond between Camille and Petra is paralleled to the developing bond between Martin (Camille's ex-fiancé) and Tory (the ex-girlfriend of the circus director). The film seems to suggest that, as long as lesbians couple and are committed to each other, there is not much difference to heterosexuals. Which raises the question of what would happen if the lesbians were not to couple.

It is impossible to determine whether the "resurrection of the dog" leaves the spectators questioning the "ideology of reconciliation" or whether it leaves them affected by it. Theoretically speaking, we are confronted with a parody of bracketing and parallelism, or a kind of "deconstruction," a deconstruction of the well-known codes of happy-ending marriages, which could be identified as a "feminist," or "emancipatory," or "alternative" politics. I would hold the sole incident of the dog's resurrection as only partly responsible for such an undertaking: forty seconds of parody could not deconstruct ninety-odd minutes of classical codification. But, as I will argue in the following, the resurrected dog is just a part in the project of constructing female desire in *When Night Is Falling*.

After demonstrating how the mainstream works in *When Night Is Falling* I want to return to the representation of autonomous female desire. Many critics have argued that such a project, the representation of female desire, can only be achieved in destructing the cinematic apparatus and building up an alternative one which allows images and meanings that could not be found within the apparatus of the mainstream. Mulvey argues that Hollywood cinema is "integrally bound up with aspects of patriarchy, particularly with unconscious mechanisms related to the construction of images, erotic ways of looking, audience identification, and the Hollywood editing style. "According to Mulvey, woman stands in patriarchal culture as a signifier for the male Other, as symbol of what woman represents to men, that is, as a symbol of their fantasies and obsessions" (Erens 1991, p. 3). In Mulveyan terms, woman becomes the victim of voyeurism and scopophilia, her representation functions for the satisfaction of the male drive to exploit woman sexually, or in psychoanalytical terms, to regard her as the *other*. *When Night Is Falling* employs Hollywood standards and techniques (as I have shown above) but does not act upon the matrix of patriarchal objectification. The film portrays female desire within a discourse that subverts the mainstream.

Woman in command of language

> "I want to see you in the moonlight with your head thrown back and your body aflame."

Film history is full of examples of how women are not only looked at but also talked at by men in an objectifying manner. The spectacle "woman" is usually a passive participant in discourse, one who does not speak the words of desire, who is not in command of the language of active approach.

> "The female subject [...] is associated with unreliable, thwarted, or acquiescent speech. She talks a great deal; it would be a serious mistake to characterize her as silent, since it is in large part through her prattle, her bitchiness, her sweet murmurings, her maternal admonitions, and her verbal cunning that we know her. But her linguistic status is analogous to that of a recorded tape, which endlessly plays back what was spoken in some anterior moment, and from a radically external vantage." (Silverman, 1990, p. 309 f)

Silverman points out that woman's talkativeness serves to keep her outside the discourse but has nothing to do with language in terms of the emergence of a subject according to Lacan. It is only from the place of language that woman can "know" herself, that identity can emerge in correlation to the achievement of the symbolic order (Silverman, 1990, p. 309). Only a subject is capable of desire and to become a subject means to participate in discourse. In classical film this process is denied to women.

Language in terms of romance film culminates in a very particular speech situation, the "proposal." The proposal marks the transformation from the state of "wooing" into the state of "consummation" and it is awaited with anticipation by both heroine and audience. Classical romance fiction, take Jane Austen's *Pride and Prejudice* as an example, builds up the whole narrative to this one scene[5], and the same holds true for the classical romance film. The proposal scene is constituted by the presence or absence of language: "Will he pop the question?" – as the colloquial euphemism goes – signifies the sole act of uttering a question; whether he will speak or not is the objective. In this moment of utter narrative importance, speech represents desire not body language or the gaze. And it is male speech that represents both male and female desire: convention bids the woman to wait for the utterance of love; her awaiting constitutes a (successful) proposal. She is to wait whereas he is to speak: Examples from Jane Austen up to *Sleepless in Seattle* (Nora Ephron, 1993) give ample proof.

The proposal(s) in *When Night Is Falling* are of a different nature. Not only is there a lesbian proposal – which does not involve a man in any way – but there is also a heterosexual "proposal," which is fundamentally different from the classical version: Martin does not propose to Camille but tells the reverend – when he is confronted with the fact that only a married couple can take the vacant position – that both he and Camille are "really committed to each other" (sequence 4, shot 95). His speech is not aimed at the "object" of his desire but at the representative of the system he wants to work in, or, in more general terms, at the patriarchal system. Camille is mere witness to this proposal but not its addressee, one could say she is almost "less" than an object. This is problematic in the sense that the audience is well aware of who it is that Martin is committed to, and by not even talking to her he objectifies her even more. On the other hand, Camille was not part of the procedure, in the subject-object dynamics: she has not waited for the proposal and has not anticipated it; on the contrary (as we learn later), she has tried to block it off.

The significance of this scene becomes all the more obvious when put in context with the sequence that follows it: the second "proposal." Petra, who has tricked Camille into coming to the circus by exchanging the laundry, makes a completely unexpected proposal to Camille, using a clichéed but still very powerful choice of words: "Camille, I want to see you in the moonlight with your head thrown back and your body aflame!" In contrast to Martin's words, Petra's are directly spoken to Camille, her piercing gaze underlining the urge with which they are spoken. This time, Camille is unmistakably the object of desire. Without hesitation, she refuses the "proposal" by reminding Petra of conventions: "This was completely uncalled for." Again, the rhetoric of this scene appears in a different light when analysed in context with the next: Camille unexpectedly invites Petra into her house for a kiss. The subversion of the object-subject dynamics immanent to the conventional proposal lies in the use of speech: "uncalled for" words stimulate and represent desire and not a long awaited ritualistic sequence of sentences.

It is the woman in possession of powerful language whom Camille turns to in the end, a woman who likes the name "Camille" because it "sounds like 'come here'" (sequence 5, shot 160). And there are several more scenes that illustrate the film's awareness of speaking women. When Camille confesses her affair with Petra to the reverend but shies away from naming it ("lesbian," for example) in sequence 13, he advises her to say it out loud because "naming things gives us power over them." Camille replies that it also gives power to others and refuses his advice only to encounter a few scenes later how powerful the denial of naming can be: In sequence 14 she wants to tell Martin the truth about her and Petra, a truth which he already knows. He talks her into being silent because "it is selfish to relieve oneself of secrets one cannot bear to live the consequences of." What he really means is that once Camille has spoken of her desire for another woman she has deprived Martin of the sole possession of language. She would dictate the terms; she would have the power of words over him. Camille's final use of language in the end scene signifies what the power of language means in terms of agency: as she lies unconscious in the snow and Petra lies beside her, trying to awaken her with the warmth of her own body and waiting for Camille to speak again, Camille's "yes" means that she is both alive and willing to go with Petra.

Empowerment through the possession of language is definitely an agenda relevant to the representation of female desire. *When Night Is Falling* is aware of this fact and represents women who can speak, women who are in command of words, women who direct their language of desire towards women. Petra speaks from the space of symbolic order and Camille's tale in *When Night Is Falling* could be described as a story of initiation. The images of the initiating sex scene between Camille and Petra (sequence 12) is intercut with two trapeze artists performing a twin act high up under the roof of the tent: the one mirrors the other in her movements. The allusion to Lacan's mirror stage is intended, which brings us to the second principle of filmic female desire.

Woman in possession of the gaze

> "I want to *see* you in the moonlight, with your head thrown back and your body aflame."

Ever since the beginnings of feminist film theory (i.e., ever since the publication of Laura Mulvey's "Visual Pleasure and Narrative Cinema" in 1975), the critique of classical film narrative has centered around the gaze. Ever since Mulvey it has been argued that the male spectator "possesses" the woman through the gaze of the male protagonist, the spectator using the protagonist as his "surrogate" (Gaines, 1990, p. 207). Female spectators have to perform an act of transvestism or masquerade in order to identify with the male protagonist so they can "enjoy." Female spectators need a certain amount of masochism to gaze at the female characters and to see them objectified (Mary Ann Doane, 1982 and Laura Mulvey, 1979). Black feminists have pointed out that it is the white male protagonist who is in possession of the gaze and that a black spectator would not use him but maybe a black co-actor as surrogate/identification figure, a black character who is not in possession of the gaze. Thus black male spectators have to perform a similar act of masquerade in order to objectify and "enjoy" women (Gaines, 1990, p. 207). Lesbian critics, however, have pointed out that positing a lesbian spectator would change the viewing paradigm once again. A lesbian spectator would identify with a female character in the film whose gaze objectifies the female star's body, which has been eroticized (Gaines, 1990, p. 200). The viewing pleasure would be neither male nor masochistic but lesbian.

In order to put such a viewing strategy into the practice of film analysis, critics have used films like *Morocco*, *Gentlemen Prefer Blondes*, *Desperately Seeking Susan*, films which usually privilege a male gaze but can be "subtexted" with lesbian meaning and looked at from a lesbian point of view. If we look at a film that privileges the female gaze, like *When Night Is Falling*, the theoretical problem presents itself in a different light. The gaze at stake is definitely a female one; the desire is undeniably lesbian. But is the target of the gaze, the other woman protagonist, as objectified as in a heterosexual situation? A male spectator could perform an act of transvestism and use the female gaze for his heterosexual trajectory of desire. Although this argument is very valid, we must consider the filmic context in which the gaze is at work (cf. above). And the gaze has to be investigated thoroughly in order to determine whether its trajector can be termed lesbian/female or whether its paradigm has not changed from the heterosexual but just substituted the male voyeur with a female voyeuse.

The first filmic instance that I want to consider for this issue is the sequence in the laundry (sequence 3). This scene establishes the second protagonist, Petra, as a woman who is "interested" in Camille, and it does so via the gaze. Shot 31 pans from a close-up of the laundry in the tumble-dryer to a close-up of a crying Camille (establishing shot which shows the situation of a distressed Camille who looks for comfort in the routine of housework). Shot 32 is the first in a succession of the typical shot-countershot technique. The neutral camera establishes Petra in a medium shot, practising some artistic act with a ball and her elbow. The soundtrack of Camille's sobbing prompts shot 33: a close-up of Petra's face in "watching position," the classical point-of-view shot. Shot 34 shows what Petra is watching: Camille crying, in close-up, from the angle of Petra's position. This is the first shot in the film when Camille is looked at from a subjective point-of-view; she is the object of Petra's gaze but unaware of it. The next few shots depict the dialogue between Petra and Camille about Bob the dog. Usually, this dialogue would be shot in the strict point-of-view convention, privileging Petra's point-of-view, i.e., filming Camille in close-up in the camera angle of Petra's position. As Petra is standing and Camille is sitting this would mean that Camille is filmed in high angle, from the "bird's perspective." High angle implies inferiority of the filmed object and sets up a hierarchy of some sort (cf. Monaco, 1981, pp. 140ff.). Camille's distressed emotional status would add to this impression and therefore characterize Petra as the one in charge, the cool observer. But Rozema does not employ high angle: both Camille and Petra are filmed straight on. Although the dialogue clearly depicts Petra as the investigator, asking about the details of Bob's death, she is not presented as the objective "detective" who tries to make out his "victim." Through the unconventional film technique, Petra is just as involved as Camille, not privileged but equal. The camera (and the spectator) watches two women becoming involved with each other. This becomes all the clearer in the finishing shot of this sequence: Petra is shown leaving the laundry in the background of the frame while Camille, who is foregrounded, puts on her coat. Petra turns at the door and looks at Camille before she leaves. As soon as she has averted her gaze from Camille, Camille turns and looks after her. It is impossible to determine a possessor of the gaze and an object: both women are bearers of the gaze and its object at the same time.

The next filmic instance which thematizes the gaze is the metaphor of the Lacanian mirror stage in the picture that Petra "sends" to Camille with an apology written on the back. The picture depicts Petra, looking longingly at her own mirrored image. Lacan argues that the moment when a child recognizes itself in the mirror is crucial for the constitution of the ego. "[...] it is an image that constitutes the matrix of the imaginary, of recognition/misrecognition and identification, and hence of the first articulation of the I, of subjectivity" (Mulvey, 1990, p. 31). Therefore one's own image in the mirror is the classic image of subjectivity, the metaphor for the constitution of the self. With her photograph Petra seems to advertise this process. "Look at me, I am a full subject" the photograph teases, and Camille understands its meaning: She invites Petra for a kiss. Not only Camille can decipher Petra's metaphorical language; also Martin is capable of reading it. Near the end of the film he finds the photograph lying on Camille's desk and instantly knows what is happening.

The last scene I want to consider for my purpose is the first sex scene between Camille and Petra (sequence 12). Camille enters the circus-tent and watches the twin-artists on the trapeze. In a somewhat cruder way this act demonstrates again what I described in the paragraph above: identity is at stake. What other critics have interpreted as an over-harmonization of lesbian relationships (cf. Schüttelkopf, 1995, p. 31: "[...] the artists symbolize the harmony and the communication between women that suffices without words," translation A.B.), I see as a signifier for the threshold between a heterosexual and a lesbian identity. The trapeze-artists visually quote the photograph that Petra has given to Camille and invite her into a new identity. They do not suggest that women are the same, are identical with each other, but rather point to the process of constituting subjectivity. When Camille sees Petra lying on a bed of red velvet the "advertisement" strategies of photograph and trapeze act have worked: It is Camille's gaze that is desiring Petra; she has crossed the threshold.

Conclusion

A filmic gaze that on the surface seems to work completely within the conventions of the partriarchal matrix of objectifying woman through the gaze proves to be fundamentally non-hierarchical when analyzed more thoroughly. Looking and being looked at alternate in a relationship between equals. The gaze here does not objectify or abuse but rather constitutes desire. In her whole oeuvre Patricia Rozema concentrates on this problem but has never achieved its solution so well as in *When Night Is Falling*. Her debut, *I've Heard the Mermaids Singing*, depicts a woman-photographer who, in search of her identity, "develops" (literally in the photolab and symbolically in succeeding in life) an alternative gaze on women. *The White Room* is about a male character whose voyeurism becomes his fate: he is drawn into a narrative of crime and detection.

In Patricia Rozema's films and especially in *When Night Is Falling*, the gaze at the *other* works under a new set of paradigms. I have tried to show that Hollywood conventions can be deconstructed without destroying cinematic visual pleasure. Visual pleasure does not always mean an enactment of the patriarchal subconscious which objectifies women as the spectacle of the male gaze and of male and heterosexual narrative. Just like the resurrection of the dog deconstructs the heterosexual narrative principles, the "mis"use of the point-of-view technique deconstructs the male gaze. And, along the same lines as the visual aspects are presented differently, the soundtrack is revised: Women possess the language of desire and are able to gain identity within discourse. In Rozema's films they are no longer confined to the discursive outsiders who "bitch, quarrel, prattle" (Silverman, 1990, p. 309), but possessing the power of language and the gaze, constitute each other in desire.

Notes

1. Or the "Classical Hollywood Film", the term which will be used hereafter. I will come to a more detailed definition later.
2. The central source for these thoughts is Patricia Mellencamp's concept of "Made in the Fade" in Mellencamp, 1995, pp.17ff.

3 It could be argued that the "dichotomisation" into opposing qualities of two women who are sexually attracted to each other marks a kind of "heterosexualisation" of the "lesbian" romance-plot. Nevertheless I would prefer to see these dichotomies as an awareness of the heterosexual matrix that constitutes mainstream narrative.
4 Square (coll): heterosexual.
5 Which is brilliantly exercised in the quoted example: there is not one but two proposals in the novel, the first one being a desaster because of the hero's pride and the heroine's prejudice.

References

Bordwell, David and Kristin Thompson, 1979, *Film Art: An Introduction*. Reading, Mass: Addison-Wesley.

Doane, Mary Ann, 1995 (1982), "Film and the Masquerade – Theorizing the Female Spectator," in: Patricia Erens (ed.), *Issues in Feminist Film Criticism*. Bloomington and Indianapolis: Indiana University Press, 41–57.

Erens, Patricia, 1995, *Issues in Feminist Film Criticism*. Bloomington and Indianapolis: Indiana University Press.

Gaines, Jane, 1990, "White Privilege and Looking Relations: Race and Gender in Feminist Film Theory," in: Patricia Erens (ed.), *Issues in Feminist Film Criticism*. Bloomington and Indianapolis: Indiana University Press, 197–216.

Kuhn, Annette, ²1994, *Women's Pictures: Feminism and Cinema*. London: Verso.

Mellencamp, Patricia, 1995, *A Fine Romance: Five Ages of Film Feminism*. Philadelphia: Temple University Press.

Monaco, James, 1981, *How to Read a Film: The Art, Technology, Language, History, and Theory of Film and Media*. Oxford, New York: Oxford University Press.

Mulvey, Laura, Mulvey, (1979), "Afterthoughts on 'Visual Pleasure and Narrative Cinema' Inspired by Duel in the Sun," *Framework*, 10 (Spring), 3–10.

——, 1990, (1975), "Visual Pleasure and Narrative Cinema," in: Patricia Erens (ed.), *Issues in Feminist Film Criticism*, Bloomington and Indianapolis: Indiana University Press.

Neupert, Richard, 1995, *The End. Narration and Closure in the Cinema*. Detroit: Wayne State University Press.

Schüttelkopf, Elke, 1995, "Lesbian Kitch," *Sic! Forum für Feministische GangArten*, 8/9, (September), 30–31.

Silverman, Kaja, 1988, *The Acoustic Mirror: The Female Voice in Psychoanalysis and Cinema*. Bloomington and Indianapolis: Indiana University Press.

——, 1990, "Dis-embodying the Female Voice," in: Patricia Erens (ed.), *Issues in Feminist Film Criticism*. Bloomington and Indianapolis: Indiana University Press. 309–327.

Smith, Ali, 1995, "Flights of Fancy," *Diva*, (October), 54–56.

Appendix: Segmentation/Sequence Analysis of *When Night Is Falling*

1. Title sequence: titles are interspersed with shots of sparkling water, two naked women swimming in the water, touching; one woman swimming behind a wall of ice.

2. (shots 1–30) Camille is shown waking up in her bed at the side of her dog Bob. Then she is teaching a class on mythology after which she has a short conversation with Martin, her boyfriend and fellow teacher about a conference he is to go to. When they kiss, they are caught by the reverend, who asks them into his office later in the day. Back in her office Camille cannot find Bob. She goes to look for him and finds him dead in the street. She carries him home and puts him in the refrigerator.

   (min. 00:00–07:00)

   fade

3. (shots 31–61) Confused, Camille goes to the laundry to do her washing where a stranger (Petra) comforts her. Petra switches the two laundry loads and leaves the laundry with Camille's clothes in her bag.

   (min. 07:01–10:30)

   cut

4. (shots 62–100) At home Camille realizes that she has taken Petra's clothes and Petra's address in the bag. She is trying on one of Petra's daring tops when Martin fetches her to go with him to the reverend. The reverend offers Martin and Camille the to-be-vacant position of reverend of the college on the condition they get married. Martin assures him of their commitment to each other.

   (min. 10:31–15:57)

   cut

5. (shots 101–181) Camille goes to Petra, who works and lives in a circus, to exchange the clothes. While drinking whisky Petra confesses her affection for Camille. Shocked, Camille flees.

   (min. 15:58–26:54)

   cut

6. (shots 182–209) Petra shoots a photograph (with "I'm sorry. Petra" written on the back) attached to an arrow into Camille's study. After some time Camille invites Petra into the house and kisses her. Realizing what she has done she runs off.

   (min. 26:55–31:00)

   dissolve shot of pylon to shot of Camille sitting in a chair

7. (shots 210–240) Petra, who has followed Camille to the college, watches from a tree how Martin and Camille quarrel and make up again after the job interview.

   (min. 31:01–36:13)

   cut

8. (shots 241–288) Camille visits Petra in the circus to explain that she is not a lesbian but she offers her friendship, which Petra accepts.

   (min. 36:14–40:40)

   cut

9. (shots 289–344) Under protest, Camille goes paragliding with Petra. During the "flight" Camille faints and they make a crash-landing during which Camille's foot gets hurt.

    (min. 40:41–45:13)

    cut

10. (shots 345–400) They go back to Camille's flat where Petra gives Camille a massage and is just about to seduce her when the reverend calls on Camille to talk to her. Petra stays although Camille wants her to leave. Camille explains to the reverend that Petra is a "streetkid" whom she "cannot get rid of." Petra, having overheard the conversation, leaves through the window.

    (min. 45:14–50:34)

    cut

11. (shots 401–415) Camille visits Martin and, while she is having sex with him, she fantasizes about Petra. In the morning Martin leaves for the weekend and Camille, who is left alone, keeps fantasizing about making love with Petra.

    (min. 50:35–54:29)

    cut

12. (shots 416–474) Camille spends the night making love with Petra. In the morning the circus director informs Petra that they will have to leave town soon.

    (min. 54:30–63:33)

    cut

13. (shots 475–546) After confessing her lesbian affair to the reverend Camille spends the second night with Petra. Martin returns from his trip and finds the two women having sex in Petra's caravan. He waits until Camille has left and then threatens Petra. (min. 63:34–76:56)

    cut

14. (shots 547–566) Camille returns to her flat where Martin is waiting for her. She wants to tell him about Petra but he stops her and persuades her to be silent.

    (min. 76:57–81:35)

    cut

15. (shots 567–626) Utterly confused, Camille takes her dead dog and buries him at the spot where she landed when paragliding with Petra. She sits in the snow and drinks herself unconscious. The paragliding people find a half-frozen Camille, phone an ambulance and notify Petra, who comes to rescue her. Camille finally awakes to Petra's promises of eternal love. She leaves with Petra and the circus for California.

    (min 81:36–90:53)

    fade

16. (shots 627–635) End credits intercut with images of the resurrection of the dog. Bob jumps out of his icy grave and runs after the caravan of Petra and Camille.

    (min. 90:54–92:00)

Femmes autochtones, médiatrices de changement: la prise de parole d'An Antane Kapesh

Hélène Destrempes

Les populations autochtones possèdent depuis des millénaires une tradition orale au travers de laquelle ils ont exprimé et expriment encore aujourd'hui leur savoir, leur système de valeurs, leur vision du monde et leurs mythes. Cette tradition orale encadre et de fait précise les priorités sociales et individuelles de la communauté dont elle est issue. Elle explique d'une part l'origine de la culture – dont elle est bien sûr, l'une des manifestations – et présente d'autre part, l'ensemble des connaissances et des règles de conduite propres au groupe concerné. Parallèlement à ces fonctions, elle sert de cadre au récit de l'histoire, c'est à dire à la mémoire même de cette société où elle a pris naissance.

Essentiellement liée à la parole, la tradition orale et ses différentes productions, d'ailleurs appelées "littérature orale" par certains critiques, dont Paul Zumthor (1983), se présente comme un discours libre ou demi-fixé, en constante mutation, où se trouve le plus souvent conservé une part d'improvisation. De par nature, traditionnelle et collective, la tradition orale comporte aussi différents genres. D'après Diane Boudreau (1993), les catégories établies au Québec dans les traditions algonquinienne et iroquoïienne sont le plus souvent les narrations qui regroupent les mythes, les contes et les légendes; les chants qui peuvent être repris à l'intérieur de ces récits ou être intérprétés dans le cadre de circonstances particulières et les discours traditionnels.

Chez les Montagnais qui habitent le nord-est québécois et le Labrador (c.f. annexe), on distingue plus spécifiquement les "atanukan" des "tipatshimun", c'est-à-dire les récits mythiques des récits historiques ou anecdotiques où les narrateurs racontent ou commentent ce qu'ils ont vécu ou entendu. Au regard de cette composante humaine et de la variabilité qui en découle, les fonctions et la valeur du discours oral reposent en grande partie sur la performance qui en est donnée et dépend fortement de l'habileté de l'énonciateur. Dans ce contexte, communiquer ou raconter, en un mot transmettre cette tradition orale relève du social et du collectif plutôt que du privé et se distingue ainsi de l'imprimé.

Dans le discours oral, le respect des valeurs culturelles traditionnelles, le bien-être collectif et les intérêts du groupe priment aussi sur l'individu et les intérêts particuliers. Ses productions s'avèrent ainsi un lieu de consensus à l'intérieur duquel la cohésion du groupe se développe tant sur le plan de la synchronie que de la diachronie puisqu'elle permet de faire le pont entre le monde des anciens (passé mythique), le passé immédiat (qu'on peut qualifier d'historique) et le monde des vivants.

C'est dans le cadre de cette tradition finalement que sont défendues les normes sociales sur laquelle repose l'organisation même de la vie communautaire. Le développement de ce discours implique donc l'assentiment et la complicité du groupe, tout en supposant le refus d'une certaine individualité. Comme le précise Diane Boudreau dans son *Histoire de la littérature amérindienne*: "Le texte oral naît de cette volonté collective de se souvenir, de se connaître et de se perpétuer dans l'histoire. Les oeuvres ainsi créées représentent la somme des connaissances acquises par un groupe et l'expression des contraintes collectives acceptables et acceptées" (Boudreau, 1993, p. 26).

L'arrivée des Blancs en Amérique du Nord au XVIe siècle et l'établissement de la colonie française au siècle suivant, viennent perturber l'équilibre socio-économique et culturel des nations autochtones, vivant alors sur le territoire de la Nouvelle-France et de l'Acadie. La traite excessive des fourrures, le choc microbien, ainsi que les tentatives d'évangélisation et de sédentarisation forcent les différentes nations à chercher leur subsistance ailleurs, à s'isoler plus au nord ou à l'est, déplaçant de ce fait d'autres tribus ou modifiant encore les rapports de force entre adversaires et alliés autochtones. L'expansion de l'empire iroquois et le repli des Montagnais vers la Côte-Nord (c.f. annexe), après avoir occupé pendant près de cent ans les rives du Saint-Laurent jusqu'à l'est de Montréal, n'est qu'un exemple des multiples conséquences liées à l'entreprise coloniale. Seuls les tribus habitant des territoires en marge des régions colonisées ne sont pas immédiatement forcées d'adapter leur mode de vie à la présence blanche toujours plus envahissante, mais dans l'ensemble, la dépendance des populations autochtones envers les autorités commerciale, religieuse ou gouvernementale commence déjà à cette époque.

Les réserves que l'on crée à partir de 1820, deviennent le lieu de ségrégation par excellence. La discrimination qui y est d'abord d'ordre spatial, correspond de toute évidence à une mise en tutelle progressive des nations autochtones par les gouvernements fédéral et provinciaux. Les nations plus isolées et nomades, tels les Montagnais et les Attikameks, échappent plus longtemps, comme nous l'avons déjà mentionné, aux contraintes et à l'encadrement que vivent les tribus de la vallée du Saint Laurent ou des Grands Lacs. Cependant, dès la seconde moitié du XIXe siècle, le morcellement des terres, le nouvel arrivage de missionnaires – cette fois-ci, des Oblats – , la déforestation et l'afflux de nouveaux colons rendent l'interaction de ces nations autochtones avec leur environnement toujours plus difficile. Rappelons qu'au départ, elle n'était pas de tout repos, puisque leur subsistance dépendait de la disponibilité des ressources et que celles-ci variaient considérablement suivant les modifications cycliques des populations animales et les conditions climatiques annuelles. L'établissement des premiers clubs de pêche (1859), de l'industrie des pâtes et papiers (1871), puis éventuellement des compagnies minières au XIXe siècle, contribuent progressivement à déstabiliser et à marginaliser les populations autochtones vivant en périphérie.

Il serait faux de s'imaginer que les Amérindiens n'étaient pas conscients, en partie du moins, des processus d'acculturation et de dépossession dont ils faisaient les frais. Attachés cependant à une tradition orale où la parole est sacrée, ils ont cru au départ, ce que les différentes autorités leur racontaient et ne se sont rendu compte que tardivement du fait que les traités écrits allaient avoir préséance sur les ententes verbales. D'après les travaux de Sylvie Vincent et Rémi Savard, il semble que l'on retrouve dès cette époque, des récits de manipulation et de tromperie dans la tradition orale, surtout en ce qui concerne l'usurpation du territoire. Les Autochtones considéraient en fait qu'en compensation pour l'occupation de leur terres, il était du devoir de l'Etat de suppléer aux manques de l'économie traditionnelle et de respecter cette entente, tacite ou pas, sans quoi ils étaient des "voleurs de territoire". Sujet à de fortes critiques, le comportement des Blancs amène les Amérindiens déjà à s'interroger sur la question de l'autosuffisance ou plutôt sur la rupture de l'autosuffisance et ses conséquences sur leur mode de vie traditionnel, tant et si bien que ce problème devient un repère chronologique dans leur tradition orale et qu'il tient alors le rôle d'une étape historique, marquant la distinction entre le passé et le présent.

Cette constante du discours oral démontre qu'il ne faut pas attendre le vingtième siècle pour que les Amérindiens réagissent à cette situation d'exploitation. C'est aussi ce qui les pousse à s'approprier une certaine parole écrite. Ainsi, dès le XVIIIe siècle, nous retrouvons sous forme de discours, de requêtes ou de correspondance, divers écrits autochtones s'adressant aux autorités (gouvernementales, commerciales ou religieuses) du pays. Ce recours à l'écriture demeure toutefois une pratique sporadique jusqu'au XXe siècle.

La tradition orale et la langue qui la sous-tend, ne traversent pas indemnes ces transformations. Elles souffrent, tôt ou tard, d'un processus de réduction: perte de variantes, de dialectes, appauvrissement du lexique et du vivier d'images. Cette situation n'est pas sans être reliée au fait que l'organisation sociale et familiale autochtone tend aussi à se fragmenter. Si les hommes ont plus de difficulté à exercer leurs occupations traditionnelles – dans certaines régions, les Amérindiens sont parfois réduits au braconnage pour survivre – ce sont les femmes qui subissent le plus grand préjudice. Dans la plupart des sociétés autochtones, il existait à l'origine un principe de base, fondé sur l'autonomie et le mérite personnel, servant à structurer les rapports sociaux et politiques, ainsi qu'à déterminer les rôles et les relations entre les hommes et les femmes. D'après Ruth Landes et Eleonor Leacock qui ont étudié respectivement les Ojibways et les Montagnais, la division du travail dans ces tribus, était d'abord et avant tout basée sur la nécessité. Bien que l'homme par exemple, ait été responsable de la chasse, il pouvait arriver que les femmes y participent ou qu'en l'absence de la mère, le père s'occupe des enfants. L'autorité revenaient d'emblée aux Anciens, hommes ou femmes, et les fonctions politiques dépendaient beaucoup plus de la valeur d'un individu que de son sexe. La survie des clans et par extension, de la tribu dépendait de cette coopération et de cette obligation mutuelle au respect.

Au contact de la société américo-européenne, les femmes se sont trouvées marginalisées. Et pourtant, dans la société traditionnelle, leur position, dérivant de leur travail, était essentielle à l'économie autochtone. Non seulement étaient elles responsables de la nourriture et des vêtements, mais en plus, de par leur rôle et responsabilité en tant que porteuse et éducatrice d'enfants, elles se voyaient octroyer une autorité considérable à l'intérieur de la nation; alors que les hommes, par la guerre et la chasse, apportaient avec eux la mort, elles demeuraient essentiellement porteuses de vie. Le rôle de la mère était considéré de façon telle qu'il représentait davantage une source de pouvoir et de reconnaissance que de subjugation. La femme autochtone n'était ainsi non seulement mère de ses propres enfants, mais aussi mère de la nation, assurant entre autres sa survie spirituelle et culturelle.

Au cours d'un long processus d'acculturation, la femme indienne se voit retirée ce statut spécial et sous l'influence, entre autres, des missionnaires, se trouve confinée au rôle de génitrice. Du coup, elle perd son droit à la parole et par extension, son pouvoir dans les sphères publique et politique. Elle se trouve marginalisée au sein de sa propre société et devient la victime d'un second colonialisme, interne cette fois à sa propre communauté. Elle revêt les couleurs d'une nouvelle altérité, celle qui la distingue de l'homme, qui devient l'unique figure normative. C'est lui alors qui détermine la langue, la culture et les institutions, bref le génie de la civilisation. L'homme voit alors le monde comme une réflexion de soi, alors que la femme ne s'y retrouve que dans son envers, sa représentation en miroir.

Les femmes issues des sociétés autochtones traditionnelles, doivent ainsi apprendre à faire face à un nouvel ordre social, étranger à leur héritage culturel. A cette situation, s'ajoutent deux lois qui réduisent encore davantage les droits et les libertés de ces femmes et en institutionnalisent l'oppression: la loi sur l'affranchissement du statut indien de 1869 et la loi cadre du gouvernement canadien, votée en 1876. Alors que la première impose aux femmes autochtones le statut et l'appartenance à la bande du mari, l'interdiction d'hériter de droits territoriaux et d'occuper des postes de nature politique dans leur bande, la seconde les force à se plier à l'ensemble des autres règlements auxquels sont soumis les Autochtones. Il est à noter que ce cadre législatif des plus discriminatoires ne sera corrigé qu'en 1985, suite à l'adoption du Bill C–31 et à l'inscription de l'égalité des droits entre les hommes et les femmes autochtones dans la Charte des Droits et des Libertés du Canada (1982) à la demande de l'Association des Femmes Autochtones du Québec.

La disparition partielle ou totale des langues et des cultures autochtones suit de près la perte ou le réaménagement du territoire, ainsi que la déstabilisation des structures sociale et familiale. Cet état des choses ne peut guère étonner compte tenu du fait que la tradition et la culture perdent leurs porte-paroles et voient les femmes réduites au silence. Pourtant, nous dit Foucault: "Là où il y a oppression, il y a résistance" et de fait, lorsque la première atteint un niveau intolérable, la seconde prend son envol. Au Canada, tant anglais que français, la goutte qui fait déborder le vase est le fameux Livre Blanc, proposé par le gouvernement fédéral en 1969. Ce document qui proposait entre autres l'égalité, la liberté et ... la citoyenneté canadienne aux Autochtones et cherchait en fait à réduire l'ensemble de la problématique indienne à la question de l'égalité des droits, secoue le pays comme un vent de tempête. Les "premières nations" perçoivent rapidement dans ce projet de loi une nouvelle stratégie d'assimilation globale. C'est la naissance du mouvement de contestation, de la Renaissance autochtone, du "printemps indien" comme l'ont appelé certains. Ce phénomène qui crée un précédent au Canada, n'est toutefois pas sans rappeler les révoltes indiennes aux Etats-Unis, Wounded Knee, les "fish-in" et le "Red Power" américain.

Au nord du 49ième parallèle pourtant, la révolution autochtone n'est pas de nature terroriste; on pourrait la qualifier même de "Révolution tranquille" puisqu'elle s'est d'abord manifestée par la création d'organisations non gouvernementales, devant représenter les différentes populations autochtones du pays. C'est ainsi que naissent l'Association des Autochtones du Québec, celle des femmes autochtones, du Conseil Montagnais-Attikamek, etc. Ces nouveaux porte-paroles culturels et politiques rejettent d'emblée l'idéologie blanche et les institutions qui la sous-tendent. Ils prônent d'abord et avant tout le retour aux valeurs traditionnelles et l'autonomisation des populations autochtones.

Cette renaissance amérindienne se caractérise aussi par l'émergence d'une écriture et de réseaux d'édition autochtones. Tant les Hurons que les Algonquins, les Abenaquis que les Attikameks et les Montagnais commencent à développer un discours écrit appelé à concurrencer celui des Blancs. Les femmes autochtones ne tardent à revendiquer leur autorité traditionnelle en matière de culture et se font à nouveau les avocats du maintien des traditions et d'un changement d'attitude au sein de leurs communautés. C'est le début d'une décolonisation culturelle: "Native women were forced to adapt to Euro-American gender expectations, but more often, they sought alternatives and created a new understanding of their roles by merging traditional beliefs with cultural innovation" (Sands, 1991, p. 8).

Elles ressentent plus que jamais la nécessité de réfléchir et de clarifier l'expérience vécue en tant qu'activité signifiante. Après des décennies de répression et d'effacement, elles veulent raconter leur version du conflit culturel au cours duquel elles ont vu leurs valeurs traditionnelles et leur estime de soi disparaître. Les critiques américains qualifient ce récit de leur dépossession culturelle "a tale of near-death experience". Elles ramènent leur culture du monde des morts vivants afin d'y retrouver sens et dignité. Elles sont des survivantes et cela est d'une importance capitale pour leurs nations car dans l'esprit autochtone "une nation n'est pas conquise jusqu'à ce que les coeurs de ses femmes soient écrasés. Alors, c'est fini; peu importe la bravoure de ses guerriers, ou la force de ses armes, l'ennemi a triomphé" (dicton cheyenne). L'engagement des Amérindiennes, tant sur le plan culturel que politique, témoigne de ce désir qu'elles ont de se réapproprier leur droit inhérent et inaliénable à la parole. La tradition autochtone affirme d'ailleurs que c'est par elles que la parole voyage.

La littérature issue des initiatives autochtones, au cour des années '70, demande à être lue comme une critique du racisme, du colonialisme et de l'exploitation économique dont les nations les plus diverses ont été et sont encore les victimes à cette époque. Le retour des Autochtones au discours signale finalement le découpage d'un nouvel espace-sujet, où les femmes se trouvent dans une position stratégiquement plus favorable afin d'agir sur leur conditions socio-économique et culturelle. Les années '80 viendront d'ailleurs consacrer cet activisme et leur présence renouvelée en matière de culture et d'engagement social, avec la révision de leur statut politico-légal en 1985.

Le discours autochtone en émergence s'offre donc au départ comme une réflexion critique du discours blanc officiel qui les a si longtemps marginalisés et "indigénés". Cherchant à renverser les rapports de domination par le biais desquels ils ont été maintenus au silence et l'apparente universalité du récit de l'histoire blanche – histoire qui les a affublés d'une représentation fixée par l'idéologie coloniale – les auteurs amérindiens dénoncent les pratiques d'appropriation et d'exploitation du territoire et font l'apologie d'un mode de vie traditionnel.

Bien que toutes les avenues littéraires soient explorées, le genre de prédilection demeure l'autobiographie. Intégrée au discours amérindien, celle-ci se développe de façon telle à se distinguer rapidement de ses homologues européen et américain. Elle se présente entre autres comme un amalgame de ce genre et de la tradition orale, et plus particulièrement de la tradition du conteur. Les femmes autochtones, car ce sont surtout elles qui s'expriment par ce médium, font d'un genre à la base assez individualiste, la voix de la nation. Leurs oeuvres relèvent ainsi plus de la rétrospection que de l'introspection. Comme dans la tradition orale, le moi se trouve subordonné au nous et le bien-être commun passe avant l'intérêt personnel.

Par le biais de l'écriture, les femmes autochtones vont encore une fois chercher à préserver les valeurs traditionnelles et la solidarité tribale. L'autobiographie devient ainsi le lieu d'une redéfinition de soi et du groupe, d'une revalorisation de la différence et de l'indianité. Plus qu'une simple déconstruction du discours des Blancs, leurs oeuvres constituent une tentative de dépassement, une réappropriation de la mémoire collective, une nouvelle source de savoir et une figure de résistance: "We are reclaiming our pride and traditions. We are asking for opportunities to practice our culture. To transmit the braiding of our past, present and future into terms others can understand and respect" (Kane/Maracle, 1989, p. 5).

Il est à noter qu'il n'y a pas à proprement parler de discours féministe autochtone à cette époque, car les femmes amérindiennes qui écrivent alors, associent d'abord leur discours au sort de leur nation et à leur condition d'autochtone. La thématique de la violence envers les femmes et celle de préoccupations plus spécifiquement féminines, ne commencent à proprement parler qu'au cours des années '90.

Alors que certains auteurs, hommes ou femmes, prônent une politique se rapprochant du multiculturalisme canadien ou bien d'un métissage conscient des cultures dominante et dominée, nombreux sont ceux qui choisissent et encouragent les Amérindiens à la révolte. Exaspérés par des siècles de colonisation et de marginalisation, ils ressentent toute forme de collaboration comme une nouvelle avenue d'exploitation. C'est l'amertume et la colère qui motivent leurs oeuvres. Elizabeth Cook-Lynn (une Sioux-Crow), exprime très clairement ce sentiment lorsqu'elle affirme: "C'est la colère qui me poussa à écrire. Ecrire pour moi, alors est devenu un acte de défiance, né de ce besoin de survivre. Je suis moi-même, j'existe, j'écris" (Cook-Lynn, 1987, p. 57).

Au Québec, An Antane Kapesh, est la première à emprunter ce ton et à composer des textes de résistance et de dépossession, comme les appelle Diane Boudreau. Née dans le bois, près de Kujuuak (Fort Chimo) en 1926, cette Montagnaise, mariée à l'âge de seize ans, pratique avec son mari et ses huit enfants, une existence nomade jusqu'en 1953, année de la création de la réserve de Malioténam, sur la côte près de Sept-Iles. D'abord conseillère pour une durée de deux ans, elle devient de '65 à '67 chef de bande à Matimekosh (Shefferville) où elle réside encore aujourd'hui.

Témoin des changements qui ont marqué sa nation, An A. Kapesh, qui n'a jamais fréquenté le système scolaire des Blancs et est demeurée unilingue montagnaise, décide en 1975 de rompre le silence et l'inertie des siens en publiant jusqu'en 1983 des contes, des lettres et surtout un essai autobiographique des plus percutants intitulé: *Je suis une maudite sauvagesse*. D'un couvert à l'autre, elle décrit l'acculturation des Montagnais, le démentèlement de leur organisation sociale et de leur mode d'éducation traditionnel, la dépendance et la tutelle gouvernementale, ainsi que la grande misère économique et spirituelle qui les frappent tous.

Publié en 1976 et dédié à ses enfants, *Je suis une maudite sauvagesse* coincide avec la ratification de la Convention de la Baie James et du Nord québécois (1975) et les premières revendications territoriales autochtones. Ce texte se veut pour eux le témoignage d'un combat à la fois extérieur à leur culture et intérieur à celle-ci. A ce sujet, elle précise dans la préface: "Après avoir bien réfléchi et après avoir une fois pour toutes pris, moi une Indienne, la décision d'écrire, voici ce que j'ai compris: toute personne qui songe à accomplir quelque chose rencontrera des difficultés mais en dépit de cela, elle ne devra jamais se décourager. Elle devra constamment poursuivre son idée, il n'y aura rien pour l'inciter à renoncer, jusqu'à ce que cette personne se retrouve seule" (Kapesh, 1976, p. 9).

Tout comme chez Elizabeth Cook-Lynn, la motivation profonde qui pousse An Antane Kapesh à écrire est l'exaspération: l'exaspération devant la prétention des Blancs, les changements qu'ils ont imposés à la population montagnaise, les fourberies et les mauvais traitements dont ils ont été et sont encore la source, au moment de la rédaction.

Présenté en version bilingue, *Je suis une maudite sauvagesse* a d'abord été écrit en montagnais, puis traduit en français. Les deux versions qui se trouvent juxtaposées dans le même volume, laissent supposer que l'auteure avait au départ deux lecteurs cibles: d'une part le Blanc, à qui elle veut faire prendre conscience de tout le mal dont il est la cause et les Montagnais d'autre part, qu'elle voudrait inciter à défendre leur culture, à réagir et à résister à l'assimilation.

Très proche de la tradition orale, le texte présente une structure circulaire ayant pour noyau la culture montagnaise et tout autour, en orbite, neuf épisodes, indépendants les uns des autres, commentant chacun un aspect de l'acculturation autochtone. Basés sur des événements plutôt que sur la vie privée de l'auteur, ils décrivent et commentent l'arrivée du Blanc sur le territoire et la dépossession qui s'en suit, la découverte de minerai, le développement d'un réseau scolaire blanc, la présence d'agents du gouvernement, tels le garde-chasse et la police-montée, la police locale et les tribunaux, sans oublier les journalistes et les cinéastes (manipulateurs de médias), ainsi que la construction des maisons et les déplacements imposés à la population.

Tout au long du récit, la rancoeur accumulée se lit et se ressent. Elle ne cesse de dénoncer la dépossession territoriale et socio-économique des siens, les conséquences néfastes de la civilisation blanche et de sa gestion abusive. La pollution, l'immobilisme gouvernemental, le système scolaire: autant de problèmes prouvant à ses yeux l'échec des Blancs en terre indienne. Dès la première phrase, sa position est sans équivoque. Elle commence en déclarant: "Quand le Blanc a voulu exploiter et détruire notre territoire, il n'a demandé de permission à personne, il n'a pas demandé aux Indiens s'ils étaient d'accord... il songeait à les tromper" (Kapesh, 1976, pp. 13-15). Elle dénonce sans relâche la fourberie et l'attitude mensongère des Blancs, incitant les siens à reconnaître ces défauts et à ne pas se tromper eux-mêmes. Le coeur du premier chapitre est à cet effet composé d'un long monologue où un Blanc fictif exprime ses intentions réelles et rappelle constamment aux Montagnais: "Attention que je vous trompe et attention de vous tromper vous-mêmes" (Kapesh, 1976, pp. 19-23-25). Elle ajoute d'ailleurs dans un chapitre ultérieur: "Depuis que je vis la vie des Blancs, tout ce que j'y trouve personnellement, c'est le mensonge et l'injustice. C'est tout ce qu'il y a" (Kapesh, 1976, p. 167).

Fidèle à la tradition orale, elle exprime sa propre vision du monde par le biais des paroles de son père qu'elle cherche à se remémorer, tant pour légitimer ses propos que pour attirer l'attention des générations plus jeunes sur la richesse et la diversité du patrimoine autochtone. C'est par ses lèvres qu'elle commente donc la pratique de la chasse, la découverte du minerai, l'importance des croyances et des nourritures traditionnelles, bref tout ce qui constitue la civilisation montagnaise et peut être opposé aux pratiques blanches qui ont corrompu sa tribu et ses enfants. Il va sans dire qu'il lui tient à coeur de redonner aux gens de sa nation l'estime de leur culture et l'idée que les vrais barbares ne sont pas autochtones: "Avant qu'un seul Blanc ne vienne ici sur notre territoire, nous étions déjà civilisés. Depuis que le Blanc est notre voisin, presque chaque jour nous l'entendons dire: 'les Indiens ne sont pas civilisés'. Depuis qu'il est notre voisin sur notre territoire, nous les Indiens nous constatons souvent que le Blanc est moins civilisé que nous" (Kapesh, 1976, p. 129).

Ecrire pour elle n'est pas un jeu ; c'est un devoir et s'est aussi l'expression de son indianité. Autre raison pour laquelle son texte demeure très proche de la littérature orale. Le conteur y est clairement identifié, son style est court, direct et surtout concret. Les formules semi-figées y abondent et les répétions aussi. Elle commence par exemple son texte en disant: "Quand le Blanc a voulu exploiter et détruire notre territoire" et l'utilise au début de chaque segment du premier chapitre. On retrouve aussi plusieurs récits anciens inscrits dans le récit initial. Le temps ne se laisse aussi mesurer qu'à partir des notions d'avant et d'après l'arrivée des Blancs, c'est-à-dire avant et après la rupture de l'autosuffisance, comme nous l'avons déjà mentionné.

Si la description des conditions de vie imposées aux Montagnais et la sincérité apparente de l'auteure éveillent la sympathie du lecteur, il n'est pas évident, pour ce dernier, de garder à l'esprit que le texte qu'il lit n'est qu'un effet de réalité et une reconstruction du passé. Il y aurait sûrement pour l'ethnologue ou l'historien quelques inexactitudes historiques à corriger, mais cette question demeure hors du domaine du littéraire et un faux problème dans le cadre de cet essai, car l'auteur ne se réclame d'aucune vérité sinon d'une certaine continuité culturelle: "Avant que le Blanc nous enseigne sa culture, nous les Indiens, n'avions jamais vécu de telle manière que nous écrivions pour raconter les choses du passé... L'Indien n'a pas de livres mais voici ce que je pense: chaque Indien possède des histoires dans sa tête" (Kapesh, 1976, p. 37).

La lecture de son texte requiert donc une certaine distance par rapport au point de vue du narrateur, afin de pouvoir interpréter l'information selon des critères qui ne sont pas nécessairement identiques aux siens. Les questions d'hygiène et de propreté par exemple gagnent en signification lorsqu'ils sont interprétées sur un mode différent de celui proposé par l'auteure. Le fait qu'elle s'indigne de la réaction de l'institutrice de ses enfants, lorsque ceux-ci ont des poux ou encore lorsque les Blancs au bar de l'hotel ouvrent, sans mot dire, les fenêtres de l'établissement à l'arrivée d'une bande de Montagnais, laissent supposer que la cohabition culturelle ne dépend pas seulement de l'absence ou de la présence de bonne volonté.

De par sa forme et son contenu, *Je suis une maudite sauvagesse* est d'abord et avant tout un acte politique; une "Défense et Illustration" de la culture montagnaise où sont à peine mentionnées les conditions de vie difficiles et la misère qui étaient souvent le lot de cette nation, même avant l'arrivée des Blancs. Dans l'ensemble de la production autobiographique autochtone, il y a peu de textes qui soient aussi rebelles que celui-ci. Une exception peut-être, l'autobiographie de Lee Maracle, justement intitulée: *Bobbi Lee: Indian Rebel. Struggles of a Native Canadian Woman* et publiée en 1975 qui dénonce la même oppression et propose un renouveau du pouvoir politique et guerrier autochtone afin d'assurer la survie de sa nation.

Si An Antane Kapesh se distingue par son amertume et son refus de tout métissage culturel, sa production littéraire, tout comme elle en exprimait le désir dans la dédicace de son autobiographie, ne demeure pas un événement isolé. Depuis les années '70, plus d'une trentaine d'auteurs autochtones ont publié des livres en français (en tout, une soixantaine d'oeuvres) et une centaines d'autres ont signé des articles dans des revues et des journaux. De nombreuses femmes autochtones ont suivi son exemple, pris la plume ou choisi l'objectif d'une caméra afin de défendre et décrire leur cultures. Même si la critique anglophone canadienne ignore encore, dans l'ensemble, cette production et ne la mentionne ni dans ses études, ni dans ses anthologies, il existe déjà un document bibliographique, assemblé et édité par Diane Boudreau et Charlotte Gilbert, pour le compte du Centre de Recherche en Littérature et Arts autochtones du Québec, comportant une introduction sur la littérature autochtone au Québec, un index des auteurs, ainsi qu'une liste des maisons d'éditions, des centres culturels autochtones, etc.

Les efforts d'An Antane Kapesh pour défendre et faire reconnaître les droits de sa nation et par extension, ceux de tous les Autochtones, ne sont donc pas restés sans fruits: depuis 1976, les pressions exercées par les différentes organisations autochtones ont forcé le gouvernement canadien à adopter le projet de loi C-31, à reviser la loi cadre sur les Indiens, ainsi qu'à négocier une entente concernant les revendications territoriales et la participation des Montagnais à l'exploitation des ressources forestières sur leur territoire. Les vingt dernières années ont aussi été le témoin d'un transfert de pouvoir et de responsabilités en matière de services sociaux et d'éducation dans les communautés autochtones. Le fait que les femmes montagnaises se mobilisent en outre aujourd'hui afin d'exprimer leurs besoins, leurs critiques et de discuter des problèmes qui les touchent de près (violence, chômage, sida, etc.) sur l'autoroute de l'information, nous renvoie à l'audace et à la persévérance d'une Mère Courage montagnaise qui, par le biais de son engagement politique et littéraire a, la première, tenté de mobiliser les hommes et femmes de sa nation à se révolter contre un mode de vie colonial et à constituer de nouveau leur identité autochtone.

Dans la postface de son autobiographie, An Antane Kapesh déclare: "*Je suis une maudite sauvagesse*. Je suis très fière quand, aujourd'hui, je m'entends traiter de sauvagesse. Quand on entend le Blanc prononcer ce mot, je comprend qu'il me redit sans cesse que je suis une vraie indienne et que c'est moi la première à avoir vécu dans le bois. Or toute chose qui vit dans le bois correspond à la vie meilleure. Puisse le Blanc toujours me traiter de Sauvagesse" (Kapesh, p. 241). Après avoir lu son oeuvre, nous ne pouvons lui souhaiter mieux, ni croire qu'il puisse en être autrement.

Annexe
Informations générales sur les Montagnais

Montagnais
– L'appellation "Montagnais" remonte à Champlain qui a rencontré pour la première fois des membres de cette nation aux abords du Saguenay, où le paysage est montagneux et escarpé par endroit.

Innu
– Les autochtones de cette région s'appellent eux-mêmes "innu", ce qui signifie "humain"; à ne pas confondre avec les "inuit" (esquimo), qui sont de culture différente et avec lesquels ils ont eu des rapports peu amicaux, au cours des siècles.

Sous-nations
– La population innue, qui fait partie de la famille algonquinienne, est répartie en trois sous-nations, soit celles des Montagnais, des Naskapis et des Attikameks. Les premiers habitent sur les rives du Saint-Laurent, entre la Rivière Saint-Maurice et Sept-Iles. Les seconds sont établis au Labrador, alors que les derniers vivent au nord de Montréal, dans le haut de la Mauricie.

Territoire
– Ils appellent leur territoire "Nitassinan".

Population
– Avant l'arrivée des Blancs, on estime leur population à 10 000. Vers 1884, elle baisse à 2 000, pour remonter et se maintenir aux alentours de 16 à 20 000 aujourd'hui, ce qui en fait la nation la plus importante après celle des Mohawks. Il y aurait 13 000 Montagnais au Québec et 800 au Labrador; 600 Naskapis au Québec et 500 au Labrador et 4 600 Attikameks au Québec. – L'ensemble de la population innue du Québec est répartie en 9 communautés montagnaises, 1 communauté naskapie et 4 communautés attikameks. Au Labrador, il existe deux communautés innues: une à Goose Bay (Sheshatshiu) et l'autre à Davis Inlet (Utshimassit) qui ne sont pas soumises à la loi cadre sur les Indiens dû au fait qu'il aurait perdu le droit de vote qui leur était déjà acquis, lorsque Terre-Neuve s'est joint à la confédération canadienne en 1949.

Conseils de bandes
– Depuis la dissolution du Conseil Attikamek-Montagnais en 1994, il existe trois conseils tribaux qui représentent les Innus lors de négociations territoriales. Il s'agit de Mamuitun (Rassemblement) pour Les Escoumins, Betsiamites, Meliotenam, de Mamit Innuat (Gens de l'est) pour Mingan, Natashquan, La Romaine et Pakuashipi et du Innu Nation, pour les Innus du Labrador. (Depuis 1994, les Attikameks ont leur propre représentation officielle).

Langue
– La langue maternelle des Innus est l'"innu-eimun". Elle est encore parlée dans la plupart des communautés, sauf aux Escoumins et en partie à Mashteuiatsh. La langue seconde est le français, sauf à Pakuashipi et au Labrador où l'anglais est privilégié. Il est à noter qu'en basse Côte Nord, certains ainés parlent encore difficilement le français.

Occupations traditionnelles
– Compte tenu de la pauvreté du sol et de la courte saison de culture, les Innus sont traditionnellement des chasseurs et des cueilleurs. Avant l'arrivée des Blancs, ils passaient les étés sur la côte et l'hiver dans les bois. Ils se nourrissaient d'orignal, de phoque, de

saumon et d'anguille. Un faible pour les porcs-épics leur a valu le surnom anglais de "Porcupine Indians". Les Naskapis qui habitent presque la tundra, vivaient en petites bandes, essentiellement nomades et suivaient les migrations de caribous.

Histoire
i) arrivée des Blancs
− L'histoire des Innus est marquée par l'arrivée des Blancs et leur entreprise de colonisation. Intéressés à consolider leur emprise en territoire iroquois − elle se terminera quand même à la fin du XVIIe siècle − ils acceptent de s'allier aux Français. Ils espèrent aussi que cette alliance leur procurera des métaux et des fusils. Progressivement, ils adoptent une économie mixte d'exploitation commerciale (traite des fourrures) et de subsistance.

ii) exploitation du territoire
− A partir de 1840, l'octroi de concessions forestières au Saguenay et sur la Côte Nord, la découverte de minerais, ainsi que l'exploitation de la chasse et de la pêche de loisir sur leur territoire, forcent les Montagnais à délaisser une partie de leur terres, puis à se sédentariser (première moitié du XXe siècle). L'établissement d'un système d'éducation obligatoire, la construction de maisons et de dispensaires sur les réserves, ainsi que la distribution de pensions sociales, familiales ou de vieillesse accélèrent ce processus.

iii) Livre Blanc
− Après la publication du Livre Blanc, les Innus se mobilisent et créent le Conseil Attikamek-Montagnais, l'Institut Culturel et Educatif Montagnais et plus récemment, la Corporation de Développement Economique Montagnais. C'est le début de la prise en charge par les communautés des divers programmes fédéraux dans les secteurs de l'éducation, de l'habitation et des services sociaux.

Négotiations territoriales
− En décembre 1994, le gouvernement du Québec présente une offre globale aux Montagnais en matière de négotiations territoriales. Ne reconnaissant ni les droits ancestraux, ni le droit inhérent à se gouverner, cette offre est rejetée. En novembre 1995, Mamit Innuat fait néanmoins une contre-offre qui a servi de base à l'entente cadre de mars 1996.

Problèmes actuels
− Les problèmes actuels auxquels la population innue doit faire face, varient de région en région mais concernent toutes, jusqu'à un certain degré, le taux de participation qui leur est ou non accordé dans les projets concernés, que ce soit dans le domaine de l'hydro-électricité, de l'industrie minière ou des vols à basse altitude. En marge des revendications territoriales, les Montagnais cherchent donc à recouvrer un plus grand niveau d'autonomie.

− Depuis 1995, il existe un site web en trois langues, représentant Mamit Innuat et Innu Nation. On y traite de culture, d'histoire, de luttes politiques et des problèmes touchant les différentes communautés. Les femmes y sont très présentes, avec des créations littéraires et des rubriques d'information. La prise de parole montagnaise étant un fait accompli, elles se concentrent davantage sur les difficultés causées par l'exploitation abusive (chômage, harassement sexuel, déplacement prolongé des hommes, etc.), le développement du Nord par des étrangers et la fréquentation de populations blanches de passage (abandon des femmes, grossesses indésirées, MTS, etc). Les problèmes frappant les femmes autochtones sont nombreux et commencent à peine à faire surface; si le discours montagnais féminin a changé d'objet, il n'a toutefois rien perdu de son actualité, ni de sa pertinence.

LES PEUPLES AUTOCHTONES AU QUÉBEC

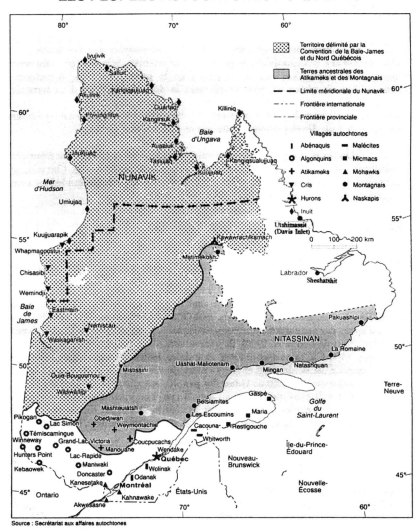

Source : Secrétariat aux affaires autochtones

Bibliographie

Kapesh, An Antane, 1976, *Je suis une maudite sauvagesse*. Montréal, Leméac.

——,1979, *Qu'as-tu fait de mon pays?* Montréal, éd. Impossibles.

Boudreau, Diane, 1993, *Histoire de la littérature amérindienne au Québec*. Montréal, Hexagone.

——,1996, "Native Writers of Quebec: Ignore no more," *Sshare/Erassh*, 4:1, (Printemps-été), p. 1, p. 8, 21–24.

Cook-Lynn, Elizabeth, 1987, *I Tell You Now: Autobiographical Essays by Native American Writers*. Lincoln, University of Nebraska Press.

Gilbert, Charlotte (éd.), 1993, *Répertoire bibliographique: Auteurs amérindiens du Québec*. CRLAAQ.

Godard, Barbara T., 1985, "Talking About Ourselves: The Literary Production of Native Women in Canada," in: *CRIAW Reader*, 1992, Ottawa, 49–108.

Lamothe, Arthur (dir.), 1991, *Archives culture amérindienne*. Production Ateliers Audiovisuels du Québec, Documents 45–46–47.

Maracle, Lee, 1975, *Bobbi Lee: Indian Rebel. Struggles of a Native Canadian Woman*. Sterling, Liberation Support Movement Press.

Ruppert, James, 1995, *Mediation in Contemporary Native American Fiction*. Norman, University of Oklahoma Press.

Sand, Kathleen M., 1991, *American Indian Women: A Guide to Research*. New York, Garland Publishing.

Vincent, Sylvie, 1983, "Mistamaninuesh au temps de la mouvance," *Recherches amérindiennes au Québec*, 12:4, 243–253.

——,1975, "L'espace montagnais non pas pays mais peau de chagrin," *Recherches amérindiennes au Québec*, 5, 4–5.

Zumthor, Paul, 1983, *Introduction à la poésie orale*. Paris, Seuil.

"We Appear Silent To People Who Are Deaf To What We Say": Women of Colour Speak Out

Pamela Z. Dube

> We form our alliances as sisters by creating a group who are strangers; but each group shifts and interacts with others, refuses to remain constant or reliable.
> (Patricia Duncker, *Sisters and Strangers*, 1992)

> Your silence will not protect you [...] it is not difference which immobilizes us, but silence.
> (Audre Lorde, *Sister Outsider*, 1984)

The aim of this paper is to explore the interaction and the limits of sisterhood among the various groups within (and outside of) the Women's Movement of the 1980s in Canada. By voicing their complaint against the Women's Movement's preoccupation with gender as the sole determinant of women's oppression, women of colour made a relevant contribution to the awareness of the interlocking structures of gender, class and race. Subsequently the concept of shared sisterhood and solidarity of women's community forming the foundation of the radical feminist movement of the early 1970s and generally regarded as providing, "both a refuge *from* and a challenge *to* the oppressive facets of a patriarchal society" (Palmer, 1989, p. 126) had to be questioned. The attention paid to the common aspects of female experience by virtue of gender had to be diverted to the specificity of women's individual circumstances in terms of class, race as well as sexual orientation. Since this discussion, by virtue of referring to 'women of colour' draws attention primarily to the issue of race and seems to suggest 'otherness', the term, "women of colour" whose complexity and ambiguity have provoked political popularity needs to be briefly explored. Saloni Mathur's essay, "bell hooks Called me a 'Woman of Colour'" will provide a basis for exploring this term and its complexities. Mathur in this essay initially reflects on this term with ambivalence, attempts to distinguish between the Canadian and American contexts for this term and seeks to locate herself as a "middle class woman of South Asian origin, born in India and raised in Canada" (in: Silvera, 1994, p. 273). She asserts:

> Initially implicit in the term "women (or people) of colour" was an attempt to gain visibility in the blanched universe of a dominant Euro-Western society. But it has become a hyper-visible term, made into a commodity and slightly over-determined. One of the effects within feminism has been the creation of a dubious dichotomy that posits the category of "white women" in opposition to those who are presumably "of colour"[...] Often it has been used to identify otherness in a way that lumps it together, in a familiar inventory of "other," with terms such as "gay," "lesbian," "working class women." Even more often it is posited as a singular opposition: white feminists versus women of colour. As a category, then, "women of colour" has become increasingly constructed as the "other" to feminism, replacing earlier formulations in which the "other" was Men [...] (in: Silvera, 1994, p. 277)

Thus for Mathur questions such as what such a formulation signifies or serves, how this otherness is "being inscribed and reproduced, and whose interests does it ultimately serve?" need to be looked into, and examined whether, as Chela Sandoval has asked provocatively, women of colour are, in fact, being "othered," seperated, segregated in feminism for the safety of white women (ibid.). Furthermore, she belives that the reluctance of most people of colour to being classified as such is part of a fear that "one's individual history and one's experience of being on the cultural periphery will become erased under the rhetoric of chromatic solidarity" (p. 278). Therefore, Mathur's criticism of the term basically lies in how while the category "women of colour" is used to privilege difference and multiplicity, "it does this through provisional contexts, by marking an essential conceptual unity...It is this particular reliance on essentialist definitions that was (and still is) the source of my discomfort" (p. 284). However, arguments from Diana Fuss' *Essentially Speaking* (1989) on how "the radicality or conservatism of essentialism depends, to a significant degree, on *who* is utilizing it, *how* it is deployed, and *where* its effects are concentrated," as well as Gayatri Spivak's recognition of a historical reliance on essentialism within feminism and the irreducibility of this moment in any given discourse, contribute to Mathur's conclusion that "'Women' or 'women of colour' can occupy these categories within a specific social field, remembering that the context defines its political effectiveness" (p. 285). In line with Spivak's belief that one "*cannot not* be an essentialist" Mathur presents an argument for a strategic use of essentialist claims for political ends and re-emphasizes that:

> ...the tensions within the concept "woman of colour" do not call for its dismissal. On the contrary, the many ambiguous meanings it can have demonstrates that, at the very least, it is an important site for a strategic politics. It is on these terms that "women of colour" continually need to interrogate their place and function in feminist discourse, need to look at the political implications of "naming" their experience and need to persistently expose the social and ideological contexts within which their names, labels and categories of identity are produced. (p. 287)

While this paper acknowledges the contradictions and complexities implied in the umbrella term "women of colour" and by no means suggests a kind of uniformity in these women's individual experiences as opposed to white women's experiences (which also obviously are not necessarily uniform), it nevertheless seeks to address the common struggle shared by various women of colour as the "other" in various situations of not only racial, but also gender, class and sexual politics. Makeda Silvera in the introduction to *The Other Woman* (1984) referring to the subtitle of this book *(Women of Colour in Contemporary Canadian Literature)* also confirms:

> "Women of colour" is a much debated term. After all, names have been imposed on us, and since colonialism we have been fighting to name ourselves. Some think the term "women of colour" shouldn't exist, that people should be named specifically [...]that view makes it harder to wage common struggle. I think of the term as a large, colourful quilt, a resting place, a place to form alliances. I do not think of it as where we live, as really our home. But I also don't think that calling ourselves "women of colour" diminishes the identity or power of any of us or that makes us invisible. We know who we are: women of the First Nations, South Asians, African Canadian, East Asians, Indo Caribbean, Afro Caribbean, Latin American, Japanese Canadian, Black, Chinese Canadian, African ... (Silvera, 1994, p. x)

However, the reference to women of colour in this paper will purposely exclude women from the aboriginal First Nations People of Canada. While First Nations women and other women of colour obviously interact at many levels and share a number of common problems in terms of racial, class, sexual orientation, gender discrimination, and triple oppression and exploitation from the men of their own race as well as from the men *and* women of the dominant white race, their story deserves a broader space of its own that explores the historical traces of their subjection to colonial domination and their strategies of survival. A variety of examples depicting this theme of the limits of sisterhood and/or interaction and shared experiences among women in Canada will be drawn primarily from poetry, symposium discussions, interviews and essays by or about women in Canada. As a starting point then, while this discussion will not look at First Nations women's situation in detail, this shared common experience and interaction among people of colour and First Nations people is shown in the following lines from Maxine Tyne's *Chameleon Silence* (1987):

> I feel very Indian tonight
> very Micmac
>   Kuakiutl
>   Huron
> and Black
> my tongue growing back 200, 500 years.
> I speak in beauty
> the truth of earth and sky
> virgin breath of
> who I am
> what I feel
> (*Fire on the water*, vol.2, 1992, p. 75)

Evidently immigrant and Canadian-born women of colour each deserve a space of their own too as cultural and historical specifics cannot be ignored. There is no homogeneous block of issues which necessarily have the same concerns, but for the purposes of this discussion it is worth exploring the common grounds of their shared sense of displacement, as well as immigrant experience from those people of colour who are of immigrant generations. It is this sense of displacement which serves as a catalyst for reaffirmation of similar kinds of consciousness, for instance, the heritage and solidarity on the basis of race or skin colour which exposes the non-white Canadian as a visible minority. A sense of pride and celebration of uniqueness in being a visible minority is evident in the following lines from Maxine Tynes:

> We wear our skin like a fine fabric
> we people of colour
> brown black tan coffee coffee cream ebony...
> we wear our skin like a map
> chart my beginning by my colour
> chart my beginning by my profile
> read the map of my heritage in
> my face

my skin
(1980, ibid. p. 74)

Furthermore, this sense of alienation or unbelonging, is also often perpetuated by the constant remarks from white Canadians as expressed in the complaint and warning in Dionne Brand's *Winter Epigrams*:

If one more person I meet
in an elevator in july says to me
'Is it hot enough for you?'
or when standing, cold, at a car stop in november,
'How could you leave your lovely sunny country?'
I will claw his face and cut out his tongue.
(in: Elliott, *Other Voices: Writings by Blacks in Canada*, 1985, p. 14)

One of the most distinctive features reflected in a number of fictional, poetical, theatrical, autobiographical and critical works by women of colour is the interplay between various feminist theories and their practical application to the cultural specifics and individual demands of each group within the larger arena of the Women's Movement comprising mainly of white women. Subsequently there have been on-going subdivisions and modifications of labels deemed to be politically correct and accurate enough to address specific group demands. These labels or categorizations, for example have ranged beyond the ideas of radical feminism that confine women issues solely within the politics of gender oppression to distinctive separatist terms such as, among others, 'Radical' and 'Political' Lesbians, and culminating in somewhat either woman-identifying or extremely separatist concepts, depending on the way one looks at them, implied in terms like Womanism. Although this paper concentrates mainly on poetry, most other literary works by women of colour also seek to redress the imbalance in the politics of representation within the Women's Movement. As Makeda Silvera, Nila Gupta, Himani Bannerji, Dionne Brand and Prabha Khosla who guest edited the 16th issue of *Fireweed* in 1983, on Women of Colour, after a year and a half of fruitless attempts to convince the members of *Fireweed* collective to allow them to work on an issue on women of colour, confirm that they edited this issue "first to reach out to women of colour and second, to educate white feminists" (Editorial, *Fireweed*, 1983, p. 6). The editors assert that this particular issue was 'herstoric' in Canada as it was the first of its kind to be published. For contributions to this issue the editors did not look at one target group of women of colour but distributed flyers and letters of invitation to writers and non-writers from all over the country; to feminist publications, various community organisations of women of colour, prisons, "in shopping areas, laundromats, restaurants, book stores, day care centres, universities and other places where women of colour are to be found" (ibid. p. 7). This successful search for contributions to this issue served to create a space for recognition of the women of colour's voices, to erase the invisibility and the stereotype belief in the silence of women of colour; as the editors state in their challenging accusation, "We Appear/ Silent/ To People/ Who Are/ Deaf/ To What/ We Say" (ibid. p. 9).

The general feeling among women of colour within the feminist movement has been that of exclusion or the refusal to acknowledge their presence; as Himani Bannerji asserts:

> We are made invisible in the mainstream. And there is talk about "coming from the woman's perspective, coming from the woman's standpoint." It seems to me very empty, this standpoint, because I do not know who this woman is that they are talking about. It never comes down to a specific group of women. They talk about women as a (sic) empty category. They will not talk about women as class, about a particular type of woman, about women as race, so it leaves you very empty at the end. (*Fireweed*, 1983, p. 10)

When addressing the issues of women of colour, when and if at all, the mainstream would deal with the concerns of these women in a token fashion, and refuse to let the women of colour have full control over the exploration of the issues that affect their lives as women of colour. When dealing with issues of women of colour they would accuse them of being silent; yet the women of colour believe white feminists, "have their own idea of what we should be saying and until we say those things they pretend to be deaf" (*Fireweed*, 1983, p. 11). Challenging the notion of the silence of women of colour and the refusal to acknowledge the presence of actively organised women of colour whose creative and literary works are not recognised, Makeda Silvera, confirms:

> There are many of us who write, they just don't want to read it; they don't want to publish it. Reading and publishing our work would definitely force white women to look at themselves, at racism, and at what has been laid on us for years...

And on the question of what then to do with a women's movement that is mostly white and tends to expose the limits of sisterhood when it comes to issues that concern women of colour and their under-representation, Silvera asserts:

> ...we don't want them to speak for us. What do they know about our oppression? I'm saying that they *do* have a responsibility if they claim that they are feminist and political. They have to struggle on all levels and *not* just around what is of primary concern to them. I'm saying that they have to take responsibility for their white skin privilege, take responsibility for the power they wield in this society. Do we have a woman's press? Can we publish our own stuff? Who controls the women's presses? Isn't it white women who claim to be feminist and "politically correct"? Well, if that is so, then they have responsibility to work to create a new vision of the world which includes women of colour. *(Fireweed,* 1983, p. 24)

Although there seem to have been subsequent attempts at including and involving women of colour in discussions or publications that deal with their issues, there exists seperate community based organisations of women of colour/ immigrant women's movements, and while solidarity work and interaction between the white women's movement and these movements does occur at times, the women of colour's movement feel it is incumbent upon them to organise and address specific issues that affect them. Taking time to look at herself, her experiences and issues that affect her as a woman, and black artist, Lillian Allen's *It's Not Apathy,* presents a picture of a worn out woman taking time for herself and indulging in the search for and assertion of the self from inside:

> I pause
> To ease the load
> Take a rest
> A quiet inbreathe
> Love a little
> Nurture myself
>
> Battered
> All these years Struggling
> Struggling physically
> Struggling mentally
> Struggling emotionally
>
> It's not apathy
> I just want to ease the load
> and take a rest
> Close my eyes for a minute
> (*Other Voices,* 1985, p. 5)

Himani Bannerji believes that the situation of black feminists is more complicated since they feel attacked by the society at large and this makes it hard for them to turn in their men, "yet, at home we have horrible relationships. These men not only have patriarchal values, but they take out the pressures from the society on us" (*Fireweed,* 1983, p. 14). So, these women feel it is appropriate to deal with this double oppression alone within their own societies:

> When you are in your own society with no question of racism or imperialism between the two sexes, then you can freely fight out the fight of patriarchy. But here, our fight with patriarchy is really compounded with the issue of racism. The women's movement here is historically unable to state that position, because it isn't their headache – except politically in an intellectual sense of the word – a moral commitment. At home, when they (the white women) fight a white man, they don't fight imperialism. (ibid.)

While women of colour are also aware of class divisions and diverse interests among people of colour as a whole as well as within the women of colour's movement, what Dionne Brand calls, a kind of feminist nationalism (*Fireweed,* p. 15), the shared experience of racial injustice provides for formation of a coherent voice. Therefore any woman of colour analyzes her situation in the world beyond the point of being a woman, as Brand asserts; "we cannot analyze the world as though men of colour are not oppressed too, because that way of analyzing the world gives us no way out of it" (ibid.). Using their community based women's movements as a mouthpiece, women of colour strive to revive the spirit of fellowship, share their experiences through various political or cultural, creative and literary activities and affirm their strength in unity. They also seek to have their voices heard by forming small presses for publication and documentation of their work, and they do guest editing in journals and anthologies seeking to address their issues[1]. Language seems to play an important role as an aspect of assertion of identity, and/ or as a means to combat tyranny and control since nationhood, racism, class and sexism are intertwined in the official languages. As Andrea Fatona in *diaspora* comments:

> Language is located as one of the most powerful sites where class, racial and gender privileges are embedded in its syntaxes and become institutionalized. Myths of difference are shrouded and coded in language as metaphors and metonyms, hence facilitating the propagation and mediation of a Western world view. (Fatona, *diaspora,* 1993, p. 24)

However it is not necessarily only an act of resistance against the inherent power relations in "master's" language that paves the way for some works to be written in Creole or Patois, and others to include bits of the vernacular language of the writer. The intentions could vary from the need to reinforce one's own cultural memory for construction of self identity to mere exploration and exploitations of the power inherent in language, for instance the often polemic recognition of difference or 'otherness'. Afua Cooper, in the spirit of women's strengths celebrates women in the following lines of "A New Creation:"

> She wail an bawl
> as she destroy but
> she create again
> she wail and shriek
> as she bring forth
> a new being/ a new way to be
> a new way of thinking
> a new understanding
> a new creation
> (*The Skin On Our Tongues*, 1993, p. 25)

Theresa Lewis' "Motherhood" does not just celebrate birth and the ambiguity of a mother's joy and pride in giving birth to a baby boy, but also raises the questions on the cultural stereotypes of gender and patriarchy, especially as traditionally held and reinforced by both men and women of her own society:

> Her eyes were shining brightly
> A glow was stretched
> around her skin-tight face
>
> She laughed out brashly
> when they said
> 'You've had a boy'
>
> A boy? she queried wildly
> (as though the specie
> had a dozen kinds)
>
> A boy... a boy?
> She laughed again in wonder
> But when they placed him
> in her arms

> she cried
> and cried
> and cried!
> (*Other Voices*, 1985, p. 108)

This paper would be incomplete without raising another issue which unfortunately seems to always come last in any discussion of the heterogeneous nature of the Women's Movement in the 80s in Canada; and this is the growth of lesbian feminism. This issue posed another challenge (and still does) to the ideas of sisterhood and female solidarity as shifts started to occur between hetero and lesbian feminists. Exactly like the challenge to the women's movement on racial and class issues had done, lesbian feminists started to define their own terms beyond notions of universal sisterhood as their cause shifted and became embedded in sexual politics. For lesbians of colour the struggle went beyond discrimination in terms of race, class and gender to homophobic encounters, from all sides if not extreme from and among their own people. The demand for recognition and acceptance of lesbians as women beyond the static categories of womanhood is also evident in most creative and literary works by lesbians; and of particular relevance to their writing are personal narratives, testimonies or confessions in the form of poetry, short stories or fiction. The following lines from Suzette Mayr's "Love:Homosexual" presents a further problematization of the notion of sisterhood, not only on the basis of gender and race this time, but also of the struggle of lesbian relationships:

> Her name is Yvette
>
> She slips bright white thoughts into plain brown wrappers
> drives needles into walls to prove their points and kisses
> me straight on the mouth homophobia and all with thick
> brown lips and a thick pink tongue.
>
> I thought that it was through race we were related brown skin
> and all but I couldn't touch her. I thought that by tearing off
> her skin I might find more earth. Nothing but
> a hot bloody centre.
>
> How funny...
> (Mayr, *Oralanthology*, 1991, p. 39)

Evidently the problematization of all the already discussed challenging factors within the women's movement in the 1980's in Canada provided a space for recognition and acknowledgement of these shifts as essential, and either led to creations of networking and cooperative structures or to an adoption of an extreme separatist stance. Multiple other identity constructs that go beyond the normal partriarchal construct of "woman," a concept that implies a uniformity between all women, have had to be defined through theory, through various voices of protest within the women's movement to expose the ambivalence in the fixity and fluidity of categorisations and borderlines[2]. Ultimately, borderlines have to be redrawn, and naming and mapping remain in constant shifts between the need for identity with a similar group and being specified as an individual. Ultimately "colour" is not a unifying end in itself in the issue of women of colour politics[3]. So, the question of coalition politics, and if there is a necessity for motivation of a common point of view in the women's movement[4] in Canada can be addressed by pointing out that while a common point of view cannot be be always established due to the diversity of the women's experiences and political orientations, the process of coalition can nevertheless begin with learning to listen. And on the basis of the collective experience of women as being marginalised (according to whatever class category, racial and sexual orientation hierarchical order) it should not be a matter of one group of women "teaching" another about themselves but a question of all learning to listen to others speaking. The categorisation of women's oppression is evidently situated differently within different national, cultural and ideological frameworks, and as Mathur confirms "one of the challenges to feminist politics is to delineate a practice that shuttles between the necessary use of certain labels and categories, while simultaneously bracketing them for critical interrogation" (in Silvera, 1994, p. 287). Basically, the current recognition of the heterogeneous nature within women's politics in Canada allows for an on-going exploration and interrogation of the contradictions inherent in the approaches to the notion of sisterhood and constructions of feminist theory.

Notes

1   Incidentally, Sister Vision Press celebrated their 10th anniversary. This first autonomous Feminist press founded by two women of colour artists gave birth to Sister Vision: Black Women and Women of Colour Press, and has published a lot of firsts in Canadian literary history, e.g., the first Black woman playwright, the first anthologies of mixed race women, as well as first lesbian of colour and of writings by Asian and Pacific Islander lesbian and bisexual women. The editorial director, Makeda Silvera points out that even though "lack of money and resources, lack of publicity and a

general lack of awareness in society about the legitimate right and place for publishers of books by women of colour, often made the trip more difficult, sometimes even painful [...] when we look on this side of the ten years, even during the most difficult of times, we sustained the necessary amounts of humour and hope, and have managed to keep a business just above water, while nurturing writers of many colours and nations, many of whom were publishing for the first time. Our alliances over the years have been with Black, Asian, Mixed Race women; and Aboriginal women, with whom we have recently been working, as publishers and as a resource in their endeavour to found a publishing house" (Words from the Publisher, Sister Vision Press, Fall 1995 catalogue)

2   One recent example of this phenomenon is Sister Vision Press' publication of *Plural Desires: Writing Bisexual Women's Realities*, an anthology that emerges from an "anti-racist, feminist framework that links struggles against homophobia and heterosexism with other liberation movements" and includes themes "that explore the plurality and fluidity of desire and identity [...]" (Sister Vision Press, Fall 1995 Catalogue).

3   Carol Camper's anthology of works by women of "mixed race," called *Miscegenation Blues* (1994), confirms this by not generally referring to these women as "women of colour" but by specifying their primarily European and African/ Asian immediate background as of a "mixed race". Although most of these women do acknowledge their "white heritage," they nevertheless identify more with their "black self" which often has shaped most of their experiences in life. They do not see themselves in parts but as one whole and the paradox of this existence in two or more races is cited by Camper from Faith Adiele's poem "Remembering Anticipating Africa" in the lines; "crowds of children churning up the dust/ they chase me shouting/ white lady! white lady!/ at me/ a nigger for 25 years."(Camper, 1994, p.xix). These often very fair or light-skinned women feel isolated and mostly excluded from white communities either for being "partially black" or totally undefinable, or are privileged to some extent in comparison to black or dark- skinned women for being exotic, and by black communities for being too fair, for having caucasian connections and not coming from a totally black experience and for being priveleged by whites.

4   An example of the difficulty of a common viewpoint in the women's movement is evident in the interview by Makeda Silvera, Dionne Brand with Himani Bannerji, published in *The Other Woman* (1994). Asked how Bannerji relates to the woman's movement in Toronto, she admits having learnt more about women's experience; issues around violence, women and political economy, women's work, and the wonderful thing about these issues for Bannerji was that, "they showed there wasn't a cutt-off between our lives as we live them and thinking through intellectual lives." One controversy was that, "white women were feminist, but we were not. We were concerned with race, so we were anti-racists, but they were feminist. So, my relationship with the so-called women's movement is and was really quite complex. I did benefit initially from understanding just a general gender analysis, a kind of an inter/ intra-sexual analysis of patriarchy. It is reading Black women's writing that I began to fully understand the huge outreach of this something called 'patriarchy' as socially structured, state-organized organization of people's lives" (in Silvera, 1994, p. 197).

References

Camper, Carol (ed.), 1994, *Miscegenation Blues: Voices of Mixed Race Women*. Toronto: Sister Vision Press.

Clarke, George, E., (ed.), 1991, *Fire on the Water: An Anthology of Black Nova Scotian Writing*. Vol. 1, Nova Scotia: Pottersfield Press.

——, 1992, *Fire on the Water: An Anthology of Black Nova Scotian Writing*. Vol. 2, Nova Scotia: Pottersfield Press.

Duncker, Patricia, 1992, *Sisters & Strangers. An Introduction to Contemporary Feminist Fiction*. Oxford: Blackwell.

Elliott, Lorris (ed.), 1985, *Other Voices: Writings by Blacks in Canada*. Toronto: William Wallace Publishers.

Fatona, Andrea, 1993, "Distance of Distinct Vision," in: Peter Hudson (ed.) *diaspora, Black?* 1:1, Vancouver: The Point Five Cultural Society, 23–25.

Goto-Tongu, Hiromu/ Mathur, Ashok/ Mayr, Suzette (eds.), 1993, *The Skin On Our Tongues: A Collection of Work from Writers of Colour and Aboriginal Writers*. Special issue of *absinthe*, Calgary: McAra Printing Ltd.

Lorde, Audre, 1984, *Sister Outsider: Essays and Speeches*. New York: Crossing Press.

Silvera, Makeda/ Gupta, Nila (eds.), 1983, *The Issue is 'ism': Women of Colour Speak Out*, *Fireweed*, 16, Toronto: Sister Vision Press.

——, (ed.), 1994, *The Other Women, Women of Colour in Contemporary Canadian Literature*. Toronto: Sister Vision.

Mathur, Ashok/ Wah, Fred (eds.), 1991, *ORAL ANT interventing the text HOLOGY: a reading*. Calgary: Printcomm, Inc.

Palmer, Pauline, 1989, *Contemporary Women's Fiction. Narrative Practice and Feminist Theory*. New York: Harvester Wheatsheaf.

Über die Langsamkeit des Blicks in Suzanne Jacobs *Maude*

Doris Eibl

> L'autre appelle à venir et
> cela n'arrive qu'à plusieurs voix
> Jacques Derrida, *Psyché*
>
> Je vis en détail(s)
> Suzanne Jacob, *Le temps passant*

An den Überlegungen poststrukturalistischer Philosophie und feministischer Theorien der 70er und mehr noch der 80er Jahre ist die Fassade der großen Wahrheiten des abendländischen Denkens und deren Fürsprecher endgültig zerbrochen. Der in der Moderne seit dem 18. Jahrhundert viel bemühte Begriff der "Freiheit" des Individuums entpuppte sich Schritt für Schritt als Begriff, der in dogmatischer Manier vor allem die Freiheit des EI-NEN auf Kosten des ANDEREN bezeichnet, eine Freiheit des Selben, die das Andere stets auf das Selbe zurückbringt. Freiheit wäre somit ein Begriff, der einen unendlichen Regreß auf das Selbe, einen perpetuiert unkritischen Akt der Identifikation des Selben benennt (cf. Lévinas, 1993, S. 50f.). Die Begegnung des Selbst mit dem Anderen in den Konventionen abendländischer Denk- und Erkenntnismodelle[1] erweist sich als systematisierter Moment spontaner Selbsterkenntnis, als Akt der Assimilation des Anderen durch das Selbst, und, wie dies etwa von Emmanuel Lévinas in *Ethik und Erkenntnis* formuliert wird, liegt "letztlich [...] im Bereich der Erkenntnis [so wie diese gemeinhin praktiziert wird] eine Unmöglichkeit, aus sich selbst herauszutreten; [...]. Auch die überraschendsten Entdeckungen werden schließlich absorbiert, aufgenommen, mit allem, was an 'Nehmen' im 'Aufnehmen' liegt" (Lévinas, 1992, S. 46f.). Jede Infragestellung des Selben durch sich selbst wird von der egoistischen Spontaneität des Erkennens des Selbst im Anderen vereitelt. So kann eine Infragestellung des Selben nur durch den Anderen geschehen. Emmanuel Lévinas bezeichnet eine solche Infragestellung der erkennenden Spontaneität des Selbst durch die Präsenz des Anderen als Ethik (cf. Lévinas, 1993, S. 51). Der Sprache muß in dieser Infragestellung des Selben durch den Anderen eine besondere Bedeutung zukommen, was wiederum impliziert, daß der Andere zu seiner Sprache kommen muß, um seine Andersheit als anderes Selbes zu artikulieren und der tatsächlichen Vielheit der Seienden zu ihrem Recht zu verhelfen.

Die Jahre 1975/1976 markieren einen zentralen Moment im literarischen "Zur Sprache kommen" des weiblichen Anderen in Québec. Im internationalen Frauenjahr 1975 werden in Montréal die "Éditions de la Pleine Lune" gegründet, gibt die Zeitschrift *La Barre du jour* eine Sondernummer zum Thema "Femme et langage" heraus, wird in einer 'rencontre des écrivains' die Problematik "La femme et l'écriture" diskutiert. 1976 entsteht ein weiteres feministisches Verlagshaus, die "Éditions du remue-ménage", erscheint die erste Nummer der feministischen Zeitschrift *Les Têtes de pioche*, beginnt das "Théâtre expérimental des femmes" seine Aktivitäten, wird das im Kollektiv entworfene, feministische Stück *La nef des sorcières* uraufgeführt und erhitzt die Gemüter in der allgemeinen öffentlichen Diskussion über Frauenfragen. Louky Bersianik publiziert 1976 ihren Roman *L'Euguélionne*, der am Anfang einer sich erneuernden, radikal-feministischen Prosaliteratur steht, welche der Frauenliteratur im weitesten Sinne eine neue Dimension geben wird.

Das feministische Schreiben in Form der "nouvelle écriture féminine" wird in der Quebecker Literatur insofern zu einem wesentlichen innovativen Faktor, als sie der geradezu suizidären Entwicklung der formalistischen Schreibexperimente neue Impulse gibt. So ist etwa bei Laurent Mailhot zu lesen: "Après quelques années de langage pour le langage, ou de jeux de mots pour le fun [...], on passe, notamment grâce aux femmes à un nouveau plaisir de la parole dans et par le texte" (Mailhot, 1997, S. 214). Es scheint, als verdanke die Quebecker Literatur im speziellen den Frauen die Etablierung der neuen Gattung "Text", oder vielmehr des Texts als "Anti-Gattung", über die sich eine ganze Reihe von Transgressionen und Infragestellungen vollziehen; als sichtbarste zunächst die Infragestellung der Validität der traditionellen Gattungsgrenzen oder Gattungsdominanten überhaupt, indem sie Poesie, subjektive Prosa, theoretische Abhandlung und andere Textformen ineinander verschreiben. Louise Dupré betont, daß gerade in Québec "écriture féminine" und "texte" zusammen zu denken sind, "[...] pour se penser différement, en dehors de la rupture absolue, en dehors d'un intellectualisme cherchant la neutralité du corps, l'évacuation du sujet et du sens. Autrement dit: c'est principalement le féminisme qui a permis le passage de la modernité à une postmodernité, de la pureté à l' impureté [...]" (Dupré, 1989, S. 18). Vertreterinnen der "nouvelle écriture féminine" in Québec wie etwa, allen voran, Nicole Brossard, France Théoret, Madeleine Gagnon und Louky Bersianik bemühen sich mit ihrem Schreiben um die Bloßstellung des die Literatur dominierenden phallozentrischen Codes, der die Perpetuierung gegebener Gesellschaftssysteme zu sichern sucht, und führen in diesem Sinne die subversive Auseinandersetzung des Formalismus mit der Sprache als Grundfeste der "einen" symbolischen Ordnung fort, allerdings nicht mehr unter den Vorzeichen der Zerstörung des "einen" Sinns, sondern durch die Infiltrierung des "Einen" durch das Andere, wobei hier klar unterschieden werden muß zwischen dem vom "Einen" erdachten Anderen und dem hier relevanten Anderen, wie sie und er sich als Andere leben und schreiben. Durch dieses Procedere erarbeiten bzw. erschreiben jene Autorinnen eine Öffnung des literarischen Codes für das Andere, für das Reale, und vollziehen so jene Verunreinigung des "Einen", auf die Louise Dupré hinweist, wenn sie von einer Entwicklung von der "pureté" zur "impureté" spricht.[2]

Textuelle Schreibpraktiken, insbesondere die feministische in ihren unterschiedlichsten Ausprägungen, haben die Entwicklung des Romans seit Mitte der siebziger Jahre und speziell in den 80er Jahren wesentlich beeinflußt (cf. Frédéric/Allard, 1987, S. 8; Beaudoin, 1991, S.81; Mailhot, 1997, S. 216), denn, obwohl etwa die Bedeutung experimenteller Texte mit Beginn der achtziger Jahre mehr und mehr in den Hintergrund tritt, bleibt ihr ideelles Vermächtnis in seiner ganzen Breite wirksam. Wenn heute in Studien über den Roman seit 1980 als dessen Charakteristika Diskordanz, Öffnung, formale Subversion, Pluralität, Verspieltheit, Ungläubigkeit, Laizismus, Mißtrauen, Subjektivität, Körperlichkeit und die bereits zitierte "impureté" genannt werden, so sind dies nicht zuletzt Elemente des feministischen Diskurses der späten 70er Jahre und wurden durch ihn zum fixen Bestandteil des literarischen Begreifens der aktuellen Gesellschaft. Nicht selten diagnostiziert die Quebecker Literaturwissenschaft für die Zeit nach dem Referendum ein allgemeines "désengagement" der Literatur. Gilles Marcotte spricht gar von den jüngeren AutorInnen als einer "génération en deuil de ce qui la précède et de ce qui ne pourra pas advenir", von einer "génération qui refuse une conscience historique ou un 'horizon'", und wirft dieser ein Dahinvegetieren in einer "sorte de bonne humeur tranquille dans le malheur même, dans le dénuement, l'absence de raisons" vor (Marcotte, 1992, S. 26). Gilles Marcottes Bewertung der SchriftstellerInnengeneration der 80er Jahre mag auf dem Hintergrund eines nationalistischen Projekts wie der Unabhängigkeit Québecs seine Berechtigung haben. Für dieses bedarf es einer Identität, die sich über den nationalistischen Mythos "Québec" definiert und diesen in die Zukunft weiterträgt. Dabei darf aber nicht vergessen werden, daß im Rahmen eines solchen Projekts mit Diskursen operiert wird, die Anderes unter den Tisch kehren; und das, was Marcotte sehr negativ konnotiert die Verweigerung eines Geschichtsbewußtseins oder eines Horizonts in der Zukunft nennt, beinhaltet gerade in Québec Möglichkeiten für eine sich verändernde Auseinandersetzung mit Vergangenheit, Gegenwart und Zukunft, die wie jeder Prozeß der Loslösung nicht schmerzlos verläuft. Das fehlende Geschichtsbewußtsein ist vielleicht nur ein anderes, ebenso wie das Engagement der aktuellen Literatur und im speziellen des Romans ein anderes ist. Mit Sicherheit kann hinsichtlich des Romans der letzten zwei Jahrzehnte nicht von Ideologie konstituierender Literatur, sondern muß – mit Ausnahmen natürlich – von ideologiekritischer Literatur gesprochen werden, und die Form der Ideologiekritik, auf die hier verwiesen wird, artikuliert sich auch nicht essentiell in plakativer, didaktischer Thesenhaftigkeit, die gesellschaftliche und nationale Zukunftskonzepte entwirft, sondern über die gezielte Wahl von Themen und Formen, die Vergangenheit und Ist-Zustand der Gesellschaft hinterfragen und nicht selten mit beeindruckender Subtilität dekonstruieren.

Ich möchte an dieser Stelle auf Emmanuel Lévinas und sein Verständnis von Ethik zurückkommen. "Die Fremdheit des Anderen, der Umstand, daß er nicht auf mich, meine Gedanken und meinen Besitz zurückgeführt werden kann, vollzieht sich nur als Infragestellung meiner Spontaneität, als Ethik" (Lévinas, 1993, S.51). Es bedarf also der Gegenwart des Anderen, des Fremden, sei dieser nun Frau oder – wie dies in Québec seit Beginn der Achziger Jahre von essentieller Bedeutung ist – Immigrant oder Ureinwohner, und dessen sprachlicher Präsenz, um die Totalität des Selben infragezustellen, um der Assimilation des Anderen an das Selbe entgegenzuwirken, und somit eine ethische Begegnung des Selben mit dem Anderen zu ermöglichen.

Eine ethische Begegnung mit dem Anderen impliziert aber nicht nur eine Infragestellung des Selben durch den Anderen, sondern auch die Notwendigkeit eines überraschten Verweilens in der Begegnung mit dem Anderen. Wenn das Selbe dem Anderen begegnet, nimmt es dieses, laut Lévinas, im Moment des Erkennens in seine Erkenntniskategorien auf, absorbiert es, ordnet es ein. Vor dem Moment des Erkennens ereignet sich aber etwas wie ein Augenblick der Verwunderung vor dem Anderen. René Descartes spricht in den *Passions de l'âme* von der "admiration" [ins Deutsche übersetzt als "Verwunderung"] als erster aller Leidenschaften.

> Lorsque la première rencontre de quelque objet nous surprend, et que nous le jugeons être nouveau, ou fort différent de ce que nous connaissions auparavant ou bien de ce que nous supposions qu'il devait être, cela fait que nous l'admirions et en sommes étonnés; et parce que cela peut arriver avant que nous connaissions aucunement si cet objet nous est convenable ou s'il ne l'est pas, il me semble que l'admiration est la première de toutes les passions; et elle n'a point de contraire, à cause que, si l'objet qui se présente n'a rien en soi qui nous surprenne, nous n'en sommes aucunement émus et nous le considérons sans passion. (Descartes, 1953, S. 723f.)

In ihrer 1984 erschienenen Arbeit über eine *Éthique de la différence sexuelle* präsentiert die französische Psychoanalytikerin Luce Irigaray die Ergebnisse einer Reihe von philosophischen Relektüren, von Platon über Descartes bis Lévinas, in denen sie versucht, mögliche Auswege, Ausgänge anzudeuten, auf denen und durch die die Frau zu sich selbst im Sinne eines anderen Selben und so zu Selbstliebe finden mag, und greift den Descartes'schen Moment der "admiration" als zentralen Moment in der Begegnung mit dem Anderen auf. Sie fordert uns dazu auf, diesen zu kultivieren, diesen Kreuzungspunkt, an dem sich die Differenz zeigt. Luce Irigaray sieht in der "admiration" einen möglichen Moment des Ausbrechens aus der Umklammerung des Selben. "Die 'admiration' ist keine Umschließung. Sie entspricht der Zeit, dem Zeit-Raum vor und nach allem, was eingrenzen, einkreisen, umschließen kann. Sie konstituiert ein Offenes vor und nach dem, was umfaßt und umschließt" (Irigaray, 1991, S. 100). Sie ist der Schlüssel zu Wachstum und Entfaltung, welche nur durch ein "Festhalten an der fortwährenden Erneuerung von sich, dem anderen, der Welt" möglich sind. "Festhalten am Werden, an seiner Unberührtheit, seiner Antriebskraft, [...]" (Irigaray, 1991, S. 100). Um sich wundern zu können, bedarf es der Bewegung, aber auch des Verweilens, bei sich selbst und vor dem Anderen. Für den Menschen ist es von wesentlicher Bedeutung, in einer Geschwindigkeit zu werden, die mit seinen Sinnen und Empfindungen vereinbar ist. Um im positiven Sinne zu werden, muß sich der Mensch das Verweilen im Moment der Verwunderung zugestehen, muß er "hinschauen, betrachten – sich wundern [...]" (Irigaray, 1991, S. 89), muß er sich die Zeit nehmen, die Frage zu stellen, wer der Andere als Anderer ist.

> Wer bist du? Ich bin und ich werde dank dieser Frage.
> Verwunderung, die über das, was uns angenehm ist oder nicht, hinausgeht. Der andere ist uns niemals einfach angenehm. Würde er uns ganz und gar zusagen, hätten wir ihn uns auf irgendeine Weise angeglichen. Aber etwas geht darüber hinaus und widersetzt sich: seine Existenz und sein Werden als Ort, der das Bündnis und/durch die Resistenz gegen die Assimilation oder die Reduktion auf das Selbe. (Irigaray, 1991, S. 91)

Während nun allerdings Descartes auf den ersten Moment der Verwunderung den des Urteils folgen läßt, die Verwunderung zerebralisiert und ein Übermaß an Verwunderung als Leidenschaft der Jugend abtut, das durch die erkennende Vernunft in Kategorien kanalisiert werden muß, erdenkt sich Luce Irigaray eine Verwunderung, die andauert, die den Menschen in Bewegung setzt "in Richtung auf" den Anderen, den er streift und berührt, aber niemals ergreift und erkennt und somit auf das Selbe reduziert.[3]

Gemeinhin ist es nicht die Langsamkeit des verwunderten Blicks auf das Andere, auf die Welt, sondern die Schnelligkeit des erkennenden Blicks, der das "Umgehen" des Anderen und das "Umgehen" mit dem Anderen in der Gesellschaft charakterisiert. Suzanne Jacob gehört zu jenen Autorinnen, die sich den erkennenden Kategorien des Selben verweigern. "La lecture des textes de Suzanne Jacob n'est pas de [sic] tout repos" (Saint-Martin/Verduyn, 1996, S. 217) im Selben, im Erkannten, denn sie versetzt den Leser immer wieder in einen Zustand der Verwunderung, indem sie in ihren Texten selbst, den Moment der Verwunderung kultiviert, ihn in die Begegnungen zwischen ihren Charakteren einschreibt und ihn zum wesentlichen Bestandteil des Welterlebens bzw. der Lebenserfahrung vor allem ihrer Protagonistinnen macht. Die Momente des Verweilens in der Verwunderung, die es erlauben, Details und Besonderheiten und den Anderen in seinem ganz anderen Dasein zu sehen, sind bei Suzanne Jacob Voraussetzung für den von ihr eingeforderten Ungehorsam gegenüber den "structures de perceptions", die die Permanenz der "structures d'organisations" einer Gesellschaft erst erlauben. Von diesen sagt sie, daß sie nichts anderes als eine normierte Fiktion der Realität des Selben seien (cf. Jacob, 1988). Den Blick ihrer Protagonistinnen auf die Umwelt strukturiert die Autorin in einer Weise, daß man mit Réginald Martel und Christl Verduyn sagen kann, "[elles] voient le monde comme s'il n'avait pas été déjà fabriqué par d'autres et au profit des autres" (Martél, 1979, S. D-3; Verduyn, 1996, S. 239). Der Blick der Jacobschen Protagonistinnen entdeckt immer das Kleine, das, was man fast übersieht, das, was der ordnende Blick verleugnet. Der langsame Blick der Verwunderung ist somit selbst schon immer ein Akt des Ungehorsams und bei Suzanne Jacob Voraussetzung für ein positives, kritisches Werden.

Der von der Literaturwissenschaft wenig beachtete Roman *Maude* (1988) scheint mir den Jacobschen Ungehorsam des Blicks und dessen Langsamkeit besonders gut zu illustrieren. Was den Leser zunächst frappiert, ist die konsequente Aneinanderreihung von kurzen Sätzen, die wie Pinselstriche ein Portrait des Verweilens und Werdens erstellen, von dem man weder sagen kann, was es motiviert, noch daß es mit dem letzten Satz des Textes in irgendeiner Weise abgeschlossen ist. Die Autorin unternimmt auch keinen Versuch, die Psychologie der Figuren zu erklären oder festzulegen. Alles, was der Leser über diese erfährt, erhellt und verdunkelt sich gleichzeitig im langsam schweifenden Blick des Erzählers, der in Form der freien indirekten Rede bald den Blickwinkel Maudes, bald den Blickwinkel ihres Freundes Bruno einnimmt, bald in indirekter Rede die Aussagen und Gedanken der Protagonisten widergibt oder unabhängig von der Perspektive einer Figur beschreibt. Die Übergänge von einer Perspektive zur anderen sind an vielen Stellen so unklar, daß der Leser häufig erst nach mehreren Sätzen erkennt, daß der Erzähler die Perspektive gewechselt hat.

Der Blick als solcher wird im Text zunächst von Maude thematisiert, die ihre Tage damit verbringt, von einem Stuhl aus einen Flieder zu betrachten, um ihre Impressionen dann als Zeichnung auf Papier zu "speien" (cf. Jacob, 1988, S. 12). (Mit Maudes intensivem Betrachten der Lichtspiele im Flieder assoziiert der Leser mitunter den Beginn von Marguerite Duras *India Song*, der uns in eindrucksvoller Weise spüren läßt, was die Langsamkeit des Blicks bedeuten kann.)

> Maude est assise dans la chaise jaune, dans le jardin. Le jardin, vite dit, le jardin: un rectangle d'herbes mal rasées entouré d'une haie de troènes. Au coin nord-est, le cerisier. Devant lui, planté seul, le lilas. C'est lui que Maude regarde. C'est devant lui qu'elle se cale dans la chaise jaune. Maude regarde foncer les feuilles du lilas. (Jacob, 1988, S. 9)

Maudes langsames Betrachten des Flieders zieht sich als Leitmotiv durch den gesamten Text. Es gibt das eine Bild des Flieders nicht, denn er ist in jedem Augenblick ein anderer, verändert sich mit dem Licht – "[...] suivre le déroulement de la lumière dans le lilas, son enroulement jusqu'à la fin. Elle ne voulait rien perdre. Elle perd toujours un glissement, ou un état, une fraction d'un état des choses, au moment où la lumière se dissout, jusqu'à l'encre" (Jacob, 1988, S. 19). –, und nie gelingt es Maude, das eine Bild des Flieders in einer Zeichnung festzuhalten; sie kann sich ihm nur annähern. Die Unfaßbarkeit des Bildes des Flieders in der Bewegung des Lichts, die dem Betrachter nur im Verweilen bewußt wird, erhält vor allem durch eine Textstelle ihr besonderes Gewicht in einem breiteren gesellschaftlichen Zusammenhang: Die hochgewachsene Hecke verwehrt Maude und Bruno den Blick auf den Sonnenuntergang.

> Si le soleil se couchait tous les soirs au même endroit, on pratiquerait un trou dans la haie de troènes. Le voisin comprendrait qu'on veuille trouer la haie pour voir le soleil disparaître chaque soir au même endroit. Le voisin comprendrait qu'on est des gens ordinaires, des gens qui regardent la disparition quotidienne du soleil. Il cesserait de se méfier. (Jacob, 1988, S. 28)

Der normierten Wiederholung desselben Blicks auf dasselbe, sich nicht verändernde Objekt und die Suggestionskraft des Selben wird mit dieser Textstelle unterstrichen, und suggeriert gleichzeitig die subversive Bedeutung des immerwährend nach dem anderen Bild suchenden Blicks von

Maude. Maudes Art und Weise ihren Blick auf Dinge oder andere Personen zu richten, sich an das heran zu tasten, was diese wirklich ausmacht, hinter ihrer Maske nach den Abgründen des Lachens zu suchen, macht diesen zu einem ungehorsamen Blick, ebenso wie sie auch Blicke auf sich zieht, die nicht sie, aber ihre Betrachter entblößt (cf. Jacob, 1988, S. 24ff.). In jedem Fall stört sie: sie fragt, hinterfragt, wundert sich.

Eine zentrale Rolle spielt der Blick auch in der Begegnung zwischen Maude und Bruno. Um sich dem erkennenden Blick des Anderen – hier ist zunächst von Bruno die Rede – zu entziehen, versteckt sich Maude hinter der Maske der Zustimmung. Wenn Bruno Entscheidungen trifft, mit denen er seine eigene existentielle Angst zu überwinden sucht – z. B. indem er Bekannte einlädt, um Maude aus der Kontemplation des Flieders herauszureißen, weil sie ihm Angst macht –, schützt sie sich mit einem Ja, das ihre eigentlichen Bedürfnisse maskiert: "Le oui sort du visage, flotte devant lui, se rabat sur lui, se couche dessus, le masque" (Jacob, 1988, S.12). Wenn Brunos Blick sie von oben herab wie eine Order überfällt, verspürt Maude Angst:

> Quand la tête de Bruno s'encadre à la fenêtre de la cuisine, à l'étage, Maude a peur. Elle regardait foncer les feuilles du lilas, elle désirait qu'il n'y ait plus d'événements, quand la tête s'est encadrée, quand Maude a eu peur.
>
> Lorsque la tête s'encadre ainsi, Maude a peur qu'ils soient enfermés ensemble, elle et Bruno. C'est possible: comment savoir s'ils ne sont pas enfermés dans ce lieu, précisément, où tout reste ouvert toute la nuit, tout le jour, même lorsqu'ils partent ensemble faire une course ou vendre un dessin quand on en est là et qu'on n'a plus rien? C'est possible: comment savoir s'ils ne sont pas des aliénés. [...] (Jacob, 1988, S. 13)

Brunos Gesicht im Fensterrahmen erinnert unweigerlich an ein eingerahmtes Bild, an etwas, das sich als unveränderliches Erkanntes postuliert, und das macht Maude Angst. Sie erlebt sich selbst und Bruno als zwei Masken, die sich begegnen, einander in der Wiederholung des Selben entfremdet. "On ne sait rien de l'âme, ici. Maude disparaît sous la fenêtre où le visage de Bruno reste encadré" (Jacob, 1988, S. 18). Brunos Blick auf Maude lassen sie zu einem Bild erstarren, einer Maske der Zustimmung, hinter der Maude Müdigkeit und Aggression verbirgt.

Im zweiten Teil des Romans konkretisiert sich die Geschichte von Brunos eingerahmten Gesicht. Bruno erlebt sich bereits als Kind als Erkannter, Benannter, dem eine fixe Rolle in der Gesellschaft zugedacht wird. Seine Mutter, die Lehrerin, "l'inspecte de là-haut comme s'il faisait partie de son histoire à elle" (Jacob, 1988, S. 84). Unter dem wachsamen Auge seiner Mutter fühlt sich Bruno in jedem Augenblick erkannt, bekannt, und vergißt, ständig auf das Selbe reduziert, sein Werden. Alles für die Zukunft Mögliche ist bereits in fixen Bildern festgeschrieben, und Brunos Leben gestaltet sich zu einem Warten auf deren Erfüllung. Er wird zum ewig Wartenden. So wartet er auch darauf, daß Maude die Details ihres Blicks auf weißes Papier speit, daß etwas passiert, was ihn aus seiner Immobilität herausholt. Er selbst hat den Augenblick der Verwunderung vergessen. Zunächst will der den Leser und sich selbst noch glauben machen, Maude wäre der Grund für seine Immobilität: "Bruno aurait pu devenir chef d'État, mais il brosse longuement les cheveux bleus de Maude chaque fois que ses propres bras frêles pèsent trop à Maude. Bruno pourrait encore devenir chef d'État, on ne sais jamais" (Jacob, 1988, S. 41). Im dritten Teil des Romans wird aber klar, daß Maude sehr wohl alleine in der Lage ist, ihre blauen Haare zu kämmen (cf. Jacob, 1988, S. 97).

Der zweite Teil des Romans wirft auch ein neues Licht auf Maudes Maske der Zustimmung. Maude bastelt sich eine Maske gegen die erkennenden Blicke ihrer Mutter, die die Tochter auf ein Bild festlegen, das dem mütterlichen Narzißmus entspricht. Die schwarzen Brillen, die sie fast ständig trägt, werden zum sichtbaren Symbol für diese Maske. Die Rede ist von ihrer Mutter, wenn da zu lesen ist: "L'air de rien, ce gras sur les lèvres, ces jambes qu'elle étirait sous le coffre à gants, ces bouffées d'odeur qui s'échappaient du sac et du porte-monnaie, de la bouche aussi, finissaient par constituer un danger contre lequel Maude ne pouvait rien si ce n'était de porter ses lunettes noires" (Jacob, 1988, S. 72). Maude wird in ihrer Jugend zunehmend von ihrer Mutter vereinnahmt, und "elle glisse sans ses lunettes noires dans les avenues dorées que cette femme protégée par sa beauté, sa mère, ouvre pour elle" (Jacob, 1988, S. 78). Maude reagiert auf den Blick ihrer Mutter wiederholt mit plötzlicher, überdimensionaler Aggression, indem sie etwa einen Autounfall provoziert und ein Motorboot beinahe zum Kentern bringt. "Un matin, Maude a pris la fuite avant de céder au désir de débrancher sa mère et Georges [deren Lebensgefährten] en faisant sauter tout le système d'allumage et de sécurité" (Jacob, 1988, S. 80). Maude bricht in ebenso radikaler Art und Weise mit ihrer Mutter wie Bruno mit seiner, der ebenfalls eines Tages beschließt, das Weite zu suchen: "Un matin, il s'est levé. Un rêve lui avait durci la nuque à son insu. Il a plié les draps au pied du lit, il a pris la route" (Jacob, 1988, S. 86). Die räumliche Distanzierung hat aber das konditionierte Verhalten der beiden Protagonisten in der Begegnung mit anderen Menschen nicht verändert. Bruno wartet weiterhin darauf, daß man ihm sagt, was er zu tun hat, und prolongiert in seinem Verhalten den Wunsch, sich mit dem Selben zu identifzieren und von ihm identifiziert zu werden. Maude trägt weiterhin ihren "masque du oui", der ihre Wut und Sehnsucht nach Selbstzerstörung und Zerstörung des Blicks, der sie minimisiert, in Zaum hält. "Nous sommes tous les deux nés attachés devant des images destinées à nous faire croire que la mort était résolue, [...]" (Jacob, 1988, S. 109). Maudes Verweilen vor dem Flieder, ihre Verwunderung vor der nuancierten Bewegung des Lichts, entpuppt sich für beide als ermüdender Rettungsanker.

Im dritten Teil des Romans kommt es im Verhalten der beiden Protagonisten zu einer entscheidenden Wende. Auf einer Fahrt ans Meer überwindet Maude ihre Angst vor den Anderen, und Bruno sieht sich zum Handeln gezwungen, als ihn seine Ersatzmutter Laurence im Regen stehen läßt (cf, Jacob 1988, S. 97 u. S. 101ff.). Was ihnen bleibt, ist die Nostalgie nach einer nicht reduzierenden, symbiotischen Einheit, nach etwas, das vor den Bildern des Selben existiert hat, nach einer Existenz außerhalb der Bilder, außerhalb der Ordnung:

> Il [Bruno] aurait voulu être tout dans le monde, comme il était tout dès le début, avant d'être happé par les opinions arrêtées de l'institutrice. Il s'en est sorti. Il a touché à tout. Mais cette nostalgie d'être tout dans le monde, ou d'occuper entièrement cet oeuf qu'est le monde, ou d'en tenir une fois toute la connaissance, reste en lui comme un poids d'eau sèche au fond d'un puits au-dessus duquel, penché, il observe son propre vertige. Maude a mis sa tête dans sa bouche et il est devenu tout pour elle. Il se serait arraché les dents une à une pour ne pas égratigner la tête de Maude se baignant dans sa bouche. (Jacob, 1988, S. 108)

Die Sehnsucht nach einem symbiotischen Urzustand vor jeder symbolischen Ordnung kommt hier klar zum Ausdruck, gleichzeitig aber auch die Unmöglichkeit, diesen in der Realität herzustellen, außer in der Fiktion der Realität – Maude legt ihre Maske vor Bruno immer nur dann ab, wenn er ihr Lebensentwürfe erzählt –, oder im Moment der Verwunderung des Verliebtseins, was dem letzten Satz des Romans sein ganzes Gewicht verleiht: Ils sont l'un pour l'autre ce rêve qui n'aurait jamais dormi" (Jacob, 1988, S. 114).

Réginald Martel schreibt in einem Artikel über Suzanne Jacob: "L'auteur est à l'écoute, dirait-on de tout ce qui parait se taire, de ce qui semble n'avoir rien à dire, en tout cas de ce qui échappe à l'oreille commune" (Martel, 1984, S. E1), oder dem gemeinen Blick. Das, was dem synthetisierenden, normierten Blick des Selben entgeht, steht in Suzanne Jacobs Roman im

Zentrum des Interesses und dekonstruiert auch die Logik des erzählerischen Procedere. In *Maude* erweitert das Detail nicht das Ganze, sondern nimmt den Platz des Ganzen ein, disseminiert das Ganze in alle Richtungen. Durch die optische Vergrößerung des Details verliert das eine Ganze seine Kohärenz. Suzanne Jacob wird in Bezug auf ihren Roman *Maude* unter anderem poetischer Manierismus vorgeworfen (cf. Martel, 1988, S. K–3). Aber gerade darin läßt sich der Ungehorsam ihres Blicks erkennen, zwingt sie den Leser zur Verwunderung. Und ... "Die Verwunderung wäre die Ankunft oder das Ereignis des anderen. Der Beginn einer neuen Geschichte?" (Irigaray, 1991, S. 92), ... eine Infragestellung des Selbst durch den Anderen (cf. Lévinas), ein anderes Erzählen.

Anmerkungen

1 "Vom Anderen nur annehmen, was in mir ist, als ob ich von Ewigkeit her besäße, was mir von außen zukommt! Nichts annehmen oder frei sein! Die Freiheit hat nichts zu tun mit der launischen Spontaneität des liberum arbitrium. Ihr letzter Sinn liegt in dieser Permanenz im Selben; die Permanenz im Selben ist Vernunft. Die Erkenntnis ist die Entfaltung dieser Identität. Sie ist Freiheit. Die Vernunft ist letzten Endes die Erscheinung einer Freiheit, die das Andere neutralisiert und einnimmt; dies kann nicht mehr überraschen seit es heißt, die souveräne Vernunft kenne nur sich selbst, sie sei durch nichts anderes begrenzt. Die Neutralisierung des Anderen, das Thema oder Gegenstand wird, das erscheint, d. h., seinen Platz im Licht einnimmt, ist nichts anderes als seine Reduktion auf das Selbe. Ontologisch oder in seinem Sein erkennen heißt, an einem gegenüberstehenden Seienden dasjenige überraschen, wodurch es sich in gewisser Weise verrät, ausliefert, dem Horizont ergibt; in dem Horizont erscheint es, verliert es sich, bietet Angriffspunkte, wird Begriff" (Lévinas, 1993, S. 51f.).

2 Louise Dupré entlehnt hier den Begriff der "impureté" ganz offensichtlich bei Guy Scarpetta. Während er bei Louise Dupré positiv konotiert ist, bezeichnet er bei Guy Scarpetta einen Zustand der Unreinheit als "symptôme d'une crise, d'une fin d'époque" (cf. Scarpetta, 1985, S. 18).

3 Einer der zentralen Kritikpunkte in Luce Irigarays Denken wendet sich gegen das Verdecken von konstruierten Differenzen im totalisierenden Selben, das Differenzen nur immer dann enthüllt, wenn sie das Selbe als Positivum bestärken und so das Andere als Negatives, als Mangel erscheinen lassen. Gertrude Postl faßt dies wie folgt zusammen: "Das heißt das Selbe kann seinen Charakter als solches nur wahren, wenn es eine radikale Differenz konstruiert, diese aber nicht ausweist, nie explizit macht, sie im Verborgenen beläßt und ihr jede Möglichkeit einer eigenen Ausdrucksweise nimmt. Im strengen Sinn genommen handelt es sich dabei eigentlich nicht um eine Differenz, sondern um die Wiederholung des Gleichen, allerdings mit negativen Vorzeichen. Mit anderen Worten, die Frau wird zwar in all den männlichen Systemen als das Andere festgelegt, die Qualität dieser Andersheit steht aber immer in direkter Relation zu männlichen Qualitäten. Insofern gibt es kein Entkommen aus diesen Systemen –

das Andere, Abweichende ist nie in seinen je spezifischen Eigenheiten relevant, sondern wird immer schon als Ergänzung zum Einen konstruiert" (Postl, 1992, S. 124).

Literatur

Beaudoin, Réjean, 1991, *Le Roman québécois*. Montréal: Boréal.

Descartes, René, 1953, *Oeuvres et Lettres* (= Bibliothèque de la Pléiade). Paris: Gallimard.

Dupré, Louise, 1989, *Stratégies du vertige. Trois poètes: Nicole Brossard, Madeleine Gagnon, France Théoret*. Montréal: Éds. du remue-ménage.

Frédéric, Madeleine/Jacques Allard (dir.), 1987, *Modernité/Postmodernité du roman contemporain. Actes du Colloques international organise par le Centre d'études canadiennes de l'Université libre de Bruxelles* (= Les cahiers du département d'études littéraires, II). Montréal: Service des publications de l'Université du Québec à Montréal.

Irigaray, Luce, 1991, *Ethik der sexuellen Differenz*. Frankfurt/Main: Suhrkamp.

Jacob, Suzanne, 1988, *Maude*. Outremont: Éditions *nbj*.

Lévinas, Emmanuel, 1993, *Totalität und Unendlichkeit, Versuch über die Exteriorität*. Freiburg/München: Verlag Karl Alber.

Mailhot, Laurent, 1997, *La Littérature québécoise depuis ses origines*. Montréal: Typo.

Marcotte, Gilles, 1992, "Génération", in: Lise Gauvin/Franca Marcato-Falzoni, (Hrsg), *L'Âge de la prose. Romans et récits québécois des années 80*. Montréal/Roma: VLB/Bulzoni, 19 – 27.

Martel, Réginald, "La passion et la distance", *La Presse* (29 septembre 1984), E1, E3.

—, "Quand le maniérisme étouffe la matière ...", *La Presse* (14 mai 1988), K3.

—, "Sur le fil très tendu d'une humeur simple", *La Presse* (3 mars 1979), D3.

Postl, Gertrude, 1991, *Weibliches Sprechen. Feministische Entwürfe zu Sprache & Geschlecht*. Wien: Passagen.

Saint-Martin Lori/Christl Verduyn, "Présentation", *Voix et Images*, Nr. 62, 216–217.

Scarpetta, Guy, 1985, L'impureté. Paris: Grasset.

Verduyn, Christl, 1996, "'Être est une activité de fiction.' L'écriture de Suzanne Jacob", *Voix et Images* , Nr. 62, 234–242.

'When you are a new immigrant you are just half and half:' The process of becoming Canadian among post-World-War-Two German Immigrants

Christiane Harzig

During the decades following World War Two Canada embarked on a journey of recreation; in the process the nation redefined her "self" and her relationship to "others." Major social, economic, and political changes brought forward an altered societal outlook and a different perception of herself among the world's nations. Along with these changes came an ever shifting sense of her own identity. The change in Canada's population composition, the ethnic diversity induced by mass immigration, was a crucial factor in this recreation process and the 1950's and 60's were an important period of transition.

A new immigration policy, the emerging concept of a Canadian citizenship, and burgeoning ethnic communities were social variables operating in this process of recreation and the immigrants themselves were leading actors. Based on the narratives of post-war German immigrants coming to Toronto, this paper seeks to show how these factors were interrelated and how immigrants negotiated the variables. At first, these immigrants were confronted with boundaries created by tradition and cultural difference. In the process of adjustment, however, all participants came to reconfigure these boundaries, and more often than not they became more permeable. Listening to the immigrants' stories we not only learn about the immigrants' hopes and disappointments, their successes and failures but we are able to connect the public decision making and the private experience. Through their comments, insights and opinions we will gain a better understanding about the process of becoming Canadian, about the changing contours of "us" and "them."

In 1977–78, the Multicultural History Society of Ontario (MHSO) launched a campaign to collect oral testimony of immigrants. The Society employed more than fifty community researchers, who "tended to be either older people who had been active in the ethnocultural life of their community or recent University graduates who had not lost contact with their origins" (Harney, 1986, 8). The results of these efforts were, by 1979, "several thousand hours of oral testimony in more than forty languages," forming the basis of what was becoming the largest bank of oral testimony about ethnicity and immigration in North America (Harney 1986, p. 11).

I have used interviews from the German collection, which were conducted by two female interviewers. One interviewer had sought out only women who were loosely associated with the German School in Toronto. The other interviewer conducted lengthy interviews with men and women involved with the German community in the Kitchener/Waterloo area. Since the interview partners presented their stories from the vantage point of a broadly perceived middle-class background, "class" as an analytical category provides no means of distinction and hence is not considered in the following. "Gender," however, influenced their perception and we will thus be able to examine the gendered forms of adjustment.

Mr. K.'s account introduces us to the post-war German (male) immigration experience. His individual process of becoming Canadian may serve as an example. Mr. K. considered himself to be a "modern immigrant" because he came on a Lufthansa flight Hamburg-Toronto in February 1958, having paid DM 1,300 for his one way ticket (a little more than two month's salary). He had received his immigration papers -- he still treasures his "important white slip" indicating his landed immigrant status -- from the Canadian consulate in Hamburg after having been questioned about membership in either the Nazi or the communist party. "Reine Formsache," a mere formality, he would later recall. Because he was a tool and dye maker by trade, the consulate also supplied him with a number of addresses of metal shops in Toronto. The officers assured him that he would have no difficulties finding employment.

He remembers the thousands of immigrants arriving every evening by train from Montréal, laden with backpacks, suitcases and "Persilkartons" (the carrying device epitomising the ultimate migration/ refugee experience in Germany). They were met at Union Station by clergymen from every denomination as well as by runners and other scoundrels, trying to rip off the unwitting.

Mr. K. thought to be well prepared for his immigration experience: he had the address of a young German in his pocket, in addition to $ 200 borrowed from his parents, an English dictionary and some measuring tools. His mind was framed by pride in "having done it," having immigrated, that is, and the knowledge that he had to start at the very bottom. After finding room and board in the same boarding house as his young German friend he began looking for a job. Since the job provided by the Hamburg consulate did not materialise he checked out every business in the Yellow Pages starting with the word 'metal'. He was thrown out of his first job after a day and a half for being too slow, he flunked his first driver's test because he had failed to acknowledge the degree to which Canadians were law-abiding and self-disciplined people, but he relished in a sense of freedom, realising that he could live up to his potentials. Soon enough he was infested with the "Canadian virus."

Mr. K. found a job working 70 to 80 hours a week, earning very good money; he saved as much as possible by continuing to live in the boarding house run by a Swiss immigrant family; he enjoyed the Jazz scene of Toronto, which included listening to Oscar Peterson (envy on my part, the listener); he was not very impressed by Toronto's amusements, which were non-existent compared to Hamburg's Reeperbahn; and finally, he was able to fulfil a long cherished dream: he embarked on a lengthy trip through North America, together with two friends, in the proverbial VW Beetle. He returned to Hamburg with the intent to settle down but did not like it anymore. He found himself a wife, returned to Toronto, moved on to Kitchener, established his own business and settled down. Voilá, the ultimate post-war German immigration story. Mr. K. was everything the Canadian immigration policy makers could ask for: skilled, hard working, willing to adjust and – eventually – a family man.

Canadian immigration policy has come a long way from a British-preferred attitude in the 19th and early 20th century, to the no-Jews-need-apply-administration during Word War Two, to the multicultural, non-racially-discriminatory procedures of today. When, after the war, it became necessary to reconsider the immigration policy, one of the most immediate concerns was emergency measures with regard to refugees and displaced persons in Europe. A cautious broadening of admission categories was also discussed. In May 1947, Prime Minister Mackenzie King presented a statement outlining the criteria upon which Canada chose her immigrants for the next twenty years.

The main objectives of the policy were to make immigration an integral part of Canada's national development: immigration was to foster population growth and encourage economic development; immigration to Canada had to be selective and related to the "absorptive capacity" of the country; policies regulating immigration were subject to parliamentary control; and last, immigration must not distort the present character of the Canadian population (Hawkins, 92-93). This statement became the basis of the Immigration Act of 1952. Since it was not revised until the introduction of the point system in 1967, it was the law upon which most post-World War Two immigration from Germany took place.

Canada experienced a number of social and economic changes in the late 1940's and 50's, which made immigration a particularly crucial aspect of social development. The country had come out of the war with, on the one hand, increasing industrial output and, on the other hand a population development which did not keep up with the growth. During the 1930's a very low birth-rate and negative net migration, – more people left Canada, mainly for the United States than entered, – had reduced Canada's rate of population growth substantially. Though we know today that fertility increased again in the post-war years (baby boomers), policy makers of the 1940's had the numbers of the previous decade to draw upon.

Mackenzie King's 1947 statement and the Immigration act of 1952 were thus made and enacted under the strong impression that Canada needed more people to support her economic development and to sustain her growing significance in the international arena. Despite this urgent need, politicians maintained that immigration to Canada was a privilege, not a right, and thus the country could pick and chose who she wanted to let in. People could be excluded for moral reasons (homosexuals, prostitutes, common criminals), for security, i.e., political reasons (spies, traitors, members of so-called subversive, i.e. communist groups), for cultural reasons (peculiar costumes, habits, methods of holding property), or geographic reasons, that is, coming from a climate which would make assimilation to Canada particularly unlikely.[1] This last ground for exclusion was, of course, just a euphemism for colour and mainly directed against people from the West Indies.

It was assumed that people living in Britain and northern and western Europe would make "good immigrant stock" and thus this region became the main source of potential immigrants. In addition to "preserving the national character," immigration policy makers felt responsible to the labour market and "the family." The idea that only those people should come to Canada who would fill an economic niche and who were needed in the labour market, was to appease union leaders and employers alike; and the idea of family reunification and sponsorship ensured that the existing ethnic composition of the country was maintained. All these objectives, as racist and selective as they may sound today, operated in favour of Germans who wanted to immigrate to Canada.

Though restricted by anti-enemy-alien regulations during the first post-war years, Germans began to immigrate in large numbers as soon as orders were revised in September 1950. Of the approx. 74,000 people immigrating to Canada in 1950 2.4 percent were of "German Nationality." A year later the number of immigrants had increased by 163 percent (194,400) and the number of people of German nationality had risen from 1,772 in 1950 to 25,813 in 1951. That year they made up 13.2 percent of total immigration. Though total immigration figures fell slightly in the following five years, Germans continued to be a large part of this group, their share rising up to 19.7 percent in 1953, by 1956 it was down to 15.5 percent. During the mid-1950's Germans were surpassed by immigrants from Italy and together with people from the Netherlands these three groups constituted the largest immigrant contingent in the 1950's (Canada Year Book). Obviously the impact of German immigration in the post-war period becomes relativized by the rising number of Italian immigrants in the early 1960's.

This early post-war immigration wave was dominated by men. In 1951 only 35.7 percent of the adult immigrants over eighteen were female. In the subsequent years women constituted about 45 percent. A number of policy decisions, such as restricting assisted passages to male heads of families, and giving preference to the needs of the male labour market influenced the sex ratio.

In Germany there were visa offices in Hanover (1951-1956), Bremen (1953-55), Hamburg and Munich (from 1954 on), West Berlin (1955), Stuttgart (1956) and immigration headquarters moved from Karlsruhe to Cologne in December 1956 (Hawkins, p. 243). Immigration officers in the various European outposts had a well-defined task on their hands: they were to promote immigration to Canada vigorously among people who were needed in the Canadian labour market. Immigrants were to be young and able bodied, and they were to have family responsibilities. The family would help the immigrant to settle down and pursue stable employment. Assistance could be given to those people especially in demand (agricultural labourers); others received at least an address of a potential employer when they came to pick up their visa, after successfully passing a personal and health examination.

These were the ideas of immigration policy makers. Now, let us look at how the personal experience of some German immigrants related to policies designed by politicians and how these immigrants reflected upon their own process of adjustment to life in Canada. Not all interview partners in our oral history sample can recall such a rich migration experience as Mr. K. By listening to these interviews a number of key issues such as work, language, citizenship, social relations, "the old country," emerge. The ways in which women and men dealt with these issues, giving them form and content in their everyday experience ,will provide us with a better understanding of the relationship between "us" and "them" in the immigration experience. Being born and raised in Germany and living most of their adult life in Canada forced them to be constantly aware and reflect upon encounters and borders.[2] Their "Germanness" as much influenced the way they experienced Canada as their subsequent "Canadianness" changed their perceptions of the home country.

They all remember their first encounter with Canada, but the impression is not necessarily a key experience from which they interpret their future attitude toward the country. These first encounters truly were a mixed bag of feelings. Some immigrants, coming from big cities in Germany, were disappointed by either the urban wilderness or the village backwardness. They could not appreciate the Canadian vastness of landscape, but rather thought the three-day-train ride from Halifax to Edmonton boring and uneventful. The streets in Toronto looked all alike, the houses were shabby and the girls wore too much make-up and funny dresses. But the white bread was delicious and the fruit, – all this abundance of apples and oranges -, was straight from heaven. As varied as these first impressions may have been, all interview partners constructed their narrative around the memory that people were marvellously friendly and helpful.

Finding a place to live, seeking work and tackling the language were the next important steps in establishing a life in Canada. Buying a house in an agreeable neighborhood was something almost all immigrants aspired to and those who could draw upon the resources of two incomes were able to fulfil their dream very early on. Many ended up in High Park, on the very west side of the city. High Park once was a fairly well-to-do neighborhood settled by Anglo-Canadians, with medium size houses and small gardens. In the 1950's the neighborhood underwent changes: many Canadians left when immigrants began to move in. And the "Europeans" – Ukrainians, Poles, Jews, Austrians, Germans – turned it into an attractive neighborhood of European charm with stores, cafes, bakeries and well tended front gardens. This is how one interviewee recalls her first years in High Park.

Learning the language became the next major concern for the newcomers from Germany. Since most of them headed directly for Toronto and the very few who stayed in Montréal lived in the English-dominated quarters of the city, the French language never was an issue for these German immigrants. For all they knew and cared, living in Canada in the 1950's and 60's meant speaking English. French-English bilingualism was a far removed concept; German-English bilingualism, however, was part of their everyday life.

Many had some knowledge of English upon arrival, but soon they realised that their "School English" was not enough and that they would have to fall back on their own wits to improve language skills. One found a helpful employer who taught her the first steps, others visited night classes which sometimes offered more than they had bargained for -- one teacher just assumed that his German adult female student wanted to knit him a sweater. Since she dared not refuse him, she stayed away.

The issue of language developed along the family cycle. It confronted the children when entering school. They sometimes had traumatic experiences for not knowing any English. When they grew older and lost their German language skills, the question whether to send them to German School on Saturdays was debated. The issue arose again when children introduced English-speaking in-laws. Whether they were able to pass the language on to their grandchildren was the final question.

The ability to master the language shaped the relationship with "others" and had its impact on the well-being in Toronto ("When I came to speak better, I felt better"). Sometimes it led to a deliberate retreat from Canadian friends for fear of insulting them. The most important issue, however, was access to employment. Depending on the gender, better language skills were a means to earn more money (the male version) while the lack of language skills prevented them from applying for better jobs (the female version). Women, more than men, remained torn between retaining the knowledge of German and feeling comfortable in English. The issue was never resolved.

Work, of course was a very gendered experience. As we have seen, Canadian immigration officials tried to select (male) immigrants on the basis of skills and labour market demands, thus most of the men who have assumed some presence in our sample, either as interviewees or as husbands of interview partners, came with an address provided by immigration officials and an understanding that work was readily available. However, some were misused as strike-breakers or misinformed about opportunities in far away cities. But even when first encounters with the labour market were less painful, they were nonetheless disappointing. In none of the cases referred to here did immigration officials make a successful match. The jobs they promised never materialised. The men always had to, and were able to, find their own employment, sometimes with a little help from a friend, but often just through perseverance, guided by the concepts of mobility and opportunity. Obviously the supply and demand aspect of the labour market needed much flexibility and a more versatile definition of skill than policy makers and immigration services were able to foresee. German immigrants, for the most part, were able to supply this.

Witness the student of the University of Heidelberg who seized the first opportunity to immigrate in 1951. He was placed by immigration officials in Karlsruhe as a farm labourer. The government paid him $250 for his passage, the young man earned $40 a month in his first job and repaid the government $10 per month. Not surprisingly he left his position as a farm labourer at the first possible instance. In the 1970's, he was a professor at Wilfried Laurier University at Waterloo.

German women seldom came to Canada considering their working skills as a resource and in the female narrative of adjustment to Canadian life "work" did not take centre-stage. But they all worked in gainful employment and they ventured into areas they would have never dreamed of at home. That they would contribute to the wage earning efforts of the couple was self-evident to them, if not always to the husbands. Those women who were willing to work as domestics never had any problems finding employment. But there were secretaries, teachers, journalists and book editors.

When they sought work in their line of business the lack of "Canadian experience" mounted huge barriers. Here, the institutions of the German community, the two newspapers *Die Torontoer Zeitung* and *Der Kurier* as well as the German School could help. They provided opportunities to gain "Canadian experience." Other women drifted into employment, turning it into a working career only later on. Working "downtown" as a sales-lady, becoming a highly qualified manageress of a duplicating department, running a bakery store, working as a looper, (a skill so high in demand that she could fix her own hours and choose her employers), becoming the principal of the German School and later a teacher in the Canadian public school system – these are just some of the opportunities they pursued.

They had to learn rules about working in Canada: that it was better to show up in person rather than apply in writing; that pay raises were not awarded automatically upon achievement, but had to be asked for; that Germany's 9-5 workday and five weeks of vacation (of the late 1960's) were unheard of. But they also learned to rely on their own potential and realised quickly that their working lives could grow and develop with experience. They did not follow the German work pattern by staying with one company until the end of their working lives (though they may have shown more persistency than their Canadian colleagues). Much rather they seized opportunities, changed places, tried out new jobs, obtained different skills or – stayed home, for a period of time, to take care of the children.

They also enjoyed the informality of working relationships. Hardly anybody felt discriminated against as a German, though sometimes notions of traditional women's jobs prevented them from finding employment for which they felt qualified. Gainful employment was taken up when the family needed money – and more often than not things needed to be purchased (a house, furniture, a trip to Germany, a car) but it was discarded when other priorities were set. Even those (divorced) women who became breadwinners of the family remembered gainful employment as enrichment ("I love my work, I like being with the girls") rather than stress, with a never-failing notion of opportunity.

While these newcomers were busy finding a place to live, learning the language, and working, social life took shape in an immigrant yet Canadian environment. If we want to find out to what extent social integration took place we also have to ask: integration into what?

In 1961 the larger Toronto area had a population of a little more than 1.8 million, of which more than one third (33.3%) was foreign born. In the city proper the foreign born accounted for 41.9%.[3] Next to the British, the Italians were the largest ethnic group but Germans came in a strong third with 22.7% of Toronto's ethnic population and 13.6% of the foreign born. Unlike the Italians, who were a highly segregated and concentrated group,

Germans were much less concentrated, although they seemed to prefer the area bounded by Keele, Dundas, Jane and Bloor Streets, that is, the larger High Park area (Richmond, 1967, p. 6). In addition there was a large number of Dutch, Poles Ukrainians, Scandinavians and "Jews."

The history of the German community in Toronto still needs to be written in greater detail, thus I can only provide a sketchy overview of its outlook in the 1960's. In 1961, it supported a wide range of organisations and services. There were nine German church congregations, four newspapers, many German doctors and lawyers, and a large number of stores provided German-speaking personnel. Several social clubs offered recreational opportunities (Richmond, p. 28). Although the group was very dispersed it nevertheless was institutionally quite self-sufficient, and thus it should have maintained a high degree of ethnic identity (Breton). However, as a study conducted in the end of the 1970's shows, German Canadians in Toronto were the least likely to retain the German language in the second generation, they were the least (ethnically) exclusive in their friendship patterns, they were not particularly eager to participate in ethnic-group functions or to support German media such as newspapers or radio programs. However, they liked to maintain their German eating and cooking habits. In short, they were, together with English and "Majority Canadians," low retainers of ethnic identity (Isajiw). Yet in the 1950's and 60's, the German community institutions were alive and well and expanding.

In a society consisting of one-third newcomers it is not surprising that our interviewees associated mainly with 'non-Canadian' friends. Sometimes "Canadian" friends would be introduced when the husband invited people from work or children introduced marriage partners. By no means, however, did the narratives indicate that people were deliberately demarcating boundaries or segregating themselves. Neither did they move exclusively in German community circles. The circle of friends was more the result of availability. Still, the feeling of ease, of being more relaxed in German circles, this obscure but pervasive notion of cultural familiarity and belonging remained strong (Ignatieff).

This brings us to the last issue in the process of becoming: the vague concept of identity. People reflected on the questions of where home is, how to relate to the country they left and what they felt about the country they had chosen to live in. The concept of half and half, and a meandering sense of belonging, best captures their feelings with regard to identity, which has a private and a public dimension. The former relates to home, the home country and their personal perception of difference, and the latter relates to national identity and citizenship.

Germany, the place they left and the place they returned to when visiting family, is obviously no unified reference point. Some interviewees had left a small town in southern Germany, escaping class boundaries. Others came from the large city of Hamburg, which imbued its citizens with a sense of mercantile openness for the cultures of business partners (seeking "Auslandserfahrung"). Again others had left East Berlin and were treated "like a queen" upon return visits, yet another had been a refugee from Sudety, living in Munich before leaving for Canada. Needless to say, they all had a different concept of "Germany" when comparing their former and their present homes.

As diverse as their backgrounds may seem, there are two common vantage points from which they perceive differences to the new country: "freedom" and "tolerance." They experienced Germans in Germany as ill-tempered, intolerant, and even arrogant.[4] They have difficulties with what they perceive as Germany's more rigid concepts of class and propriety, with its structuredness and competitiveness. By contrast they enjoy the friendliness, tolerance and open-mindedness of their host culture, and feel less captured in gossip. All of them, and here the consensus is quite stunning, refer to the greater freedom when asked what they like about Canada. However, it is impossible for the researcher to extract the essence of this vague but all-embracing idea of freedom. It may be the vastness of the landscape, the opportunities related to work, the choices on the housing market, the informality in social relations, the political liberties, or – all of the above. Though the respondents are very firm on this issue – the answers usually are given unhesitantingly – even upon further inquiry by the interviewer they are unable to fill this concept with personal content.

Most of them did, and liked to, go back to Germany for visits. The desire to maintain family ties was strong. Though they claimed to enjoy seeing their families and to feel comfortable "at home," they were also estranged from the world outside. Germany had become a static picture, the beauty of which they enjoyed very much. They liked to visits friends and family, but they did not really belong. They adjusted for the time of the visit, they made compromises, but when they stepped off the aeroplane in Canada, they felt home again. Home also was defined as "where the children grow up." For this particular generation of German immigrants children were the most obvious reason to grow roots.

When looking at the public aspect of identity we notice that, unlike in the U.S., Canadian political culture does not offer a powerful notion of Canadian identity. As a consequence it is not very obvious what immigrants are supposed to "become." This is reflected in the answers of our interviewees. Upon the question whether they feel more Canadian or German they were not only unable to decide but also unable to resolve what "Canadian" felt like.

Since citizenship defines membership in a (nation) state and establishes rights and privileges, the distinction between "us" and "them" lies at the very centre of the concept. But despite its powerful implications, it has been argued that Canadians take their citizenship for granted and have not turned it into a source and symbol of national pride (Kaplan, Introduction). Since there are very few aspects that differentiate Canadian citizens from legal residents in Canada (there is no general conscription of Canadian males and today every resident is entitled to the same protection under Canadian law) opinion makers have difficulties to infuse the concept of citizenship with meaning. Often a Canadian is defined as someone who is not a resident of another country, a Canadian is *not* an American (Kaplan) – Canada's own version of thinking in terms of "us" and "them."

The political desire to create a genuine Canadian citizenship arose out of the experience of World War Two (Granatstein). The task was to design a citizenship that would neither offend those who did not want to give up their status as British subjects and at the same time accommodate the growing sense of Quebec uniqueness and patriotism. It also had to cater to provincial vanities. Aboriginals, however, at that time were a non-issue. The act that came into force in January 1947 defined Canadian citizenship by right of birth on Canadian territory, it set up rules and regulations for naturalisation procedures, it put British subjects on a (somewhat) equal footing with other immigrants and it gave married women the right to determine their own citizenship. An attempt was made to celebrate the new status in a grand symbolic act which was to help generate a new Canadian identity. The first Ukrainian farmer who settled on the western prairies was invited to participate in a public ceremony alongside the mother of a soldier who had died heroically in World War Two. Throughout the country ceremonies were staged during this official "Citizenship Week" (Martin).

It is almost impossible to determine what citizenship meant to our group of immigrants. The question, at what point, if at all, they took out citizenship has very little to do with voting, with exercising one's democratic rights or with the possibility to sponsor other immigrants.[5] Rather, despite its public dimension it was a very personal decision. Sometimes it was related to an event in the family cycle. When a new baby was born, a Canadian, the rest of the family may have decided to become Canadians, too. Or the German citizenship was kept for fear of forgoing German pension rights and claims. A daughter, who was described as "the most German of the family" also was the only Canadian citizen of the family. Most of them did not seem to worry one way or the other. There may have been this one point in life, where they thought it was the right time to make the decision – the baby, a job, any event. If this point did not come up, they lived happily without Canadian citizenship.[6] Citizenship, such a highly contested concept in present day debates about migration, to those post-war Germans was not an important issue. The attempt to utilise citizenship in the process of creating a national identity failed with them.

Due to the circumstances of the interview the politics of multiculturalism was something they considered as important. However, they also voiced doubts. On the one hand, they appreciated the opportunities it created for ethnocultural activities. They saw how the country as a whole profited from the input of immigrants. On the other hand they also believed that it had little to do with them as individuals. They had adjusted without receiving any support, nobody had guided them. They were pleased in having arrived. At this point they clearly had "become" Canadians, despite their feelings for the home country, despite their small regard for citizenship.

By way of conclusion a methodological note is in order. When trying to appreciate these interviews it is important to notice the number of actors involved in the show and the various historical times which come into play. First of all, there is the person who is interviewed, the interviewee, who reflects upon his or her first years in Canada. Then there is the interviewer who asks all these questions at the end of the 1970's; and there is the listener to the interviews, the author of this paper, who listens to the interviews in the mid-1990's. Each of them/us bring a variety of assumptions to bear in this plot. The interviewee has some notions about what the interviewer wants to hear; the interviewer has some preconceptions about what she expects to hear; and the listener, I, have some hypotheses I want to prove, some point I want to make.

The interviewees, the immigrants, came to Canada in the 1950's and 60's, they experienced their most active exchange with Canadian society in the 1950's to 70's and they are interviewed at the end of the 1970's. For most of them it was the sunset after a very crucial period in their lives, when they had to adjust to a vast number of changes. These changes, however, took place during a period of great economic expansion and opportunity in a country which, though sometimes unwittingly, needed to accept change, socially and politically. The immigrants interpret their lives, the choices they made, the opportunities they seized and the experiences they went through within the framework of this change-prone environment.

The interviewers, on the other hand, worked for the Multicultural History Society, which had just received a large grant as an expression of and in accordance with the policy of multiculturalism. They bring enthusiasm to their job, most likely being in favour of the policy and eager to recount a (successful) immigration narrative.

Listening to these German immigrants telling their stories has provided me (and hopefully the reader) with a better understanding of the relationship between the personal and the political; of the way people create opportunities for themselves within, or if necessary, outside the contours of political wisdom; and how the concepts of "us" and "them" are forever changing, depending on the respective points of view. It also made me realise how illusive the concepts of home and identity are, and how they almost defy any structural analysis.

The Immigration Act of 1952 certainly favoured immigration of these individuals but beyond that they were left alone, with enough manoeuvring space to make their own decisions. Having realised that the policy of laissez-faire best suited this group of immigrants, I am awed by the powerful sense of never-ending opportunities which was the prevailing attitude among men and women alike; an attitude fostered by the economic boom and beginning political liberalism of the post-war years.

The mid 1990's, however, the times in which I am listening to the tapes, is a period equally full of change, but changes of which I am/we are often fearful. Only very few people think of the globalising economy and the neoconservative demands for change in terms of expanding and growing opportunities for themselves. It is a small minority which profits and a large majority which is hesitant if not scared. Political uncertainties, unemployment, declining wages and horizontal rather than vertical career moves mark change in the 1990's. And as much as the post-war immigration experience was influenced by socio-economic conditions in the receiving culture, creating a large array of opportunities, the 1990's migration (and refugee) movements have to be seen in socio-political context of a globalising economy and exclusionist demands. For the migrants the results are painfully different.

Notes

1 See Immigration Act, Sect. 61 and Order in Council from Sept. 17, 1954. Corbett, pp. 41–43, 50–52.
2 The analysis is based on interview log forms: 3280, 6701, 0048, 6706, 6709, 1118, 5827, 6830, 5814, 0285, 6697, 6708, 6835, 5825, 5828, 1112.
3 According to the 1971 Centus Metro Toronto continued to have a majority of "British Stock," whereas the city of Toronto has a non-British majority.
4 "Many Germans think they know better and do better. You act like that for a year, than you realize that the Canadian way of doing things is good, too, than you stop criticizing."
5 Richmond (p. 28) pointed out that very few Germans, in this wave of immigration, came under the sponsorship programme.
6 Surprisingly, the question of travel never arises in this context. Most of them travel frequently between Germany and Canada, sometimes to the U.S., but hardly anywhere else. Thus the question of passports and visas does not come up.

References

Raymond Breton, 1964, "Institutional Completeness of Ethnic Communities and the Personal Relations of Immigrants," *American Journal of Sociology*, 70, 193-205.

Canada Year Book, 1947-1957, Ottawa, Queens Printer.

Corbett, David C., 1957, *Canada's Immigration Policy: A Critique*. Toronto: University of Toronto Press.

Fulford, Robert, 1993, "A Post-Modern Dominion: The Changing Nature of Canadian Citizenship," in: Kaplan, *Belonging*, 104-119.

Granatstein, J.L., 1993. "The "Hard" Hobligations of citizenship: the Second World War in Canada," in: Kaplan, *Belonging*, 36-49.

Harney, Robert, 1984, "Toronto's People," *Polyphony* 6:1, 1-14.

——, 1987, "History of the Multicultural History Society," *Polyphony* 9:1, 1-16.

Hawkins, Freda, 1988 (1972), *Canada and Immigration: Public Policy and Public Concern*. Kingston: McGill-Queen's University Press.

Ignatieff, Micheal, 1993, *Blood and Belonging: Journey into the New Nationalism*. Toronto: Viking.

Isajiw, Wsevolog W., 1990, "Ethnic Identity Retention," in: Raymond Breton, Wsevolod W. Isajiw, Warren E. Kalbach, Jeffrey G. Reitz, (eds.), *Ethnic Identity and Equality: Varieties of Experience in a Canadian City*. Toronto: University of Toronto Press, 34-91.

Kaplan, William, (ed.), 1993, *Belonging. The Meaning and Future of Canadian Citizenship*. Montréal, Kingston: McGill-Queens.

Martin, Paul, 1993, "Citizenship and the People's Word," in: Kaplan, *Belonging*, 64-78.

Richmond, Anthony H., 1967, *Immigrants and Ethnic Groups in Metropolitan Toronto*. York University: Institute for Behavioural Research.

Whitaker, Reg, 1987, *Double Standard: The Secret History of Canadian Immigration*. Toronto: Lester and Orpen Dennys Ltd.

Vision und Transgression – "La femme au volant" in Monique Proulx' *Le sexe des étoiles*

Ulrike C. Lange / Marion Schomakers

> "Etre soi, c'est incarner ce qui n'eut jamais lieu d'exister. À partir de l'instant que la poésie comprend qu'elle *sera en avant* ou ne sera plus, elle devient philosophie de la création. Avec sa puissance d'utopie, la poésie entre dans son âge politique."
> Claire Lejeune, *Le livre de la sœur*

> "Où exactement, dans quelles cellules précises du cerveau l'identité sexuelle des individus s'imprime-t-elle? Le savez-vous? [...] Moi, je ne le sais pas, et pourtant, j'ai été un grand scientifique, j'ai fouillé dans l'infiniment petit. Qu'est-ce qui fait que l'on SAIT que l'on est un homme, ou une femme, les attributs physiques mis à part?"
> Monique Proulx, *Le sexe des étoiles*

> "Je est un autre."
> Arthur Rimbaud, *La lettre du voyant*

Die Definition eines Selbst erfordert, so scheint es, die Abgrenzung zum anderen, die zumeist in einer Gegenüberstellung des Selbst und des Anderen geschieht. So werden in unserer westlichen, patriarchalen Welt die Geschlechter Mann und Frau in einer Binäropposition konfrontiert.[1] Wie in vielen anderen Zusammenhängen, in denen Binäroppositionen organisieren (z. B. Weiß/Schwarz, Jung/Alt), spiegelt die Gegenüberstellung Mann – Frau eine Symmetrie vor, deren tatsächlich hierarchischer Charakter durch viele Beispiele offensichtlich wird. Man denke im kanadischen Kontext daran, daß es bis Herbst 1996 kein Gesetz gab, das Frauen und Männern einen gleichen Lohn zusicherte, man denke an die Affäre des Richters Bienvenue,[2] man denke an die Männer, die den Frauenmörder Marc Lépine als Helden feiern.[3]

Von dieser Asymmetrie ausgehend, werden wir im folgenden zunächst einige theoretische Gedanken zur Geschlechteridentität diskutieren, die wir in Beziehung setzen zu den Möglichkeiten des poetischen Aktes, woran sich unsere Analyse des Romans *Le sexe des étoiles* von Monique Proulx im Hinblick auf eben jene Geschlechteridentität anschließt. Der Text zeigt unserer Meinung nach in humor- und kraftvoller Weise die beengenden Normen unserer sozialen Realität auf und weist über deren Grenzen hinaus.

In der westlichen patriarchalen Welt stellt das Selbst des Mannes das Zentrum der Definition und somit die Norm dar, von der die Frau abweicht, so daß sie als *Andere* untergeordnet wird. Wie Guillaumin ausführlich zeigt,[4] wird die Frau vom Mann in der sozialen Lebensrealität sowohl im individuellen wie im kollektiven Sinne vereinnahmt. Sie hat demnach keine Identität: "C'est comme sujets que nous n'existons pas" (Guillaumin, 1987, S. 15). Den Prozeß dieser Appropriation der Frau nennt Guillaumin in Analogie zu den sich auf Rassen- und Klassenunterschiede beziehenden Begriffen *servage* und *esclavage* "sexage". Die einzelne Frau kann nicht, oder nur bedingt ihre Identität als handelndes Subjekt leben (ibid., und S. 17), da ihr die Macht zur aktiven Veränderung[5] im Rahmen der patriarchalen Ordnung fehlt. Wenn sie dennoch versucht, ihrer Identität selbstbestimmt Ausdruck zu verleihen, wird dies von Seiten der patriarchalen Ordnung als Transgression der Norm bewertet.

Der herrschende patriarchale Diskurs beschreibt und begründet die Rolle der Frau als passive, dem Mann untergeordnete, reproduktive Kraft in der privaten Sphäre als natürlich und sinnvoll. Durch ihre Verortung im Privaten, wo sie die materielle und psychosoziale Reproduktion zu gewährleisten hat, ist die Frau ortlos, d. h. ihr wird kein selbstdefinierter Ort zugestanden. Geschickterweise wird dabei die Rolle der Frau als Hausfrau und Mutter aufgewertet, sie ist im privaten Bereich verantwortlich.[6] Daß es sich bei ihrer Verantwortlichkeit vor allem darum handelt, die private Welt so zu organisieren, daß sie den Belangen der (männlichen) Öffentlichkeit zuarbeitet, liegt auf der Hand. Aus feministischer Sicht wird jedoch selbst die Unterscheidung zwischen privater und öffentlicher Sphäre fragwürdig, da eine jede Handlung und Entscheidung im privaten Bereich Auswirkungen auf das Funktionieren der öffentlichen Sphäre hat. Die Strukturierung des Privaten ist das Fundament, auf dem der öffentliche Bereich aufbaut, eine Trennung der Sphären führt also zwangsläufig zum Einsturz des (Gedanken-)Gebäudes, woran sich spätestens die politische Dimension des Privaten zeigt.

Die Unterscheidung zwischen biologischem und sozialem Geschlecht, zwischen *sex* und *gender* bzw. *sexe* und *genre*, ermöglicht es jedoch, die vermeintlich unumstößliche "Natürlichkeit" der Frau zu entkräften. "Gender can no longer be treated as a simple, natural fact" (Flax, 1990, S. 44). Spätestens seit Simone de Beauvoirs berühmtem Satz "On ne naît pas femme, on le devient", sind sich viele Feministinnen einig, daß die Kategorie Geschlecht als Binäropposition zwischen weiblich und männlich ein soziales

Konstrukt und *nicht* eine natürliche Größe darstellt.[7] Dem biologischen Geschlecht steht eine soziale Geschlechtsidentität gegenüber, deren Form durch das soziale Umfeld beeinflußt wird. Sich auf anthropologische Forschungen stützend, unterscheidet Mathieu (1989) zwischen drei verschiedenen Identitätsstufen. Die "identité sexuelle" stellt eine homologe Beziehung zwischen *sexe* und *genre* heraus, die "identité sexuée" eine analoge, während die "identité de sexe" auf einer politischen Basis aufbaut. Mathieu erläutert die verschiedenen Stufen am Beispiel der Homosexualität. So wird Homosexualität im Rahmen der ersten Identitätsstufe als Anomalie oder Perversion verurteilt (ibid., S. 114), innerhalb der zweiten Identitätsstufe wird Homosexualität am Rande der Norm, aber in der Einheit einer Gruppe erlebt (ibid., S. 119ff.), während die dritte Identitätsstufe Homosexualität als politische Wahl beschreibt (ibid., S. 136). Wir sind mit Massé der Ansicht, daß für die in unserer Gesellschaft lebenden Charaktere des Romans *Le sexe des étoiles* noch gilt: "Le rapport homologique est encore celui qui nous semble sévir le plus souvent dans l'établissement du comportement de nos sociétés occidentales [...]" (Massé, 1990, S. 81). Es würde unserer Meinung nach einen entscheidenden Fortschritt darstellen, zum Konzept der dritten Stufe zu gelangen, in der die Beziehung zwischen *sexe* und *genre* eine fließende, neudefinierbare Kategorie würde, eine "correspondance sociologique" für die gelten würde: "Le genre construit le sexe" (Mathieu, 1989, S. 112).

Doch die Kategorisierung von *sexe* und *genre* bringt auch Probleme mit sich. Scott beobachtet in diesem Zusammenhang das Anhaften der Kategorie *gender* an der Frau wie ein Stigma.[8] Manche Forscherinnen fordern daher, sich von dem starren Binaritätskonzept *sexe et genre* zu lösen. So meint de Lauretis: "We need a notion of gender that is not so bound up with sexual difference" (de Lauretis, 1987, S. 2, vgl. auch Butler, 1992), und Scott argumiert: "Nous avons besoin d'un rejet du caractère fixé et permanent de l'opposition binaire, d'une historicisation et d'une déconstruction authentiques des termes de la différence sexuelle" (Scott, 1988, S. 139). Dies geschieht aus der Erfahrung heraus, daß die Betonung der Differenz zwar Erklärungen ermöglichen kann, aber mit der Etablierung einer Binäropposition zwischen Geschlechtsidentität und biologischem Geschlecht gleichzeitig eine verstärkte Festschreibung der Grenzen vornimmt, so daß eine Selbstdefinition außerhalb dieser Grenzen nahezu unmöglich ist. Proulx' Text ist, wie wir im folgenden zeigen wollen, ein literarisches Beispiel für das Aufbrechen des starren Binaritätskonzepts.

Vor diesem Hintergrund stellt sich eine zentrale Frage für die weibliche Identitätssuche, die Smart folgendermaßen formuliert: "Comment se reconnaître femme, s'identifier aux traits revendiqués par le féminisme comme les marques de notre différence sexuelle, sans se trouver enfermée comme les femmes l'ont été autrefois dans des catégories qui nous coupent de notre pleine liberté?" (Smart, 1995, S. 68). Literarischen Texten kommt dabei eine besondere Rolle zu, wie z. B. das Werk der belgischen Autorin Claire Lejeune[9] zeigt. Auch Louise Dupré unterstreicht diesen Aspekt:

"[...] dans la fiction au féminin [...] se joue le devenir du féminisme comme *philosophie*. Dans la conscience féministe en effet, éthique et esthétique sont irrémédiablement liées. La forme des femmes n'ayant pas d'ancrage dans le symbolique, il n'y a que l'imaginaire qui permette de la dessiner peu à peu, de la dévoiler."[10]

Unsere Analyse will zeigen, wie eine solche "poélitique", um mit Théry[11] zu sprechen, funktionieren kann.

Innerhalb der theoretischen Diskussion finden gerade in Zeiten, in denen sich Xenophobie in wachsendem Maße Ausdruck verschafft, Begriffe wie Heterogenität und *métissage* (vgl. Smart, 1992, S. 44f.) ihren Platz, die treffender und weniger einschränkend als Binäropposionen soziale Wirklichkeiten und politische Forderungen umreißen.[12] Besonders für die Frau scheint dies vielversprechend, wie Théry herausstellt: "Le concept d'hétérogène pourrait mettre fin à cette association pernicieuse du 'féminin' avec les femmes" (Théry, 1992, S. 63). In dieser Hinsicht geht manch feministische Forschung zum Teil mit der Postmoderne Hand in Hand,[13] die den Zerfall der mit Lyotard *métarécits* genannten Normen konstatiert, wobei jedoch (mindestens) *ein* großer Unterschied besteht: Da die Frau in einem *je universel* bisher nicht eingeschlossen war, kann die Dispersion des Subjekts so nicht in ihrem Sinne sein, es geht im Unterschied dazu zunächst darum, ein *je au féminin* zu artikulieren. "This kind of deconstruction of the subject is effectively a way to recontain women in femininity (Woman) and to reposition female subjectivity *in* the male subject, however that will be defined. Furthermore, it closes the door in the face of the emergent social subject [...] constituted across a multiplicity of differences in discursive and material heterogenity," warnt de Lauretis zurecht (1987, S. 24). Aus Autorinnenperspektive bringt Lola Lemire Tostevin diesen Zusammenhang treffend auf den Punkt: "When someone pointed out to me recently the importance of ridding oneself of the 'I' in writing, I said, 'Great, I'll lose it as soon as I find it'" (1987, S. 33).

Es ist demnach (noch) ein erklärtes Ziel, dem selbstbestimmten Ich Ausdruck zu verleihen. Diese Forderung nach einem handelnden Subjektstatus für die Frau stellt jedoch – wie bereits angedeutet – aus der Sicht der patriarchalen Gesellschaft oftmals ein Überschreiten von Grenzen, einen Verstoß gegen Normen dar. Solche Transgressionen beurteilen wir aus feministischer Perspektive mit Bersianik positiv: "Transgresser, c'est progresser" (Bersianik,

1976, S. 211). In diesem Zusammenhang bezeichnen wir diejenige, die sich über die festgeschriebene Binäropposition Mann versus Frau bzw. Norm versus Andere, *sexe* versus *genre* hinwegsetzt und ihren Weg als Frau am Steuer selbstdefiniert, als *femme au volant*.[14] Wir beziehen uns mit der Wahl dieses Begriffs auf ein Zitat Cixous', das die Zweischneidigkeit des transgressiven Akts herausstellt:

> *Voler*, c'est le geste de la femme, dans la langue, la faire voler. Du vol, nous avons toutes appris l'art aux maintes techniques, depuis des siècles que nous n'avons accès à l'avoir qu'en *volant*; que nous avons vécu dans un vol, de voler, trouvant au désir des passages étroits, dérobés, traversants. Ce n'est pas un hasard si voler se joue entre deux vols, jouissants de l'un et de l'autre et déroutant les agents des sens. (Cixous, 1975, S. 178)

Das Homonym *voler* macht deutlich, daß der Freiflug der Frau aus der normativen Sicht der sie umgebenden Gesellschaft immer auch ein Kraftakt des Stehlens, ein Durchbrechen der bestehenden Machtstrukturen ist. Die *femme au volant* ist, dem Diskurs des Heterogenen folgend, geschlechtsunabhängig, sie ist dem Woolfschen Androgynitätskonzept angenähert:

> And I went on amateurishly to sketch a plan of the soul so that in each of us two powers preside, one male, one female; and in the man's brain, the man predominates over the woman, and in the woman's brain, the woman predominates over the man. The normal and comfortable state of being is that when the two live in harmony together, spiritually co-operating. If one is a man, still the woman part of the brain must have effect; and a woman also must have intercourse with the man in her. (Woolf, 1959, S.147f.)

und Woolf fährt fort: "It is fatal for anyone who writes to think of their sex. It is fatal to be a man or woman pure and simple; one must be woman-manly or man-womanly" (Woolf, 1959, S. 156f.). Die von Woolf geforderte Androgynität kommt in der Kreation von Charakteren fernab von Geschlechterstereotypen literarisch zum Ausdruck.

Wie eine solche Repräsentation der androgynen *femme au volant* auf textueller Ebene aussehen kann, zeigt Monique Proulx' Roman *Le sexe des étoiles*, erschienen 1987 bei den Éditions Québec/Amérique.[15] Proulx führt in ihrem Roman vier sich im Grad ihrer Grenzüberschreitungen unterscheidende Hauptfiguren vor. Als erste begegnet uns die engagierte, ihre Gegner mit deren eigenen Waffen schlagende Gaby, die zwei der anderen Protagonisten zusammenbringt, zunächst auditiv über die Wellen des Radiosenders, für den sie arbeitet, und dann räumlich, als sie dem Schriftsteller Dominique

Larue ihre Wohnung als Treffpunkt mit seiner transsexuellen "Muse" zur Verfügung stellt. Dominique seinerseits verbindet das Schicksal der Romanfiguren (und der Romanschriftstellerin) in seinem innerhalb von *Le sexe des étoiles* entstehenden Buch. Außerdem lernen wir die elfjährige, überdurchschnittlich begabte Sternebeobachterin Camille kennen, die die Vision des Romans verkörpert, sowie ihren Vater, die Transsexuelle Marie-Pierre, die als Ur-Mutter Marie und als Vater Pierre-Père durch ihre Ausstrahlung die Einzelschicksale der anderen Figuren zusammenführt. "En suivant le cheminement de Marie-Pierre et des autres personnages, le roman procède d'interrogations, de transgressions et de jeux permettant de dépasser le paradoxe du sexe et du genre" (Massé, 1990, S. 79).

Ohne das einzelne Subjekt aufzulösen, gelingt es Proulx in ihrem Text, die Binarität zwischen *sexe* und *genre* und zwischen Mann und Frau ins Wanken zu bringen, indem sie heterogene Charaktere entwirft, die als *femmes au volant* Grenzen überschreiten. "Dans le roman de Monique Proulx, *Le sexe des étoiles*, aucun des personnages n'est l'exemple d'une adéquation parfaite entre le sexe biologique et le genre (ou le sexe social)" (Massé, 1990, S. 70). Ihre Figuren reflektieren ihre geschlechtliche Identität und erkennen die einschränkenden gesellschaftlichen Normen. In ihrem täglichen Kampf um den Ausdruck des Selbst, so wenig normenkonform es auch sein mag, transgredieren die Figuren die Grenzen und entdecken neue Wege. Indem sie traditionell männliche und weibliche Eigenschaften "biologischen" Männern und Frauen zuordnet und die der "Natürlichkeit" angepaßten, eindimensionalen Geschlechtsidentitäten außer Kraft setzt, aber vor allem, indem sie eine Transsexuelle zu ihrer Protagonistin macht, versetzt Proulx die geschlechtlichen Identitäten in einen gleitenden Zustand, der das Binaritätsprinzip aus den Angeln hebt. Dies ist notwendig, denn die Binarität von *sexe et genre* dient vor allem der Erhaltung des Status quo, wie Proulx ihre Heldin Marie-Pierre bemerken läßt: "Y a pas à dire, vous êtes pointilleux sur la chose, vous, les Biologiques... Tout est tellement tranché au couteau pour vous, c'est tellement plus facile comme ça, hein? Les Femmes d'un bord, les Z'hommes de l'autre, et swingue la baquaisse dans l'fond d'la boîte à bois!"[16] Die Transsexualität Marie-Pierres ermöglicht Proulx, die geschlechtliche Rollenverteilung in humorvoller, aber auch umso drastischere Weise infragezustellen, wie sie in einem Interview bemerkt: "Qu'est-ce qui fait qu'on est un homme ou une femme en dedans de soi? Est-ce qu'on pense et réagit de la même façon suivant qu'on est un homme ou une femme? Évidemment, il y a la culture, l'atavisme, l'éducation, mais indépendamment de tout cela, y a-t-il quelque chose de vraiment féminin ou masculin?" (Ferland, 1987, S. C9).

Die transsexuelle Protagonistin Marie-Pierre illustriert, wie Smart (1995, S. 70) zurecht bemerkt, Beauvoirs "On ne naît pas femme, on le devient" in radikaler Weise. Erfolgreicher Wissenschaftler, Ehemann und Vater eines Kindes, beschließt Henri-Pierre Deslauriers sein Erscheinungsbild und schließlich auch seinen Körper der schon immer verspürten Weiblichkeit anzupassen, womit die körperliche Geschlechtsidentität selbstdefinierbar wird. Aus Henri-Pierre wird Marie-Pierre, eine Frau, die "s'y jette de plain-pied [dans la féminité] [...] qui ferai[t] frémir plus d'une féministe traditionelle" (Smart, 1995, S. 70). Proulx spielt sprachlich mit der Doppelung der Figur, indem sie z. B. Marie-Pierres Tochter sagen läßt: "Son père était très belle, ce soir" (151). Hier wird die französische Grammatikregel "Le masculin l'emporte sur le féminin", die besonders Camilles Logikverständnis auf die Probe stellt,[17] außer Kraft gesetzt, was zu so schönen Kreationen wie "ma trésore" (251) führt. Aus der Sicht der Gesellschaft macht Marie-Pierre-Henris Entscheidung ihn/sie jedoch zur Unperson, zum "Ex-être humain" (111), wobei die gesellschaftliche Reaktion die Unhaltbarkeit einer Trennung zwischen privater und öffentlicher Sphäre nur allzu deutlich werden läßt. Ihr Schicksal zynisch zusammenfassend, bemerkt Marie-Pierre in einem Brief an den Minister:

> Je saisis, finalement, la raison pour laquelle vos distingués fonctionnaires refusent de rayer de mon dossier ce malencontreux M qui m'empêche d'accéder au pain quotidien, et je compatis avec leur embarras. C'est que ce malencontreux M ne fait pas référence à mon ex-statut de MÂLE, comme je le croyais en toute innocence, mais à mon nouveau statut de MONSTRE, spécification que je comprends qu'ils désirent conserver, car il faut bien appeler les choses par leurs noms. (110f.)

War Henri-Pierre Kandidat für den Nobelpreis, so ist Marie-Pierre arbeitslos, mittellos und obdachlos. Was dem erfolgreichen Henri-Pierre völlig unbekannt war, trifft sein Ich als Frau umso mehr:

> Depuis maintenant presque quatre ans, Marie-Pierre se butait à l'hostilité de cette vaste confrérerie en uniforme dont elle n'avait jamais perçu, avant, l'omniprésent pouvoir ombrageux: les Cravates étaient partout, dans les universités, les laboratoires, les compagnies où l'on réfusait de l'engager, dans les ministères où l'on manipulait son dossier avec un arrogant dégoût, dans les médias où l'on se gaussait de son existence, jamais sans doute ne serait-elle absoute d'avoir osé quitter leurs rangs pour rejoindre l'arrière-garde des faiblardes et subalternes femelles. (106f.)

Der Kampf um eine offizielle Anerkennung ihrer Identität als Frau wird begleitet von Herabsetzungen unverschämtester Art ("L'une des premières

Cravates gouvernementales [...] lui avait malicieusemant lancé: 'Prouvez-moi que vous êtes une femme!' ce à quoi Marie-Pierre avait malicieusement retorqué: 'Prouvez-moi, vous, que vous êtes un homme!'", 107) und scheitert an der simplen Eitelkeit von Politikern. "Un espace entre l'esprit et le corps" (Théry, 1992, S. 70), ist sie trotz ihrer unangenehmen sozioökonomischen Situation innerlich in ihrer Selbstfindung und -definition am Ziel: "Je suis moi à cent pour cent: on ne peut pas en dire autant de beaucoup de monde" (63).

Marie-Pierre stellt das Leben der Personen, mit denen sie in Kontakt kommt, auf den Kopf, sie fragt nach, stellt in Frage. Die Wichtigkeit von Frauensolidarität und -freundschaft[18] spürend, bringt sie Gaby, die talentierte Radiorecherchistin, dazu, sie in ihre Wohnung aufzunehmen. In deren Gesellschaft deckt sie im Gespräch so manche Widersprüche und Lächerlichkeiten des "biologischen" Frau-Seins auf. So fällt ihr die Peinlichkeit der Menschen gegenüber ihren Körpern auf: "[...] les gens n'habitaient pas leurs corps, ils le traînaient derrière eux comme une maladie honteuse" (50). Als Gaby Marie-Pierres Vorliebe für Makeup und enganliegende Kleidung obszön findet, kontert Marie-Pierre treffend:

> Comment, obscène?... Mais toutes les femmes, ma petite chatte, AIMENT qu'on remarque leurs seins... Toi-même, ta blouse un peu trop transparente, et pas de soutien-gorge [...] Cette façon détournée que vous avez, vous, les Biologiques, de vous montrer en faisant semblant que vous ne le faites pas... Eh bien, OUI, je les exhibe, moi, mes seins, et fièrement, si tu veux savoir, regarde comme ils sont beaux. L'hypocrisie, c'est ça qui est obscène...
> (183)

Auch Gaby versucht ihrerseits, sich als Frau beruflich und privat zu finden, sich als Subjekt zu artikulieren. Auf ihrem Weg zum Selbst beklagt sie den Verlust ihrer Freundinnen, von denen "plus d'une encore disparaît de l'annuaire téléphonique, agglutinée à l'ombre bienveillant de son n'époux" (70). Dennoch, "il n'y avait qu'avec les femmes que pouvait naître, comme du tréfonds de ses viscères, ce fou rire infantile, d'une absolue et merveilleuse gratuité, sans lequel la vie ne vaut pas la peine que l'on passe au travers" (74). Hier spricht nicht nur Gaby, wie so oft in der *littérature québécoise au féminin* läßt auch Proulx ihre *femmes au volant* in ihrem Roman den Humor als transgressive Waffe einsetzen.

Die Beziehung zwischen Marie-Pierre und Gaby zeigt auch die Bewertung traditioneller Rollenverteilung auf. So verbringt Gaby mit ihrem ruhigen, sauberen, ordentlichen neuen Liebhaber Luc ein Wochenende, als Marie-Pierre ihr zum Dank für die Gastfreundschaft eine vollständige Wohnungssäuberung anbietet. Während Luc, der perfekte, den gesamten Haushalt führende neue Mann, Gaby zum ersten Mal anschreit, als sie einen Fuß auf den eben geputzten Boden setzt (vgl. 178), endet Marie-Pierre im Sessel, ein Likörglas in der Hand: "Le ménage, ça fait chier. Qu'est-ce qu'une femme émancipée peut bien trouver de jouissif là-dedans, peux-tu me le dire?" (178). Marie-Pierre ist es, die Gaby in einem Gespräch auf ihr "côté yang très fort" (309) aufmerksam macht, das Gaby bisher ignoriert hatte. Im folgenden integriert sie ihre weiblichen und männlichen Eigenschaften stärker und versucht, ihr androgynes Selbst zu leben. Sie gibt ihrer Subjektivität Ausdruck indem sie formuliert: "JE VEUX" (309), und findet auf diese Weise ihren Weg.

Marie-Pierres elfjährige Tochter Camille entdeckt die Ungerechtigkeiten der gesellschaftlich geforderten Geschlechtsidentitäten früh und erfährt so ihr Anderssein: "[...] au fond, l'intelligence était une malédiction en ce bas monde, l'intelligence était ce qui faisait qu'elle restait seule les heures de lunch, les soirs et les mois de vacances à regarder les autres échanger des inepties heureuses, l'intelligence était une monstruosité chez les filles et la condamnerait à passer sa vie derrière un télescope géant, seule comme une sauvage. *Elle s'était trompée de sexe et d'univers*" (Proulx, 1987, S. 98f, unsere Hervorhebung). Insofern ist sie ganz Tochter ihres weiblichen Vaters, denn auch sie wird der Kategorie der Monster zugerechnet. Sie ist sich der Differenz zwischen ihrem Selbst und den anderen bewußt: "L'ensemble avait des seins. L'ensemble portait des pantalons à fourche basse et les montgolfières en guise d'épaules prescrits par la mode. L'ensemble se maquillait. [...] L'ensemble vibrait au mêmes incompréhensibles plaisantries et partagaient les mêmes mots de passe. [...] L'ensemble avait des amis, des partenaires sexuels et de grands projets de maternité. L'ensemble avait un père en forme d'homme. L'ensemble savait toujours jusqu'où ne pas aller pour demeurer dans l'ensemble" (205f.). Auch wenn sie zunächst unter ihrer Andersartigkeit leidet, da ihre Intelligenz ihr die Zuneigung des Jungen Lucky Poitras vorzuenthalten scheint, entscheidet sie sich schließlich bewußt für die Differenz und findet darin ihr erfolgreiches Selbst: "[...] elle était condamnée à être différente? Soit. Elle le serait totalement. Sa position à la queue du peloton ne lui assurait aucune espèce d'intégration? Très bien. Elle en prendrait la tête" (206). In dieser Hinsicht unterscheidet sie sich von den anderen drei Figuren, ihre transgressive Autonomie weist in ihrem Bewußtseinsgrad über die der anderen hinaus (vgl. auch Massé, 1990, S. 73). Sie gibt der traditionellen Aufgabe der Frau, dem Schweigen, eine neue Wendung, indem sie es subversiv einsetzt. Als der Schulpsychologe und Liebhaber ihrer Mutter versucht, ihre Motivationen und Gedanken aufzuspüren, entzieht sie sich vollständig und läßt ihm nicht die geringste Chance, in ihre innere Welt einzudringen (vgl. 208ff.). Sie ist sehr alt und sehr weise, wie Marie-Pierre bemerkt (vgl. 228), aber tatsächlich auch sehr jung, so daß Marie-Pierre für sie Mutter und Vater gleichzeitig sein kann, aber ihrerseits auch Halt bei ihrer Tochter findet. Marie-Pierres Credo gibt ihrer Tochter Kraft: " – Il faut pas être comme tout le monde. Il faut marcher toute seule à la tête, pis essayer de trouver un chemin que personne d'autre a pris avant. – Pourquoi? – Parce que les chemins des autres ne mènent pas assez loin" (199f.).

Der einzige "biologische" Mann, dem der Roman eine wichtige Rolle zugesteht, ist der Schriftsteller Dominique.[19] Von Beginn an wird "Dominique Larue, spécialiste en choses molles et en fuites diverses" (82), in Situationen gezeigt, die seine Unzulänglichkeit herausstellen. In der Liebe impotent, bleibt er auch in seinem Schriftstellerdasein erfolglos. Er ist jene Figur des Romans, die am wenigsten zu einer Selbstfindung gelangt, da er nur in Marie-Pierre, über die er ein Buch schreibt, seine Verwirklichung sucht und sein Selbst nicht zu akzeptieren vermag: "Il avait besoin d'Elle pour connaître son aboutissement" (260). Seiner Freundin gegenüber verstrickt er sich in Lügen, bei seinem Vater versucht er vergeblich Zuneigung und Verständnis zu finden. Auch Dominique, dessen Name bereits auf eine weiblich-männliche Ambiguität hinweist, besitzt androgyne Züge. So hat er eine "fine calligraphie féminine" und träumt davon, mit seiner Inspiration schwanger zu gehen (vgl. 76f.). Doch zuoft bleibt er "un petit garçon" (26), sodaß es ihm nicht vollständig gelingt, seine Vielschichtigkeit positiv zu nutzen, wie Marie-Pierre unterstreicht: "Il y a en toi plein de zones troubles" (229). Erst sein Tod, der ihn auf der Suche nach Marie-Pierre ereilt, verschafft ihm Erlösung und eine späte Antwort auf seine Frage "QUI ÉTAIT-IL?" (230):

> Il ne sentit rien de douloureux, à dire vrai, rien qu'une apesanteur soudaine qui le soulagea de son corps. [...] et il vit sortir de sa gauche un petit garçon timoré, un vieillard qui marchait droit et qui n'avait pas de visage, une jeune femme gracieuse qui lui ressemblait en tous points, une jument jaune au regard de vieille dame, et il songea que c'était toutes des parties de lui-même qui s'en allaient s'éffritant une à une et qu'il avait maintenues prisonnières en dedans [...] (316f.)

Erst im Augenblick seines Todes erkennt er seine Vielschichtigkeit, die er zu Lebzeiten zu fliehen versucht hat.

Die Romanfiguren überschreiten nicht nur die Grenzen der gesellschaftlich vorgegebenen Rollen, sie begeben sich in ihren Handlungen auch in den rechtlich illegalen Bereich. So machen sich Marie-Pierre und Camille einen Spaß daraus, sich als Mutter-Tochter-Duo in den besten Restaurants der Stadt zu verlustieren, um dann im "moment M. M pour Mystification et Monopoly" (154) mit Falschgeld zu bezahlen und die Flucht zu ergreifen.

Auch Gaby setzt sich gegen ihren Kollegen Bob durch, indem sie sein auf sexuelle Anziehungskraft und Macht zurückgreifendes Spiel gewinnt, als sie sich der gleichen Waffen bedient, um ihre berufliche Stellung zurückzubekommen.[20] Ihre Vorliebe zur Kleptomanie bekommt eine positive Bewertung. "Kleptowoman de charme et de choc" (Théry, 1992, S. 70), entwendet sie jeder Person, der sie sich nahe fühlt (und nicht etwa einem Gegner), heimlich ein Stück ihres Eigentums. "Pour elle, le vol est un processus de rapprochement qui cache aussi son besoin d'identification" (Massé, 1990, S. 75), wie Massé herausstellt. Camilles Transgressionen bestehen in dem schon beschriebenen Schweigen, das sie als Waffe einsetzt, aber vor allem auch in ihrem Widerstand gegenüber der Welt der Erwachsenen, deren Sichtweise ihr zu eng erscheint. So zieht sie es vor, die Sterne zu beobachten und zu erforschen. Sie verkörpert die Entdeckerin von Neuland, einer neuen Galaxie, in der ein freieres Leben und Denken möglich ist. Camilles gen Himmel gerichter Blick ist visionär. Camille, Marie-Pierre und Gaby sind *femmes au volant*, für die das *voler* im übertragenen Sinne nicht so sehr "stehlen" bedeutet (auch wenn es in Gabys Fall die Form des Stehlens annehmen kann), sie fliegen vielmehr. Ihr "en-vol" läßt sich ebenfalls an den zahlreichen Ausdrücken ablesen, die dem Bereich "voler" entnommen sind und stets eine positive Bewertung erfahren. So lösen sich die Metastasen von Dominiques Vater Maurice in Nichts auf, sie sind "volatilisées" (270), als er dem Sohn endlich seine Homosexualität gesteht. Für Dominique liegt im Schreiben der Sinn seines Lebens: es ist "quelque chose de grand qui ne demandait que de prendre l'envol" (298). In diesem Sinne sind seine Schreibutensilien "doués d'aérodynamisme": "un gros dictionnaire voltigeait, son grévisse et son Petit Robert [...] filèrent trop vélocement" (302). Auch die Seiten seines Manuskripts fliegen bei seinem Unfall durch die Lüfte, "en tourbillant dans les airs", "[les feuilles] voltigent" (317f.). Der Ohrring in Form eines Vogels, den Gaby Marie-Pierre entwendet, symbolisiert nur zu gut das Wesen der Hauptfigur. Schon ihre Mutter "était douée pour toutes les choses aériennes."[21] Sie selbst wird mit Begriffen beschrieben, die eine leicht schwebende Leichtigkeit suggerieren. So ist sie "une créature aérienne" (328), die sich fortbewegt "en lévitant gracieusement" (54). Ihre Tasche ist "aérien", und ihr Gesicht ist fließend: "il flotte" (313).

Als einzige der vier Hauptfiguren des Romans schafft es Dominique nur bedingt, seinem Leben eine selbstbestimmte Wendung zu geben. Er lügt und erfindet, findet sich selbst aber nicht. In einem genialen Coup läßt Proulx das Manuskript seines Romans bei seinem Unfall durch die Luft fliegen und in ganz Montréal verstreuen. Von Dominique aufs Papier gebannt, entkommt Marie-Pierre, die Andere, die Fremde, dennoch. Sie fliegt auf den Papierseiten frei durch die Lüfte zu den vielen Figuren des Romans: das Fremde, das Andere ist immer bei ihnen, unfaßbar, unbezähmbar.[22] Doch

Proulx treibt die Dualität der Figuren noch weiter. Dominique, der Autor, das ist auch Monique Proulx: sein erstes Buch unterscheidet sich im Titel nur geringfügig von ihrer ersten Textsammlung (*Sans cœur et sans reproche*). In einer *mise en abyme* reflektiert Proulx ihr eigenes Schreiben und sprengt die Grenzen des Textes. Die letzten Worte von Dominiques Roman sind auch die letzten Worte ihres Textes. Außerdem finden sich ihre Initialen MP im Namen von Marie-Pierre wieder. Und auch Gaby ist Autorin des Romans, schließlich signiert sie in kleptomanischer Zuneigung Dominiques Manuskript als das ihre: "Et comme elle l'aimait bien, Dominique Larue, et qu'elle n'avait jamais eu le temps de lui dire, Gaby éprouva l'irrésistible besoin de lui dérober quelque chose, cette unique trace de lui abandonnée derrière: elle signa le manuscrit de son nom, et le porta chez un éditeur en se croisant les doigts" (323). Aber nicht nur Monique Proulx teilt die Autorinnenschaft mit ihren Figuren, auch die Quebecker Autorin Monique LaRue[23] klingt in Dominiques Namen an. Durch die Ineinssetzung der Romanautorin mit ihren Figuren und mit anderen Autorinnen spiralt sich der Text in die außerliterarische Wirklichkeit und bekommt eine besondere extratextuelle Brisanz. Proulx realisiert auf diese Weise eine "poétique de l'irreprésentable" (Théry, 1992), sie verwischt die Geschlechtergrenzen und entwirft *Le sexe des étoiles*, eine Galaxie, in der Rimbauds "Je est un autre" zu "chacun est l'autre" wird. Geschlechtliche Identität wird hier als veränderbares Kontinuum gedacht, wobei die Identität in der Vielfältigkeit des Anders-Sein, der/s Anderen liegt: "Chacun prendrait enfin le risque de l'*autre*, sans se sentir menacé(e) par l'existence d'une altérité, mais en se réjouissant de s'augmenter d'inconnu à découvrir, à respecter, à favoriser, à entretenir" (Cixous, 1975, S. 143). Hier wird ein Konzept der Heterogenität umgesetzt, innerhalb dessen das biologische Geschlecht nur eine untergeordnete Rolle spielt, und das eine multiple Sichtweise der Geschlechter bevorzugt. Die Figuren heben ab, sie fliegen: "En fait, le portrait de ces quatre personnages témoigne de l'aspect duel de l'être humain, de ses caractéristiques fluides, mouvantes et refoulées qu'il se doit de taire ou rendre visible" (Massé, 1990, S. 78).

Durch die Verwischung der Geschlechtergrenzen ist Proulx' Universum "une célébration non pas de la fixité mais du mouvement, du changement, et de la différence" (Smart, 1995, S. 75). Und so gilt für ihren Text dasselbe wie für ihre *leading lady* Marie-Pierre: "Elle était déjà rendue plus loin, elle marchait seule et victorieuse en laissant derrière elle un parfum de créature aérienne, elle s'en allait ailleurs troubler les infaillibles bien-pensants" (328).

Anmerkungen

1 Wobei wir den Begriff Geschlecht an dieser Stelle zunächst noch undifferenziert als ganzes gebrauchen, ohne zwischen biologischen und sozialen Gegebenheiten zu unterscheiden.

2 Der Richter verurteilt eine Frau unangemessen hart, die ihren gewalttätigen Mann tötet, und vergleicht ihre Tat mit der Tötung unzähliger Juden durch die Nationalsozialisten. "Même les nazis n'ont pas éliminé des millions de juifs dans la douleur, ni dans le sang. Ils ont péri sans souffrance, dans les chambres à gaz." Le Devoir, 1996, S. A2.

3 Am 6. Dezember 1989 trennt Marc Lépine an der Montrealaiser École Polytechnique mehrere Frauen bewußt von den Männern, um sie dann als Feministinnen, die ihm das Leben schwer gemacht haben, brutal zu töten. Vgl. Chalouh/Malette, 1990.

4 Guillaumin, 1987. Guillaumins Text ist nicht mehr ganz neu und mutet besonders bezüglich ihrer Beispiele veraltet an, außerdem bezieht sie sich vor allem auf die Situation von Ehepaaren. Ihre Analyse scheint uns aber dennoch das auch heute noch grundlegende Prinzip der Geschlechterbeziehungen treffend zu erläutern, denn: Wieviele Männer nehmen die Möglichkeit eines Kinderjahres wahr? Warum haben die meisten berufstätigen Mütter *zwei* Vollzeitarbeitsplätze? Warum wird Frauen in Bewerbungssituationen die obligatorische Frage nach der Versorgung ihrer (tatsächlichen oder potentiellen) Kinder gestellt, Männern aber nicht? Warum fühlen viele berufstätige Frauen sich bemüßigt, ihre Situation zu erklären oder gar zu entschuldigen, je nach Gesprächspartner? Viele andere Fragen sind denkbar...

5 Im anglo-amerikanischen Raum wird in diesem Zusammenhang von *agency*, im frankophonen Raum von *agentivité* gesprochen.

6 Gerade in Québec ist die Rolle der Mutter lange Zeit unterstrichen worden. Vgl. hierzu Smart, 1992.

7 Hier ließe sich einwenden, daß der Unterschied zwischen männlich und weiblich immer natürlich gegeben ist und von der großen Mehrheit der Weltbevölkerung als Tatsache gelebt wird. Man sollte allerdings nicht vergessen, daß viele Zwischenformen existieren und gelebt werden, die den sozial-konstruierten Aspekt der Opposition weiblich versus männlich offenlegen. Vgl. hierzu neben Mathieu, 1989, auch Badinter, 1986.

8 Scott, 1988, S. 128. So bezeichnen z. B. "gender studies" zumeist feministische Forschungen, von denen sich die wenigsten Männer angesprochen fühlen, es sei denn, sie gehören als Homosexuelle selbst einer Gruppe "anderer" an.

9 Vgl. das dem Text vorangestellte Zitat von Lejeune.

10 Dupré, 1988, Hervorhebung im Text, zitiert nach Théry, 1992, S. 64.

11 Théry, 1992, S. 65. Vgl. auch den Text *Poélitique* von Madeleine Gagnon, 1975.

12 Offener erscheinen die Begriffe u. a. insofern, als sie das Differenzerleben allgemeiner fassen, so daß Unterschiede aufgrund von z. B. Klasse, Rasse, sexueller Präferenz, Geschlecht, sprachlicher Identität – ein gerade in Kanada nicht zu unterschätzender Aspekt – etc. berücksichtigt werden.

13 Vgl. Paterson, 1993, die in ihrem Artikel Übereinstimmungen und Unterschiede der postmodernen Diskussion mit feministischen Ansätzen untersucht.

14 Zum Begriff der *femme au volant* vgl. auch Lange, 1996.

15 Die hervorragende Verfilmung des Romans von Paule Baillargeon wurde unter gleichem Titel 1993 zur Eröffnung des Festival des Films du Monde in Montréal präsentiert.
16 Proulx, 1987, S. 250. Alle weiteren Verweise auf diesen Text werden wir im folgenden durch die Angabe der Seitenzahl in Klammern im fortlaufenden Text belegen.
17 Vgl. Proulx, 1987, S. 102: "le masculin triomphant irréversiblement du féminin – trois mille femmes et un cochon sont passés."
18 "Nous allons nous revoir, avait souri, très sûre d'elle, Marie-Pierre. Nous avons des atomes crochus, toi et moi, une affinité d'âme sœur... Entre femmes, ça se sent, ces choses-là" Proulx, 1987, S. 65.
19 Zu einer detaillierten Analyse der Figur des Dominique Larue vgl. Ouellet, 1990.
20 An dieser Stelle weisen wir daraufhin, daß die Frauen, die versuchen, mit Hilfe der Männer zu Erfolg zu kommen, kläglich scheitern. Das trifft auf Michèle, Marie-Pierres Exfrau zu, der der Nobelpreis ihres Mannes wichtiger war als alles andere, wie auf Mado, Dominiques Freundin, die versucht seinen Roman als Autorin zu zeichnen, wie schließlich auf Priscille, Gabys Radiokollegin, die über Bob versucht, an Gabys Job zu kommen.
21 Proulx, 1987, S. 139. Hier handelt es sich um eine euphemistische Formulierung für die Tatsache, daß Marie-Pierres Mutter als Prostituierte gearbeitet hat.
22 Vgl. in diesem Zusammenhang auch Ouellet, 1990, S. 101.
23 Vgl. LaRues, 1989, Roman *Copies conformes*, der seinerseits Duplizität und weibliche Identität zum Thema hat.

Literatur

Badinter, Elisabeth, 1986, *L'un est l'autre*. Paris: Éditions Odile Jacob.

Bersianik, Louky, 1976, *L'Euguélionne*. Montréal: Éditions La presse.

Butler, Judith, 1992, "Contingent Foundations: Feminism and the Question of 'Postmodernism'", in: Butler, Judith/Joan Scott, *Feminists Theorize the Political*. New York/London: Routledge, 3-21.

Chalouh, Marie/Louise Malette, 1990, *Polytechnique, 6 décembre*. Montréal: Les Éditions du remue-ménage.

Cixous, Hélène, 1975, "Sorties", in: Cixous/Catherine B. Clément, *La jeune née*. Paris: 10/18.

De Lauretis, Teresa, 1987, *Technologies of Gender: Essays on Theory, Film, and Fiction*. Bloomington: Indiana University Press.

Ferland, Guy, 1987, "Monique Proulx: comme un gratte-ciel", *Le Devoir*, 31.12.1987, C9.

Flax, Jane, 1990, "Postmodernism and Gender Relations in Feminist Theory", in: Linda J. Nicholson (Hrsg.), *Feminism/Postmodernism*. New York, London: Routledge, 39-62.

Gagnon, Madeleine, 1975, *Poélitique*. Montréal: Les herbes rouges 26.

Guillaumin, Colette, 1987, "Pratiques du pouvoir et idée de Nature (1): L'appropriation des femmes", *Questions féministes*, 2, 5-30.

Lange, Ulrike C., 1996, "Femme au volant – Les héroïnes nautiques d'Antonine Maillet", in: Raoul Boudreau/Zénon Chiasson/Pierre M. Gérin/Anne Marie Robichaud (Hrsg.), *Mélanges Maillet*. Moncton: Les Editions d'Acadie, 225-235.

LaRue, Monique, 1989, *Copies conformes*. Paris: Denoël.

Lejeune, Claire, 1992, *Le livre de la soeur*. Montréal: L'Héxagone.

Le Devoir, 25.09.1996, A2.

Massé, Sylvie, 1990, "Agir clandestin, définition hétérogène et sanction sociale: La perspective ludique des transgressions reliées au sexe dans le roman de Monique Proulx, *Le sexe des étoiles*", *Féminisme et androgynie: explorations pluridisciplinaires, Les Cahiers du Grad*, 4, Faculté de philosophie, Université Laval, 69-82.

Mathieu, Nicole-Claude, 1989, "Identité sexuelle/sexuée/de sexe? Trois modes de conceptualisation du rapport entre sexe et genre", in: Marie-Claude Hurting/France Pichevin (Hrsg.), *Catégorie de sexe et constructions scientifiques*. Aix-en-Provence: Université de Provence, 109-147.

Ouellet, Bernard, 1990, "Les stations de Dominique Larue: l'écrivain (mâle) en procès", *Féminisme et androgynie: explorations pluridisciplinaires, Les Cahiers du Grad*, 4, Faculté de philosophie, Université Laval, 83-105.

Paterson, Janet, 1993, "Postmodernisme et féminisme: où sont les jonctions?", in: Koski, Raija/ Kathleen Kells/ Louise Forsyth (Hrsg.), *Les discours féminins dans la littérature postmoderne au Québec*. Lewiston, New York: The Edwin Mellen Press, 27-44.

Proulx, Monique, 1987, *Le sexe des étoiles*,. Montréal: Éditions Québec/Amérique.

Rimbaud, Arthur, (1870) 1989, *Oeuvres I. Poésies*, Paris: Flammarion.

Scott, Joan, 1988, "Genre: Une catégorie utile d'analyse historique", *Les Cahiers du GRIF*, nos 37/38, 125-153.

Smart, Patricia, 1995, "Au-delà des dualismes: identité et généricité *(gender)* dans *Le sexe des étoiles* de Monique Proulx", in: Gabrielle Pascal (Hrsg.), *Le roman québécois au féminin (1980-1995)*. Montréal: Triptyque, 67-76.

——, 1992, "Différences en conflit? Identité nationale et altérité sexuelle dans la littérature québécoise", in: *Zeitschrift für Kanadastudien*, 12:2, 37-47.

Théry, Chantal, 1992, "Sujet humain non identifié: imaginaire en souffrance", in: Simon Harel (Hrsg.), *L'étranger dans tous ses états. Enjeux culturels et littéraires*. Montréal: XYZ, 61-71.

Tostevin, Lola Lemire, 1987, "Sounding the Differences", Interview mit Janice Williamson, in: *The Canadian Forum*, 33-38.

Woolf, Virginia, [13]1959, (1929), *A Room of One's Own*. London: The Hogarth Press.

Die Rolle des Monologs für "Spectacles de femmes" und "Théâtre de femmes" in Québec oder Von Hexen, Feen und anderen Unheimlichkeiten

Birgit Mertz-Baumgartner

1. Einführung

Die Gattung des "monologue" genießt im kulturellen Leben der Quebecker im Verlauf des gesamten 20. Jahrhunderts – von Paul Coutlée über Gratien Gélinas zu Clémence DesRochers, Yvon Deschamps und Marc Favreau – einen hohen Bekanntheits- und Popularitätsgrad. "Spectacles solo", Monodramen und Monologe in Mehr-Personenstücken sind fester Bestandteil der Quebecker Theaterproduktion der letzten 30 Jahre. Schon 1976 stellte Louis Francoeur fest, daß der Monolog für die "neuen" Quebecker Theaterautoren ein beliebtes formales wie inhaltliches Gestaltungsprinzip darstellt und aufgrund seiner im Vergleich zum europäischen Theaterrepertoire häufigen Verwendung "[...] pourrait presque servir à l'identifier [...]" (Francoeur, 1976, S. 182). Die Bedeutung des Monologs für das Quebecker Theater kann jedoch nicht nur an Autoren wie Michel Tremblay, Jean Barbeau und Jean-Claude Germain festgemacht werden, sondern insbesondere an Theaterproduktionen von Autorinnen: von *La Nef des Sorcières* (1976), über Denise Bouchers *Les Fées ont soif* (1978), Louisette Dussaults *Moman* (1980) zu *Jocelyne Trudelle trouvée morte dans ses larmes* (1983) und *Oublier* (1987) von Marie Laberge, um nur einige Beispiele zu nennen. Jane Moss unterstreicht, daß für das Frauentheater in Québec neben "improvisation techniques and collective creation" der Monolog als typischstes Charakteristikum angesehen werden muß: "women's plays rely heavily on the monologue form, whether they are one-character or multiple-character plays" (Moss, 1985, S. 242).

Ich möchte daher in der Folge der Frage nachgehen, welche Funktionen der sonst häufig als "anti-dramatique", "statique" und "invraisemblable" (Pavis, 1980, S. 260) gewertete Monolog im Zusammenhang frauenspezifischer Themenstellungen und Anliegen übernehmen kann und warum der scheinbar an keinen Adressaten gerichtete Monolog zum privilegierten Medium weiblicher Kommunikation wird. Ich werde zunächst den "monologues" von Clémence DesRochers, Jacqueline Barrette und Denise Guénette "Gehör" schenken, jenen dramatisch-narrativen Kurztexten also, die von den

Künstlerinnen selbst verfaßt, inszeniert und präsentiert werden. Dabei schlüpfen die Monologistinnen in die einzige ausgeführte Bühnenrolle der Ich-Erzählerin und tragen deren komische und tragische Geschichten ohne Requisiten und Kostüme auf einer Bühne ohne Bühnenbild, dafür jedoch mit intensivem Publikumskontakt vor.[1] Im darauf folgenden Abschnitt wende ich mich dann der kollektiven Theaterproduktion *La Nef des Sorcières* zu, die man als eine Kette von acht "monologues" beschreiben kann. Im Unterschied zu DesRochers, Barrette und Guénette werden die Texte in *La Nef des Sorcières* mit Ausnahme jener von Luce Guibeault und Pol Pelletier jedoch von Schauspielerinnen interpretiert, das heißt, die für den "monologue" charakteristische Personalunion Auteur - Metteur en scène - Interprète teilt sich – wie im Theater üblich – auf mehrere Personen auf. In diesem Abschnitt komme ich auf eine weitere kollektive Theaterproduktion, *Les Fées ont soif*, zu sprechen, deren Text von Denise Boucher nachträglich verschriftlicht wurde. *Les Fées ont soif* kann mit drei ausgeführten Bühnenrollen als Mehrpersonenstück gesehen werden, in dem der Monolog als formales und inhaltliches Gestaltungsprinzip eine wichtige Rolle übernimmt; es wird jedoch von der Schauspielerin und Theaterautorin Louisette Dussault als "monologue à trois voix" (Dussault, 1981, 26) gewertet. Die schrittweise Entfernung vom "monologue" als eigenständiger Gattung und die Annäherung an den Monolog als Gestaltungselement in einem Mehrpersonenstück münden in einen abschließenden Ausblick auf die möglichen Rollen und Funktionen des Monologs im Quebecker Frauentheater am Beispiel von zwei ausgewählten Theaterstücken von Marie Laberge.[2]

2. Der "monologue québécois" und die Popularisierung geschlechterspezifischer Themenstellungen bei Clémence DesRochers, Jacqueline Barrette und Denise Guénette

Der "monologue", der aufgrund seiner volkstümlichen und oralen Tradition als "literarische Kleinform", als "Marginalie" bezeichnet und gewertet wird (cf. Mertz-Baumgartner, 1997, S. 185f.), stellt beinahe durchwegs Ich-Erzähler-Figuren auf die Bühne, die einerseits durch das enge Merkmalsbündel der Marginalität, der Naivität und der Passivität charakterisiert werden,[3] andererseits in ihrem Streben nach einer eigenen Identität in ein Geflecht von Beziehungen mit diversen "Anderen" verstrickt werden. Geht man von einer der Grundannahmen der Phänomenologie aus – "l'individu se pose en s'opposant" –, ist dieser Versuch, sich selbst über den "Anderen" zu definieren, keinesfalls außergewöhnlich: "Pour se situer lui-même par rapport à l'autre, le moi doit d'abord définir l'autre et souvent c'est en fonction de l'autre qu'il parvient à sa propre définition de lui-même" (Dion, 1987, S.

17). Die in den "monologues" beschriebenen Beziehungen von "le moi" und "l'autre" weisen jedoch nie eine symmetrische Struktur auf sondern sind asymmetrisch und auf die Pole "domination – subordination", "exploitant – exploité", "colonisateur – colonisé", "supérieur – inférieur" (cf. Dion, 1987, S. 18) ausgerichtet; die sich als "Moi" artikulierenden Quebecker nehmen in diesem asymmetrischen Verhältnis zu Anglokanadiern, Amerikanern und Franzosen des Mutterlandes immer die Position des Unterlegenen, des Minderwertigen, des sich über das Negative Definierenden ein (cf. Mertz-Baumgartner, 1997, S. 77-91). In den "monologues" von Yvon Deschamps wird das asymmetrische Beziehungsmuster an der Auseinandersetzung des Arbeiters mit seinem Arbeitgeber illustriert,[4] in den Texten Clémence DesRochers', Jacqueline Barrettes und Denise Guénettes werden stets weibliche Ich-Erzählerfiguren mit allen Facetten einer patriarchalen Welt konfrontiert, in der das Weibliche als Negativum des Männlichen, das Differentielle über den Mangel bestimmt werden. Quebecker, Arbeiter und Frauen werden in der Gattung des "monologue" als gleichermaßen "kolonisierte" und marginalisierte Bevölkerungsgruppen präsentiert, die gegen eine zentralisierte Machtstruktur das Wort ergreifen.[5] Das Themenrepertoire jener "monologues", die das hierarchische Oppositionsverhältnis Frau-Mann aufgreifen, ist breitgefächert und umfaßt viele Ansatzpunkte feministischer Literatur ganz allgemein.[6] Am deutlichsten manifestieren sich das asymmetrische Verhältnis und seine Infragestellung wohl in den Texten, die die traditionelle Rollenverteilung und das Rollenverständnis der Frau als Ehefrau und Mutter in den Mittelpunkt rücken. So schildert Clémence DesRochers in *L'art d'être femme* (DesRochers, 1969, S. 176-177) die Erwartungshaltungen, die von der Mutter und dem Mann – *qui t'a choisi* – an eine Frau herangetragen werden. *La moman* von Jacqueline Barrette (Barrette, 1972, S. 60-67) sowie *La triste collaboratrice* von Denise Guénette (Guénette, 1993, S. 57-59) erzählen vom unbezahlten, harten, bis zur körperlichen Erschöpfung führenden Alltag einer Hausfrau, dem die Gesellschaft keinerlei Wertigkeit beimißt; *La p'tite sacripante* von Denise Guénette (Guénette, 1982, S. 23-25) zeigt schließlich, wie die sozialen Rollen bereits in der unterschiedlichen Erziehung von Mädchen und Buben festgemacht werden. Die Monologistinnen kritisieren aber nicht nur die von der Gesellschaft zugewiesenen Rollen an sich, sondern weisen darauf hin, daß die der Frau zugedachten Aufgaben wie Haushalt und Kindererziehung ihr gleichzeitig auch neue Wege versperren. *La rentrée des classes* von Clémence DesRochers (DesRochers, 1969, S. 168-169) erzählt beispielsweise von einer jungen Frau mit sechs schulpflichtigen Kindern, die ihren durch die Großfamilie bedingten Mangel an Schulbildung am Abend durch Selbststudium auszugleichen versucht (*Ma grande soeur refait, par ses soirs, en cachette/Dans les livres d'enfant, sa quatrième année!*). Jacqueline Barrette leiht *Antoine* (Barrette, 1972, S. 79-80) ihre Stimme, die in Verzweiflung ihr achtes Kind erwartet und ob seines Todes erleichtert ist.

Ein zweiter großer Problembereich, der innerhalb des übergeordneten Themas der Geschlechterbeziehungen immer wiederkehrt, sind die Gewalt, die Frauen von Männerseite in verschiedenen Beziehungen entgegengebracht wird, sowie die sexuelle Belästigung und Degradierung zum Lustobjekt, die Frauen häufig erfahren müssen.[7] Mit humorvoller und zugleich schmerzlicher Direktheit schildert Jacqueline Barrette in *La vie c'est pas une chanson* (Barrette, 1972, S. 13-16) die leidvollen Erfahrungen einer Ehefrau mit der Trunksucht und Gewalttätigkeit ihres Mannes (*mon mari buvait; [...] y m'battait m'engueulait [...] on avait pas une cenne*). Nachdem sie sich lange Zeit mit einfühlsamen Chansons und dem Hören von Musik trösten kann, erkennt sie schließlich *La vie c'est pas une chanson* und verläßt ihren Mann. Eine ähnliche Atmosphäre verbreitet der "monologue" *J'y'ai dit* (Barrette, 1972, S. 20-21), der die Mutlosigkeit, Hilflosigkeit, aber auch Passivität eines Ich beschreibt, welches im Bus einen Mann beobachtet, der seine Frau gewaltsam zum Gehorsam zwingt. *J'yé tu [tout] dit*, versehen mit einer ganzen Zeile von Fragezeichen, bleibt zuletzt als beißender Selbstvorwurf des Ich zurück und spiegelt zugleich eine Einstellung der Gesellschaft wider, die solche Verhaltensweisen zwar beobachtet, jedoch unbestraft läßt. Eine der "Heldinnen" Denise Guénettes resümiert in *Quand j'aime j'aime* (Guénette, 1993, S. 15-18) die in den meisten "monologues" dargestellte Rolle der Frau sowie ihre Konfrontation mit dem "Anderen" mit einem Vokabular, wie es auch für die Charakterisierung anderer Abhängigkeitsstrukturen (der Quebecker, des Arbeiters) verwendet wurde: *je m'étais effacée, oubliée, écrasée, reniée,/transformée en robot au service de son maître*. Die Frau beschließt jedoch, nicht duldsam in ihrer Rolle zu verharren, sondern diese zu verlassen: *Là, j'ai fait mes bagages/ pis chus partie sans même le réveiller/pour y dire bonjour....* Im allgemeinen fällt auf, daß viele Texte von Monologistinnen nicht ein "je/nous immobile" darstellen, sondern einen Aufbruch der Frau signalisieren.[8]

Betrachtet man die zitierten Beispiele in ihrer zeitlichen Chronologie, so wird deutlich, daß mit Ausnahme der Texte von Clémence DesRochers, die teilweise bereits in den 60er Jahren geschrieben wurden,[9] alle zwischen 1970 und 1985 entstanden.[10] Sieht man diesen Produktionszeitraum als historischen Abschnitt, zeigt sich, daß sich die Frauenbewegung in Québec erstmals deutlich im Zuge der politischen Ereignisse 1970 manifestiert – nationale und feministische Forderungen laufen parallel -, ihren Höhepunkt gegen Ende der 70er Jahre erreicht und zu Beginn der 80er Jahre merklich an Radikalismus und Konsequenz verliert (cf. Lamoureux, 1986, S. 146ff.).

Was kann nun der "monologue" inhaltlich und formal für die Artikulation und Mitteilung frauenspezifischer Forderungen leisten? Entsprechend dem

Gattungsprofil, welches am besten durch die volkstümliche Entstehung der Gattung und deren orale Tradition beschreibbar ist, kommt es im "monologue" zu einer der "écriture féminine" französischer Prägung diametral entgegengesetzten "Schreib-Sprech-Praxis", die sich durch eine Popularisierung der Inhalte, deren häufig plakativ-einfache Darstellung und die Verwendung von mündlicher Sprache auch im nachträglich verschriftlichten Text charakterisiert. Die Rezeption bei breiten Bevölkerungsschichten scheint darin bereits angelegt zu sein.[11]

Die von Laurent Mailhot in der Anthologie *Monologues québécois 1890-1980* angesprochenen Funktionen des "monologue" treffen in besonderem Maß auch auf die Texte von Monologistinnen zu. Mailhot setzt diese Funktionen des "monologue" mit Verben wie 'appeler', 'nommer' und 'explorer'[12] in Verbindung und vergleicht ihn mit einem "cri sourd et perçant" (Mailhot / Montpetit, 1980, S. 19). Der "monologue" stellt demnach eine Möglichkeit dar, Unausgesprochenes zu artikulieren, Erfahrungen und Wahrnehmungen zu ergründen, zu benennen und "hinauszuschreien". Der "monologue" hilft dem Ich auf diese Weise, eine Realität zu bewältigen, die "une blessure qui voudrait guérir" (Mailhot / Montpetit, 1980, S.19) ist, und ermöglicht es ihm, sich selbst zu erfahren und als "Moi" zu situieren[13]. In einem zweiten Schritt führt der "monologue" das Ich aus seiner einsamen Zurückgezogenheit, seiner "jonglerie hivernale", dem "repliement méditatif sur soi" (Mailhot / Montpetit, 1980, S. 13) hinaus und ermöglicht ihm die Kontaktaufnahme mit einem Du. 'Contact' und 'ouverture' werden dabei für Mailhot zu jenen Leitbegriffen, die die für ihn zentrale Funktion des "monologue québécois" erfassen und ihn zu einem wirksamen Mittel politischer und sozialer Artikulation und Handlung machen: "Le personnage est encore seul, mais il est seul avec d'autres, solitaire-solidaire [...]." (Mailhot / Montpetit, 1980, S. 13)[14] Dabei ist diese so wesentliche Öffnung nach außen, zu einem Publikum, bereits in den wichtigsten Gattungsmerkmalen angelegt: Ein Künstler, der Autor, Regisseur und Schauspieler in Personalunion ist, und ohne Kostüm, ohne bühnenpräsente Mitspieler, auf einer Bühne ohne Bühnenbild und mit wenigen Requisiten agiert, ist beinahe zwangsläufig darauf angewiesen, über diese Bühne hinauszutreten und sein Spiel auf die andere Seite der Bühne, den Zuschauerraum hin auszurichten. Während Bühnenbild, Kostüme und verbale und nonverbale Interaktionen mit weiteren bühnenpräsenten Figuren im Theater für den Zuschauer eine andere, fiktive Welt erschaffen, bewegt sich der Monologist häufig in einem halbfiktionalen Raum, in einer "Fiktionskulisse" (cf. Vogel, 1993, S. 150). Die Fiktionalität wird dabei insbesondere durch eine größtmögliche Interaktion zwischen Publikum und Künstler (offener Dialog, Publikumsdialog) aufgebrochen[15] und durch verschwommene Grenzziehungen zwischen der realen Künstlerpersönlichkeit und der fiktionalen Erzählerfigur sowie zwischen fiktionalen und realen Rezipienten "reduziert". In jedem Fall wird dem "Moi" die Begegnung mit einem zumeist solidarischen, mitwissenden "Toi/Vous" unter Ausgrenzung des "Il/Autre" ermöglicht.

3. "Je sors du monde du silence. Ma bouche n'est plus sèche. Je parle. Je peux parler"[16]: Monolog und Sprachfindungsprozesse in *La Nef des Sorcières* und *Les Fées ont Soif*

Die 1976 im Théâtre du Nouveau Monde uraufgeführte Theaterproduktion *La Nef des Sorcières* ist eine Kette von acht Monologen, die sieben Autorinnen kollektiv verfaßten. Wenn *La Nef des Sorcières* auch von zahlreichen Kritikern und Kritikerinnen als erstes feministisches Theaterstück Québecs gelobt wurde (cf. Saint-Martin, 1992, S. 27), so verstummten aber auch jene kritischen Stimmen nicht, die aus ästhetischen und politischen Gründen an der Monologform Anstoß nahmen. Yollande Villemaire äußerte sich diesbezüglich: "Les femmes de la *Nef* n'ont pas risqué la création collective: chacune est à sa place et suit sa *track*. [...] Nous ne sommes donc pas face à un corps collectif de femmes. Mais à des femmes isolées dans leurs productions. [...] Nous avons donc affaire à six personnages de femmes isolées dans leurs monologues" (Villemaire, 1976, S. 20). Ähnliche Aussagen finden sich auch bei Nicole Brossard und France Théoret selbst, die in ihrem Vorwort zu *La Nef des Sorcières* schreiben: "Chacune isolée dans son monologue, comme elle l'est dans sa maison, dans son couple [...]" (Brossard / Théoret, 1976, S. 9); Louisette Dussault, Autorin des Monodramas *Moman* (1981) und Schauspielerin in *La Nef des Sorcières* und *Les Fées ont Soif* bestätigt: "Ça [*Moman*] reste un monologue et on a de la misère à en sortir: *Les Fées*, c'est un monologue à trois voix, *La Nef*, des monologues parallèles, mais les femmes vivent dans un tel isolement..." (Dussault, 1981, S. 26). Der strukturellen Besonderheit des Monologs – es fehlt im Vergleich zum Dialog der auf der Bühne anwesende Ansprechpartner – scheint auf inhaltlicher Ebene der Ausdruck von Einsamkeit und Isolation geradezu zu entsprechen.

Tatsächlich berufen sich zahlreiche gängige Definitionen des Begriffs "Monolog" auf seine Etymologie (*monos* 'seul', *logos* 'discours') und unterstreichen die beim Monolog im Unterschied zum Dialog fehlende Komponente des Perzipienten. So definiert der *Grand Dictionnaire encyclopédique Larousse* 'monologue' als "discours qu'un personnage se tient à lui-même, qu'il n'adresse pas directement à un interlocuteur" (Larousse, 1984, S. 7055); der Theaterwissenschaftler Patrice Pavis spricht ebenso von einem "discours d'un personnage non adressé directement à un interlocuteur en vue d'obtenir une réponse" (Pavis, 1980, S. 260) wie Tzvetan Todorov, der den Monolog als "extension de la forme linguistique d'exclamation", als "forme expressive par excellence qui ne s'adresse à aucun interlocuteur" (Larthomas, 1972, S. 374) bezeichnet. Versehen wir jedoch den Monolog nicht mit einem Mangel, einem Negativum und betrachten ihn nicht als verhinderten Dialog, sondern mit Emile Benveniste als "dialogue intériorisé, formulé en langage intérieur entre un moi locuteur et un moi écouteur" (Benveniste, 1974, S. 84f.) oder gar mit Louis Francoeur als "moyen de communication intrapersonnelle destiné à influencer, de quelque manière, le spectateur-destinataire" (Francoeur, 1976, S. 183),[17] so eröffnen sich neue Wege für das Ich zum Du, Wege, die aus der Einsamkeit heraus zunächst zur Sprach- und Selbstfindung und schließlich zur Solidarität führen. Eine derartige Sichtweise des Monologs korreliert nicht nur mit den zentralen Themen von *La Nef des Sorcières* – Sprache finden, Weibliches Sprechen, Frau-Sein und Sprechen -, sondern auch mit der von Luce Guilbeault 1976 gewählten Inszenierung, bei der die Schauspielerinnen nach der Darbietung ihres Monologs auf der Bühne bleiben und sich auf diese Weise zuletzt als solidarische Gruppe dem Publikum präsentieren. Auch Lori Saint-Martin sieht in der Aufführung eine "Nuit de la poésie au féminin, où la succession des artistes n'est pas signe d'isolement mais de richesse collective" (Saint-Martin, 1992, S. 39).

Die monologische Kommunikation zwischen einem "moi locuteur" und einem "moi écouteur" wird besonders in jenen Texten deutlich, die um die Sprachfindung und das Aussprechen bislang tabuisierter Themen kreisen. So erkennt die Schauspielerin, die gerade die Rolle der Agnès für Molières *Ecole des femmes* probt, aus einer Gedächtnislücke heraus, daß sie bislang nur "männliche Texte" auswendig reproduzierte: *Mon texte, je le savais par coeur, j'en rêvais./ Par coeur, mes coeurs./ M'écoeure [...]/ Bam, bam, bam dans la tête, les mots/ Avec le grand marteau pénis. Pénis?* (La Nef, 1992, S. 47). Sie schlüpft daraufhin in andere Rollen, zitiert aus dem Monolog der Außenseiterin Pierette Guérin in *Les Belles Soeurs* von Michel Tremblay, evoziert mit Angéline, Marie-Lou und Carmen weitere Frauenfiguren der tremblayschen Theaterwelt und spielt auf die "Außenseiter" Gauvreau und Jarry an. Nur im Gespräch zwischen "moi locuteur" und "moi écouteur", im Selbstgespräch also, gelingt es ihr, die von der männlichen Gesellschaft geforderte Sprachlosigkeit der Frau (*Femme jusqu'au bout des ongles/ Sois belle et tais-toi/Femme*; La Nef, 1992, S. 47) beziehungsweise ihre Rolle als Mimin zu überwinden[18] und zu ihrer eigenen, an die weibliche Körperlichkeit gebundenen Sprache zu finden. Ähnliches beobachten wir im Monolog der *méno-pausée*, dessen zentrales Thema – die Sprachfindung – bereits in der 20maligen Verwendung von 'parler' und von synonymen Verben deutlich zum Ausdruck kommt. "Weibliches Sprechen" wird dort zum Mittel, Frau-Sein nicht länger als Negativität und Mangel, über männliche Normen und Wertungen zu definieren[19], den weiblichen Körper anzunehmen und auszusprechen[20] und stereotype Rollenbilder zwischen madonnenhafter Überhöhung und Verhöhnung als Hure zu zerstören[21]. Neben dialogischen, an das eigene hörende Ich gerichteten Sätzen wie z. B. *Où est-ce qu'elle est ma peau pour que je sois bien dedans?* (La Nef, 1992, S. 61)[22] fordert gerade die Auseinandersetzung mit ihrem Frausein sowie mit den ihr von einer männlichen Gesellschaft zugewiesenen Rollenbildern die Ich-Erzählerin zu fingierten Dialogen mit bühnenabsenten männlichen Repräsentanten dieser Gesellschaft wie Arzt oder Psychiater auf. Daraus resultiert, wie die folgenden Beispiele zeigen, insbesondere durch die Verwendung zahlreicher pronominaler Anreden und an den bühnenabsenten männlichen Partner gerichteter Fragen eine durchaus dialogische Struktur: *On m'a toujours dit que tu étais le héros./ Tu sens-tu un héros, toi?* (La Nef, 1992, S. 57); *Parce que j'ai toujours menti pour TOI./ Pour toi./ Parce qu'il fallait que je te plaise;/ tu étais supérieur – tu possédais la Force...* (La Nef, 1992, S. 63).

Wird nun die Position des bühnenabsenten Perzipienten im Text nicht durch ein "tu/toi" sondern ein "vous" realisiert, erleben wir in der Aufführungspraxis eine Ansprache an eine nicht näher definierte Gruppe, in die das Publikum potentiell eingeschlossen ist. Die Beispiele *Excusez-moi, je ne sais plus quoi dire* (die Schauspielerin in La Nef, 1992, S. 45), *Imaginez-vous./ J'ai eu 20 ans. Hier....* (die alternde Frau in La Nef, 1992, S. 51), *Je m'appelle Lucie ou Lucy comme vous voudrez* (die Arbeiterin in La Nef, 1992, S. 67) oder *Vous m'avez trahie, vous m'avez menti, vous m'avez fait honte* (die Lesbe in La Nef, 1992, S. 119) zeigen deutlich, daß derartige Publikumsimplikationen neben den zahlreichen Textverweisen auf die neu entstehende Solidarität zwischen Frauen[23] dazu beitragen, dem zunächst entstandenen Eindruck von Einsamkeit und Isolation entgegenzuwirken und eine Begegnung mit solidarischen Anderen aufzubauen. Der Monolog wird auf diese Weise zum Mittel der Selbstfindung und der Solidarisierung von Frauen in Abgrenzung zu einer männlichen Welt. Spinnt man den Gedanken der Schriftstellerin im Sinne der *Nef des Sorcières* weiter – *Seule, je parviens à me débrouiller l'esprit. Mais à deux, je deviens isolée* (La Nef, 1992, S. 136) – so ermöglicht der Monolog Sprachfindung, Definieren und Situieren der weiblichen Differenz sowie Kommunikation und Solidarisierung, währenddessen der Dialog, der "Normalfall" zwischenmenschlicher Kommunikation, von Frauen als hierarchisierende und daher isolierende Struktur empfunden wird.

Auch *Les Fées ont Soif* von Denise Boucher (1978) schildert Sprachfindungs- und Solidarisierungsprozesse, wie wir sie in *La Nef des Sorcières* in einer Abfolge von Monologen kennengelernt haben. Die zunächst alternierenden Monologe der Protagonistinnen, Marie, Madeleine und La Statue entwickeln sich jedoch mit deren zunehmender Solidarisierung zu echten Dialogen; parallel dazu verlassen die Figuren immer häufiger ihren "lieu respectif" und sprechen im "lieu neutre", dem Bühnen-Ort der Befreiung und

Verständigung zwischen Frauen. Schildern die drei Frauen – die Mutter (Marie), die Jungfrau (La Statue) und die Hure (Madeleine) – zunächst die ihnen von einer patriarchalen Gesellschaft zugewiesenen Rollenbilder[24], ihre zerstörten und verhinderten Träume (leitmotivisch stehen dafür die Begriffe "attendre" und "peur"; Boucher, 1989, S. 57 und 62ff.), so artikulieren sie sich später zunehmend als "Moi" und finden parallel zu ihrer eigenen Sprache auch zu einer Basis weiblicher Solidarität: Ab dem Moment, als Marie auffordert *Parlons, parlons. Parlons. Paroles. Hymnes. Chants. Danses. Rires. Larmes. Tirons les murs du silence* (Boucher, 1989, S. 64), treten die Frauen zunehmend in einen Dialog ein, der ihre Solidarität stärkt und eine Befreiung von ihren Rollen-Attributen (Schürze, Kette=Rosenkranz und Sockel, Stiefel) erst ermöglicht. Zuletzt artikuliert sich ihr neues kollektives Bewußtsein als starkes "Nous", welches sich gegenüber einem männlichen "Toi" abzugrenzen versteht und mit dem leitmotivisch verwendeten "imagine" (Boucher, 1989, S. 96ff.) auf den Entwurf einer neuen weiblichen Welt verweist: *Nous voici devant toi debout, nouvelles. Imagine* (Boucher, 1989, S. 100). Wir erleben im beziehungsweise über den Monolog, wie er in den beiden besprochenen Theaterproduktionen verwendet ist, – ähnlich wie bereits in Abschnitt 2 gezeigt – eine Begegnung des Ich mit einem solidarischen "Toi/Vous/Nous", welches ein männliches "Il/Autre" ausgrenzt beziehungsweise die Konfrontation mit einem männlichen "Toi/Autre" aufnimmt.

4. Monolog und "théâtre de femmes" am Beispiel von Marie Laberge: ein Ausblick

Wie im Theater von Michel Tremblay, Jean Barbeau und Jean-Claude Germain so finden Monologe und monologähnliche Passagen auch bei der wohl bekanntesten Quebecker Bühnenautorin Marie Laberge durchgehend Verwendung. Am Beispiel von *L'homme gris* (uraufgeführt 1984) und *Jocelyne Trudelle trouvée morte dans ses larmes* (geschrieben 1980/ uraufgeführt 1986) soll gezeigt werden, daß auch in diesen Theaterstücken der Monolog ein bedeutungstragender Bestandteil der Dramenstruktur ist. Dabei können abschließend zwei mögliche Funktionen des Monologs skizziert werden, die in ihrer diametralen Gegensätzlichkeit den Monolog im Spannungsfeld zwischen Kommunikationslosigkeit und Isolation einerseits sowie Solidarität und Begegnung andererseits zeigen. *L'homme gris* ist ein Zwei-Personenstück, in dem die weibliche Protagonistin Christine zwar stets bühnenpräsent ist, jedoch nur in zwei kurzen Repliken auf den Monolog ihres Vaters, den "homme gris", reagiert (cf. dazu Laberge, 1986, S. 41f. und 56ff.). Der Rest ist ein langer Monolog des titelgebenden Protagonisten, in dem die Perzipientin in Formulierungen wie *comme tu vois* und *attends* zwar stets präsent ist, jedoch nicht zu Wort kommt. Solche oder ähnliche Formulierungen erfüllen scheinbar die phatische Funktion, zum Gesprächspartner Kontakt zu halten, können jedoch letztlich nicht über die gescheiterte Kommunikation zwischen Vater und Tochter hinwegtäuschen. Wie der Vater vergeblich in Phrasen versucht, zu Christine Kontakt zu halten und doch in einen langen Monolog abgleitet, so bleiben auch auf inhaltlicher Ebene die gutgemeinten Ratschläge und Hilfsangebote im Keim stecken und entwickeln sich zu versteckten Vorwürfen und verletzenden Bemerkungen.[25] In *L'homme gris* ist der Monolog – anders als in den in Abschnitt 2 und 3 besprochenen Texten – letztlich formales und inhaltliches Zeugnis einer gescheiterten Kommunikation: "Le langage, moyen d'approche par excellence, est manié, dégradé, pour devenir paradoxalement le chemin de l'isolement, du narcissisme le plus atroce" (Navarro Pardiñas, 1989, S. 105). Der Monolog ist in diesem Fall im Mund des männlichen Protagonisten das sprachliche Zeugnis der Kommunikationslosigkeit, angesichts dessen die Protagonistin vollends verstummt.

Dieses Thema steht auch in *Jocelyne Trudelle trouvée morte dans ses larmes* im Zentrum, in dem die Hauptfigur Jocelyne nach einem Selbstmordversuch im Koma liegt und daher – ähnlich wie zuvor Christine – ausschließlich eine "présence exprimée" (Laberge, 1992, S. 136) besitzt, wie Marie Laberge selbst feststellt; das heißt Jocelyne charakterisiert sich durch eine replikenlose Bühnenanwesenheit, ist jedoch in den Dialogen und Monologen der anderen Bühnenfiguren stark als Gesprächsgegenstand präsent. Die von der Krankenschwester Lucie verfolgte Absicht, die Figuren zu einer Kommunikation *mit* Jocelyne zu bewegen, verharrt in einem Sprechen *über* sie. Das Theaterstück führt dem Zuseher Kommunikationslosigkeit in allen seinen Facetten vor, wobei die Mutter, die von sich selbst sagt *J'sais pas parler, moi ... j'parle jamais* (Laberge, 1992, S. 36) "sprachlos" bleibt (*Ma pauv' enfant qué cé que j'pourrais ben t'dire*; Laberge, 1992, S. 36), und der violente Vater zwar in Streitgespräche über Jocelyne mit Lucie und Carole eintritt, seiner Tochter gegenüber jedoch ebenfalls schweigt. Allein ihre Freunde Ric und Carole finden das Gespräch mit der im Koma liegenden Patientin, und gerade ihnen kommen nun interessanter Weise die monologischen Passagen des Theaterstücks zu: So erzählt Ric in einem monologhaft anmutenden, stark narrativen Textabschnitt Carole zunächst von seiner zärtlichen Liebesnacht mit Jocelyne (Laberge, 1992, S. 110ff.) und überwindet daraufhin, wenn auch nur kurz, seine Ängste, mit Jocelyne nicht reden zu können. Carole läßt sich demgegenüber ganz auf ein "Gespräch" mit Jocelyne ein, in dem in einem dichten Netz von Fragen und gemeinsamen Lösungsmöglichkeiten die tiefe Verzweiflung aber auch Freundschaft Caroles zum Ausdruck kommt. In ihrem letzten Satz *[...] j'vas être là, Jocelyne, j'te lâcherai pas, lâche-moi pas!* (Laberge, 1992, S. 122) klingt dabei bereits der

Ausgang des Stückes – Carole folgt Jocelyne in den Selbstmord – an. Im Gegensatz zu *L'homme gris* entwickelt sich in *Jocelyne Trudelle trouvée morte dans ses larmes* der Monolog – hier wieder einer Frauenfigur in den Mund gelegt – erneut zum Ort der Begegnung und der Solidarität.

5. Resümee

Der "monologue", wie ich ihn am Beispiel von Clémence DesRochers, Jacqueline Barrette und Denise Guénette dargestellt habe, trägt dazu bei, Themen der Geschlechterbeziehung zu popularisieren und – gestützt durch die populäre und orale Entstehung und Tradition der Gattung – einem breiten Publikum zu erschließen. Die Gattungsspezifika, die man mit dem Begriff der "Fiktionskulisse" resümieren kann, bedingen darüberhinaus beinahe zwangsläufig eine Orientierung der monologistischen Botschaft zum Zuschauerraum hin, wodurch der Zuschauer und -hörer zum wichtigsten Kommunikationspartner der Erzählerfigur und der Künstlerin wird. Diese Öffnung nach außen erlaubt eine Solidarisierung des "Moi" zum "Nous" unter Ausgrenzung des männlichen, unterdrückenden "Il/Autre".

In *La Nef des Sorcières* und *Les Fées ont soif* scheint die von den Autorinnen gewählte Monologstruktur zunächst formal die Einsamkeit und Isolation der Frauen in einer männlichen Welt widerzuspiegeln. Die Inhalte der Monologe weisen diesem jedoch eine diametral entgegengesetzte Bedeutung zu: Der Monolog wird in beiden Theaterproduktionen zum privilegierten Ort der Selbst- und Sprachfindung, die ihrerseits die Voraussetzung *sine qua non* für eine Solidarisierung mit anderen Frauen darstellen. Während in *La Nef des Sorcières* die Skepsis gegenüber dem Dialog – als hierarchischer, männlicher Struktur – bleibt und eine Solidarisierung nur in Monologen angesprochen sowie durch die Inszenierung dargestellt wird, treten die Protagonistinnen in *Les Fées ont soif* selbst in einen Dialog ein, der ihre gemeinsame Befreiung erst ermöglicht.

Und wenn Nicole Brossard und France Théoret schreiben "Les femmes ne sont pas dans l'Histoire, elle n'ont que 'des histoires'" (Brossard / Théoret, 1976, S. 10), so scheinen "monologues" und Monologe in "Spectacles" und "Théâtre de femmes" gerade diese verborgenen Geschichten zu erzählen und zu einer weiblichen "Histoire" zusammenzuführen: "Le malaise fabrique sa transformation. Il passe à l'action (la scène). Il passe dans les mots. [...] Le monologue ramasse la voix 'maternelle', il la déplace sur scène en traces historiques" (Brossard / Théoret, 1976, S. 11).

Anmerkungen

1 Cf. zur Gattung des "monologue" in Québec Mailhot, 1983 und Mertz-Baumgartner, 1997.

2 Im Rahmen dieses Artikels können hierzu nur einige Ideen formuliert werden, die sich für eine intensivere Auseinandersetzung sicherlich anbieten würden. Auch der Bereich des Monodramas (wie zum Beispiel *La Sagouine* von Antonine Maillet und *Moman* von Louisette Dussault) mußte aus Platzgründen ausgeblendet werden.

3 Cf. dazu Kapitel 4.1. in Mertz-Baumgartner, 1997.

4 Cf. dazu *Les unions qu'ossa donne?* (1968), *La mort du boss* (1973) in Deschamps, 1973, S. 19–29 und S. 227–233 sowie *La manipulation* (1979–80) in Deschamps, 1981, S. 153–173.

5 Ich erinnere an dieser Stelle an die Theorie der Marginalität, der Subversion und des Dissidententums bei Julia Kristeva, die ja eine ausschließliche Theorie des "Weiblichen" ablehnt und Unterdrückung und Marginalität in einen größeren Kontext stellt (cf. Moi, 1989, S. 191).

   Ich teile keinesfalls die Feststellung Jane Moss', daß zwischen den "comic monologues of male performers such as Yvon Deschamps and Reynald Bouchard" und den "intimate, personal insights into private lives and emotions" von Autorinnen ein gravierender Unterschied bestünde (Moss, 1983, S. 282; Moss, 1985, S. 247). Vielmehr können auch zahlreiche "monologues" männlicher Autoren von Coutlée über Gélinas zu Favreau eine solche Innensicht bei durchaus unterschiedlichen Tonalitäten – von zärtlich-kritisch bis bitter-zynisch – belegen, und auch die Erzählerfiguren sind stets ähnlich typisiert.

6 Neben den in der Folge diskutierten Themen erscheinen auch das Altern und seine Bedeutung für die Persönlichkeit der Frau als Themenkonstante. Cf. *47 ans* von Jacqueline Barrette (Barrette, 1972, 74–76), *40 ans* von Denise Guénette (Guénette, 1980, S. 87–89), *Enfin j'ai mes 50 ans!* von Denise Guénette (Guénette, 1993, S. 64–68). Guénette übertitelt darüberhinaus einen ganzen Abschnitt mit *La reproduction* und diskutiert das Problem der künstlichen Befruchtung und der Leihmütter (Cf. Guénette, 1993, S. 147–174).

7 Cf. *L'honnêteté/Ma blonde* Yvon Deschamps (Deschamps, 1981, S. 45–50), *La topless* von Clémence DesRochers (DesRochers, 1977, S. 107–108), *Sont ben achalants!* von Denise Guénette (Guénette, 1993, S. 33–37) sowie *La fille de rien* von Denise Guénette (Guénette, 1982, S. 114–123).

8 Cf. von Clémence DesRochers *Les jeudis du groupe* (Pedneault, 1989, S. 397–398), *Monologue à trois voix* (Pedneault, 1989, S. 399–401), *La rentrée des classes* (DesRochers, 1969, S. 168–169), *La topless* (DesRochers, 1977, S. 107–108); *La vie c'est pas une chanson* von Jacqueline Barrette (Barrette, 1972, S. 20–21); von Denise Guénette *Y est parti ... chus libb* (Guénette, 1980, S. 47–51), *Quand j'aime j'aime* (Guénette, 1993, S. 15–18), *La moppeuse du quartier* (Guénette, 1982, S. 28–29); *Coupe tes ficelles* von Marc Favreau (Favreau, 1978, S. 139–141).

9 "Elle a été la première humoriste à exploiter systématiquement les thèmes féminins pour ne pas dire féministes. [...] Sur cinquante-trois chansons étudiées, trente-quatre racontent des histoires reliées aux femmes." (Cf. Tremblay, 1994, S. 532) Diese Beobachtung gilt auch für die "monologues" der Künstlerin.

10 Insbesondere Denise Guénette stellt ihr Gesamtwerk unter den übergeordneten Themenbereich Frau/sein: "Y sont représentées des femmes urbaines, issues de milieux populaires, isolées, aliénées ou naïves, épouses, mères, consommatrices avant d'être femmes" (Maziade, 1994, S. 885).

11 Zahlreiche kollektive Theaterproduktionen zu Beginn der 70er Jahre sind thematisch ähnlich ausgerichtet und zeigen dieselbe Tendenz zur Popularisierung (cf. Moss, 1983, S. 277–278).

12 "[...] ils [die Ich-Erzählerfiguren] appellent, explorent, nomment" (Mailhot / Montpetit, 1980, S. 13),

13 "Ils parlent pour s'entendre, se situer" (Mailhot / Montpetit, 1980, S. 28).

14 Cf. auch "Le monologue est individuel, personnel, cellulaire; il cherche le contact, l'ouverture." (Mailhot / Montpetit, 1980, 28); "Le monologue cherche désespérément (joyeusement) le contact" (Mailhot / Montpetit, 1980, S. 30).

15 Zu weiteren Wirkungsmechanismen der Fiktionskulisse cf. Mertz-Baumgartner, 1997, S. 152–182.

16 Cf. den "monologue" von Marthe Blackburn in *La Nef des Sorcières* (La Nef, 1992, S. 51).

17 Francoeur führt dann weiter aus: "Le monologue vise à influencer le destinataire et dans ce sens il a un interlocuteur".

18 Nach Luce Irigaray hat die Frau "als Gefangene der spekularen Logik des Patriarchats [...] die Wahl, entweder sprachlos zu bleiben, indem sie nur ein unverständliches Plappern hervorbringt [...] oder tatsächlich die spekulare Darstellung ihrer selbst als minderwertiger Mann zu inszenieren." (cf. Moi, 1989, S. 159)

19 *Jusqu'ici on a été faits l'un par l'autre./ Définis l'un par l'autre. Inventés par les autres./ Et c'est un échec* (La Nef, 1992, S. 57).

20 *[...] dire le mot sang [....]/ Du sang rejeté. Du sang toujours gardé secret./ Du sang sans poésie* (La Nef, 1992, S. 52f.).

21 *[...] je suis un MONUMENT. [...]/ Je suis la Fontaine d'amour, vous savez/ Je suis la Fécondité./ Je suis le Flambeau./ Je suis la Pietà...* (La Nef, 1992, S. 60). *Je suis la pornographie, l'écoeurant, le cochon,/ Je suis les fesses, le con, la poitrine/ Je suis le nombril du monde* (La Nef, 1992, S. 61).

22 Ein besonders deutliches Beispiel eines solchen Dialogs zwischen "moi locuteur" und "moi écouteur" stellt auch der Text von Marcelle I dar: *Ne t'effaces-tu pas pour mieux exister Marcelle? Eclate, bondis, sois méchante (il le faut tu deviendras plus humble et plus généreuse)* (La Nef, 1992, S. 109).

23 *Je pense à Elles pour la première fois* (La Nef, 1992, S. 97); *on écoute ces voix [...] de se joindre à nous* (La Nef, 1992, 116); *J'exhibe pour moi, pour nous, ce qui nous ressemble. J'écris et je ne veux plus faire cela toute seule. Je nous veux. Faire craquer, grincer, grincher l'histoire* (La Nef, 1992, S. 131). Cf. dazu auch Saint-Martin, 1992, S. 30.

24 *Je m'appelle Marie. Ils glorifient mes maternités [...]* (Marie in Boucher, 1989, S. 42); *Ils ont dit que la chair était un péché contre l'esprit. Et ils m'ont enfermé au coeur même de la chair de la pomme* (La Statue in Boucher, 1989, S. 55). *Je suis la celle au grand coeur. Qu'ils disent. Eux* (Madeleine in Boucher, 1989, S. 43). Oder etwas später: *Y disent tout' que chus folle* (Marie in Boucher, 1989, S. 61), *Y disent tout' que chus une sainte* (La Statue in Boucher, 1989, S. 62), *Y disent tout' que chus hystérique* (Madeleine in Boucher, 1989, S. 62).

25 So verknüpft sich beispielsweise die "Liebeserklärung" an seine Tochter sogleich mit der Erinnerung an den verstorbenen Sohn und an das geliebte 11-jährige Mädchen Christine: *Un ans après c'est toi qui est née. On t'a appelée Christine en souvenir de lui, pis malgré toute, on t'a aimée. [...] Mais j'ai perdu ma belle tite fille aussi... J'ai rêvé à deux choses dans ma vie: à mon fils pis à ma p'tite fille de 11 ans* (Laberge, 1986, S. 51).

6. Literatur

6.1. Primärliteratur

Barrette, Jacqueline, 1972, *Ça-dit-qu'essa-à-dire*. Montréal: Les grandes éditions du Québec.

——, 1973, *Flatte ta bedaine, Ephrème*. Montréal: Le Théâtre actuel du Québec et Les grandes éditions du Québec.

——, 1975, *Dis-moi qu'y fait beau, Méo!* Montréal: Les grandes éditions du Québec.

Boucher, Denise, 1989, *Les Fées ont soif*. Montréal: L'Hexagone.

Brossard, Nicole et al., 1992, *La Nef des Sorcières*. Montréal: L'Hexagone.

Deschamps, Yvon, 1973, *Monologues*. Ottawa: Leméac.

——, 1981, *Six ans d' monologues. 1974-1980*. Ottawa: o.A.

DesRochers, Clémence, 1969, *Sur un radeau d'enfant*. Ottawa: Leméac.

——, 1973, *La grosse tête*. Ottawa: Leméac.

——, 1974, *J'ai des p'tites nouvelles pour vous autres et des dessins*. Montréal: L'Aurore.

——, 1977, *Le monde aime mieux...*. Montréal: Les Editions de l'homme.

——, 1993, *Tout Clémence: Tome 1: 1957-1974*, Montréal: vlb éditeur.

——, 1995, *Tout Clémence: Tome 2. 1957-1994*, Montréal: vlb éditeur.

Dussault, Louisette, 1981, *Moman*. Montréal: Boréal.

Favreau, Marc, 1978, *Rien détonnant avec Sol!* Montréal/Paris: Stanké.

Guénette, Denise, 1980, *la vie...des fois*. Montréal: Les Editions de la pleine lune.

——, 1982, *m'as dire comme on dit:.* Montréal: Les Editions de la pleine lune.

——, 1993, *Des mots qui rient, des mots qui parlent*. Lachine: Les Editions de la pleine lune.

Laberge, Marie, 1986, *L'homme gris.^* Montréal: vlb éditeur.

——, 1992, *Jocelyne Trudelle trouvée morte dans ses larmes*. Montréal: Boréal.

Pedneault, Hélène, 1989, *Clémence. Tout l'humour du vrai monde: Chansons et monologues précédés d'un documentaire de Hélène Pedneault*. Ottawa: Les Editions de l'Homme.

6.2. Sekundärliteratur

Benveniste, Emile, 1974, *Problèmes de linguistique générale*. Paris: Gallimard.

Brossard, Nicole und Théoret, France, 1976, "Préface", in: Nicole Brossard et al., 1992, *La Nef des Sorcières*. Montréal: L'Hexagone, 9-19.

Dion, Léon, 1987, *Québec 1945 2000: A la recherche du Québec*. Québec: Presses de l'Université Laval.

Francoeur, Lucien, 1976, "Sémiologie du nouveau théâtre québécois: Le 'monologue' comme moyen de communication intrapersonnelle", in: Pierre Léon/Henri Mitterand (Hrsg.), *L'analyse du discours/Discourse analysis*. Montréal: Centre Educatif et Culturel Inc., 181-191.

Lamoureux, Diane, 1986, *Fragments et collages: essai sur le féminisme québécois des années 70*. Montréal: les Editions du remue-ménage.

Larthomas, Pierre, 1972, *Le langage dramatique*. Paris: Armand Colin.

Mailhot, Laurent und Montpetit, Doris-Michel, (Hrsg.), 1980, *Monologues québécois (1890-1980): Une anthologie*. Ottawa: Leméac.

Mailhot, Laurent, 1983, "De la littérature orale au théâtre. L'évolution du monologue", *Québec français* 49, 40-43.

Maziade, Linda, 1994, "La vie...des fois, monologues de Denise Guenette", in: Maurice Lemire (Hrsg), *Dictionaire des oeuvres littéraires du Québec*. Tome VI, Montréal, Fides, 885-886.

Mertz-Baumgartner, Birgit, 1997, *'Monologues québécois' oder Geschichten eines 'Monsieur qui parle tout seul': Standortbestimmung einer Gattung am Rande*. Augsburg: Dr. Wißner Verlag.

Moi, Toril, 1989, *Sexus, Text, Herrschaft*. Bremen: Zeichen + Spuren Frauenliteraturverlag.

Moss, Jane, 1983, "Women's Theater in Québec: Choruses, Monologues and Dialogues", *Quebec Studies* 1, 276-285.

——, 1985, "Women's Theater in Quebec", in: Paula Gilbert Lewis (Hrsg.), *Traditionalism, nationalism and feminism. Women Writers of Quebec*. Westport/London: Greenwood Press.

Navarro Pardiñas, Blanca, 1989, "Les masques de la communication: analyse de *Jocelyne Trudelle trouvée morte dans ses larmes* et de *L'homme gris*", in: André Smith (Hrsg.), *Marie Laberge, dramaturge*: Actes du Colloque international, Montréal: vlb éditeur, 105-118.

Pavis, Patrice, 1980, *Dictionnaire du Théâtre: Termes et concepts de l'analyse théâtrale*. Paris: Editions Sociales.

Saint-Martin, Lori, 1992, "Introduction à La Nef des Sorcières", in: Nicole Brossard et al., *La Nef des Sorcières*. Montréal: Hexagone, 21-41.

Villemaire, Yollande, 1976, "autour de la nef des sorcières", in: *Jeu* 2, 16-21.

Vogel, Benedikt, 1993, *Fiktionskulisse. Poetik und Geschichte des Kabaretts*. Paderborn/München/Wien/Zürich: Ferdinand Schöningh.

The Split Self in Margaret Atwood's Female Dystopia
The Handmaid's Tale

Dunja M. Mohr

Anticipating the approach of the new millenium, literary visions of the future, however promising or disquieting, present us with much needed food for thought. This future-oriented literature has been called by many different names and labels, such as utopia, dystopia, science fiction, speculative fiction and fantasy literature. The borders, however, are admittedly difficult to identify. Science fiction, by many critics considered to be the appropriate new name of the utopian genre and subsuming utopia/dystopia (although neither science fiction nor utopia really fit as the all-inclusive name for this very diverse genre),[1] proposes *other*, fictional extrapolations of the respective present society. Hence it has been a most popular genre with female writers influenced by feminism's challenge of the sociopolitical status quo. Science fiction and its subgenres are particularly amendable to experimentation, because "realism by definition is grounded in the actual, patriarchal world, *only* Science Fiction, with its embrace of fantasizing and the impossible, can fully sustain a feminist vision of the future" (Roberts, 1990, p. 137). Sarah Lefanu characterizes the relationship between science fiction and feminism thus:

> Unlike other forms of genre writing, such as detective stories and romances, which demand the reinstatement of order and thus can be described as 'closed' texts, science fiction is by its nature interrogative, open. Feminism questions a given order in political terms, while science fiction questions it in imaginative forms [...]. If science fiction demands our acceptance of a relativistic universe, then feminism demands, no less, our acceptance of a relativistic order. (Lefanu, 1989, p. 100)

The term utopia, coined by Thomas More in 1516, plays with the Greek word "topos" (place) and the prefixes "u" and "eu," thus creating a pun on no place/good place. Utopia then means "a non-existing good place." Following Darko Suvin's definition, utopia is a "verbal construction of a particular quasi-human community where sociopolitical institutions, norms and individual relationships are organized according to a more perfect principle than in the author's community" (1973, S. 132). Accordingly, dystopia, meaning "a non-existing bad place," voices humanity's deepest fears. Although dystopia and utopia share a discontentment with the present, their approaches are diametrically opposed. Dystopists fear the "perfect state," which is exactly what utopia strives to describe. Utopia, in fact, carries the very *other*, the dystopian seed, in its core. In the end, very often dystopia and utopia merge, depending on one's viewpoint. Calin Andrei Mihailescu defines dystopia thus:

> Dystopias are stories that contrast the failure of the main character with the unstoppable advance of society towards totalitarianism. The loss of the self is the character's final acknowledgement of, and ultimate contribution to, society's being definitely victorious. (Mihailescu, 1991, p. 215)

Up to the late nineteenth century utopias/dystopias have been mainly described by male authors, writing from the male perspective. The first wave of female fictional extrapolations (e.g., Mary Bradley Lane's *Mizora: A Prophecy*, 1889; Charlotte Perkins Gilman's *Herland*, 1915 and its sequel *With Her In Ourland*, 1916; Ayn Rand's early dystopia *Anthem*, 1938) occurred at the turn of the century, with women's fight for political rights, the vote in particular. The women's liberation movement in the 60s and 70s of our century sparked off a real surge of female utopias/dystopias.[2]

The basis of our Western concepts of reality, and thus of ourselves, is determined by our grasp of the existing order of dualities, of "the age-old distinction between the Same and Other" (Foucault, 1970, p. xv). Ever since Simone de Beauvoir's *The Second Sex* (1949) we are conscious of the argument that man is perceived as the subject and woman as the *other*. In our dualistic world man's experience is placed as central and absolute while woman is inessential and alien. It is not astonishing then for women to have no place but their traditional one in male utopian literature.

Thus writing from the position of the *other* in our society, female utopists/dystopists are especially interested in breaking this dualism, designing new ways of organizing a society, paying explicit attention to different forms of cohabitation and (co)existence of the two sexes in their imaginary alternative worlds. With the help of literary blueprints they aim at unveiling patriarchal society. In order to achieve any changes within every-day life, a human's perception of reality needs to undergo a fundamental transformation. Male utopists' perception of reality has mostly excluded the view of the *other* and thus their extrapolations remain in that sense imperfect.

However, female utopias and dystopias are mostly written from a white perspective, marginalizing yet other forms of *otherness*.[3] Sally Miller Gearhart, writer of female utopias, notes how rarely otherwise egalitarian women authors like Charlotte Perkins Gilman, Joanna Russ, Monique Wittig and even Gearhart herself escape the trap of racism: "[they make] no successful attempt to paint ethnic differences among women or to identify conflicts that might arise because of such differences. [...] [T]he action and the critical question for these writers clearly lie in the strife between women and men" (Gearhart, 1984, p. 307).

Male utopists/dystopists attempt to design a better or worse place – but for whom? They rarely concern themselves with the condition of the *other* gender (if they do concern themselves, it just is not in feminist terms) as the order within the utopian society very often reflects the dominant (patriarchal) culture of the author's society. Therefore male utopias/dystopias have dealt mainly with the distribution of power within society, while leaving gender roles and sexual division of labour the same in their projected futures (see Baruch, 1984b). These misogynist novels improve little for women, showing women as subordinates to men, assuming that women will follow their "natural instincts" (housework, maternity, subordination, silence) even in a liberal society.[4] Women remain prisoners of their bodies and their sex. Biology is destiny. On the other hand, looking at some aspects of male dystopias from a different angle, what appears to men as negative, might be judged by women as desirable (and vice versa).[5] In *Brave New World* (1932) Aldous Huxley condemns contemporary feminist concepts like the destruction of the family and reproductive control.

Science fiction novels very often lack the sociopolitical drive of utopian/dystopian novels and are more concerned with the conquest of other planets, time travel and technological gadgets. These (male) worlds are often populated by fraternities of scientists, engineers, space explorers all set upon the subjugation and conquest of new planets or galaxies, with the aid of the newest technological inventions.

Women writers reacted with creating a fictional future, a space, for free women. Their specific contribution to the genre consists of drawing feminism into utopian/dystopian literature: investigating the power relations *between* the sexes, extending the utopian postulates for freedom to *all* members of the human society, opting for non-patriarchal/non-hierarchical societies. Drawing on postmodern feminist thought in all its diversity they also introduced an increased awareness of language's phallocentric bias.[6] Their visions explore anti-hierarchical, egalitarian concepts open to the fusion of community goals with individual necessities, abolishing the nuclear (patriarchal) family.

A significant difference between male and female utopias is their respective concern for the actual achievement of the ideal future society. Jean Pfaelzer notes a curious "absence of historical process in utopian fiction" (Pfaelzer, 1983, p. 312). The actual transformation of the society is not mentioned or only referred to briefly in retrospect (as in William Morris'

News From Nowhere, 1890; Edward Bellamy's *Looking Backward 2000-1887*, 1888). For quite a few works by female utopists this is not true. Suzette Haden Elgin's triology – *Native Tongue* (1984), *The Judas Rose* (1987) and *Earthsong* (1992) – depicts the very slow alteration of a dystopian reality (as shaped by males) through a new language constructed by the linguist women of that society. Female utopists are less likely to opt for a static "perfect" state, but for a society open to process and modifications. Elaine Hoffman Baruch notes a significant shift from (male) stasis to (female) dynamics: "The fixed divisions between ideal and real, reason and madness, before and after, inside and outside, dissolve. Definitions become fluid. Either/or polarities disappear. Beginnings and endings alike are rejected. Utopia is process" (Baruch , 1984a, p. 207).

Creatively using the stock conventions of dystopia, women writers of dystopian novels expose questions of gender hierarchy, biological reproduction and women's rights in addition to the injustice of a rigid class system. They carry the patriarchal definition of society and the implicit control of women to its logical extremes, pushing the relation between class systems and existing gender hierarchies into the limelight. Hence central topics of criticism are gender roles, the relationship between the sexes, women's sexual autonomy, their reduction to "breeders," misogynist religion and literacy in connection with power politics.[7]

The opposition of the self and the *other*, the male subjective self assuming the centre of the personal experience, constructing everything alien to it as *other*, is one of the all-encompassing major dualisms female utopists/dystopists have attacked. In reality as much as in (male) utopia/dystopia women are pushed to the margin of the real or alternative (patriarchal) society and are denied the fulfillment of selfhood. If the existence of an all-defining centre which dominates all other ways of seeing reality is assumed, other values must be ignored, repressed or marginalized in order to stabilize the centre. In other words, the realities and values male (and female, for that matter) utopists/dystopists extrapolate from are perceived by them as universal but are in reality contingent upon their specific gendered perspectives. Through literary extrapolation from an*other* perspective, the existing (real) centre can be destabilized. However, *otherness* is not exclusively an external category. Psychoanalytic discourse suggests with the concepts of the self and the *other* a fundamental division not only between the sexes/genders, but also within the individual consciousness.

Margaret Atwood's female dystopia *The Handmaid's Tale* (1985) shows how concepts of duality and *otherness* do not only divide Gilead, Atwood's future society – and thus ours – but how the female protagonist Offred has internalized this dichotomy, leaving her as a fragmented fictional self. Offred's only way of survival within the totalitarian system consists of seemingly limiting herself to the role of the *other* while deconstructing exactly these concepts through her subversive use of language. In *The Handmaid's Tale* Atwood exposes several forms of the alienated *other* and the self. As so often in her novels, she analyzes on the geographical (Canada/USA), the sociopolitical (female/male) as well as the psychological and linguistic levels (Offred/Moira; Offred as narrator/survivor).

Atwood's dystopia, projected into the near future, is set in the USA after a religious right-wing takeover. The narrator Offred describes a woman's nightmare: The Republic of Gilead, located in what was formerly Cambridge (Massachusetts), the heart of puritan colonization, is a theocracy which aims to increase its population since it suffers from depopulation due to rampant sterility. The totalitarian system forcefully uses fertile women as breeders – the handmaids. While in Gilead maternity is idealized as the "ultimate" female achievement, real women are dehumanized as objectified bodies. Biblical authority is employed to maintain the political/biological subjection of women, restoring the "natural order" of female obedience to man. Only women's capacity to reproduce is scrutinized, blamed or celebrated, whereas the male capacity remains unquestioned.

Red, nun-like uniforms render the handmaids anonymous and indicate their sexual duties as well as the blood of child birth. Handmaids are subjected to collectivism; whenever in public they must be "in twos" (19), and fear of denunciation prevents any personal relationships. Gilead's patriarchal society exploits the idea of a sisterhood, playing exactly their potential ability to solidarize against them and turning the originally positive image "of two walking as one" into a metaphor for ultimate isolation.

Gilead's system of surveillance uses electronic devices and computerized technology. Obedience is enforced through abductions, beatings, hangings and silencing. Everyone lives in fear of torture, execution or deportation to the contaminated Colonies. Social life is made uniform, the autonomy of the individual is oppressed in order to maintain the rigid system. There are two types of public rituals, either ensuring progeny or obedience, centering around offences against religion or sex. The Ceremony, a communal Bible reading followed by enforced coercive copulation, and the Birth Day, centering around a handmaid giving birth, ensure progeny. The rituals of obedience are those of verbal obedience (Testifying, Prayvaganzas) and those enforcing bodily obedience (Salvagings; Particicutions).

Appended to the novel are "Historical Notes" of the year 2195, revealing that Offred's story is a recollection taped on cassettes, rearranged by male authorities (the Professors). This framing story *ad infinitum* mirrors the dystopian content; eternally women are judged and belittled – in the past, the present and the future. Atwood's criticism, focusing her dystopian novel mainly on progeny, class and gender division, legitimized by patriarchal religion, extends to sexism and marginalization of women hidden in the "Historical Notes," and refers back to sexism in Offred's past (our present). Much of the sexism is hidden in and attached to language, as language constitutes power and sexism. Writing and reading are hierarchized in Gilead: books are banned, reading and possessing books becomes a heroic and subversive act. The book ban is mainly gender-oriented: the aim is to silence all women – to monopolize literacy for the male elite. The Commanders, Gilead's top class, are the only ones who own books *and* are allowed to procreate. The Handmaids are assigned to Commanders only, sexual contact with other men of lower classes is prohibited.[8]

On the geographical level, Atwood's view of the USA as the imperialistic (male) aggressor to Canada's (female) victimization becomes clearer if one takes into account that the relationship between the two states, their two literatures, has indeed been a gendered one, marginalizing the latter: "Canada is not the fifty-first state of the United States, nor is Canadian literature part of American literature, rather it is the *other* North American literature" (Pache, 1996, p. 3, emphasis D.M.). Atwood writes as a Canadian female author from the *other* perspective about the sociopolitical status quo within the USA – and nearly every other society in the world – turning the mirror and reflecting the ultimate objectification of women by the male gaze. In *The Handmaid's Tale*, however, Canada's role is ambiguous. Atwood extends her criticism beyond scrutinizing the male self symbolized by the USA. On the one hand, Canada functions as a sheltering haven, on the other hand "the Canada of that time did not wish to antagonize its powerful neighbour, and there were roundups and extraditions of such refugees" (292). Atwood has explained in several interviews why she chose the States as a setting:

> America is a tragic country because it has great democratic ideals and a rigid social machinery [...]. But Canada is not tragic, in the classical sense, because it doesn't have a utopian vision. Our constitution promises 'peace, order and good government' – and that's quite different from 'life, liberty and the pursuit of happiness'. (Ingersoll, 1990, p. 57)

On the sociopolitical level, the hierarchical social structure clearly centers around the male subject and marginalizes the female object. In Gilead, men hold most of the power (consider the Aunts), while women are limited to the domestic sphere. Within the male hierarchy, there is a certain mobility; men can climb up the social ladder. Within the women's hierarchy only a downward movement is possible. Women are made uniform and stripped of their individuality, their names, clothes, and way of life are depersonalized, rendering them invisible. They are divided into eight groups, colour-coded according to their functions: sterile "Wives," "Handmaids," postmenopausal "Aunts," "Marthas" (sterile servants), lower-class "Econowives," widows, uncooperative "Unwomen," who have to clean up toxic waste in the Colonies. The lowest group of women is rendered invisible by the official structure, because their existence officially is denied in Gilead: the prostitutes at Jezebel's. The women sent to Jezebel's are former intellectuals, ex-prostitutes or rebels. Their very existence, though, shows Offred that Gilead has some cracks: their presence refutes the premise that sex is a mechanical act. The *other* is still there, it always is – the male self cannot extinguish the *other*, on the contrary, despite all efforts to exclude the other it is still needed to afirm the male self. Yet, only for the men the sexual act changes in so far as they foster the illusion of getting "real sex" (love has no part in it) here, meaning that *their* needs are attended to. At Jezebel's the Commanders can use women for their sexual lust without being on public display for procreation. Women, as objects of male sexual satisfaction, remain in the humiliating victim position.

The degradation of female sexuality culminates in the Ceremony and the birth ritual. This obsession to purify sex of all desire in terms of compassionate love indicates the immense potential danger which sexuality as fulfillment of love presents to Gilead's rigid system. Sex is either legally reproductive (Ceremony) or illicit and non-reproductive (Jezebel's). The monthly Ceremony perversely copies the "licensed" marital act of dutiful procreation of patriarchal Christianity. Supposedly an act of intimacy between two consenting persons, the procreational act is turned into a threesome public act of utter separation. Sex as an act of physical communication between lovers in a deeply involved human relationship is not allowed for in Gilead's seemingly "ascetic" society, officially oppressing desire and erotic sexuality but at the same time thriving as a (patriarchal) system on the very eroticization and sexualization of power.[9] In the Ceremony, Commander and assigned handmaid have intercourse in the presence of the Wife – all are fully dressed except for the body parts involved. The handmaid doubles the Wife at the Ceremony as well as on the double-decker birthing stool. Neither birth nor sex is private; both have become a collective act. With the strict laws against all other intercourse, previously non-sexual activities, such as illicit reading or playing Scrabble, become sexual. The Scrabble game played secretly between Offred and the Commander turns into a new kind of voyeurism, vividly connecting power with language and literacy. The game is doubly illegal, since it demands and promotes literacy, and because it takes place in private with distinct sexual overtones, illustrating the eroticization of power. Offred steals back language by playing Scrabble and reading magazines in the Commander's study, thus gaining knowledge and power. In the pre-Gilead era, Offred took no interest in politics, and failed to see the importance of language, not recognizing that silence adds to the oppressors' power.

Atwood holds both sexes, to varying degrees, responsible for this regime, yet she makes it very clear, that it is women who suffer from this dichotomy. Although the concept of the other is (arguably) a fundamental category of human thought, the human mind bears a cultured hostility to other consciousnesses, foremost privileging its own consciousness. Women, additionally imprinted with the "given" imbalance between the sexes, instead of reciprocally classifying men as alien, submit to men's view of them as *other* – a view applied to Gilead *and* to our society alike. Thus women involuntarily as much as voluntarily, according to Atwood, participate in their own subjugation by collaborating with the ruling system; both sexes, men and women, take part in the oppression of the *other*. In Gilead, the Aunts and Wives submit; assuming the role men have scripted for them is easier than attempting to divorce themselves from the given structure. However unjust and oppressive the society is, they cooperate as long as they maintain the top positions within the female hierarchy. In this respect, woman is the correlative of man's fragmented existence, helping him to affirm his selfhood, based on the exclusion of herself as the *alien*.

In return for their collaboration with the male elite – they control and train the handmaids – the Aunts are allowed to read and write. Ironically, the Aunts themselves believe in establishing a kind of "sisterhood," which is, in fact, a frightful parody of what the women's movement tried to establish with female networks in the 70s and 80s. Offred addresses her absent feminist mother with bitter irony: "Mother [...]. You wanted a women's culture. Well, now there is one. It isn't what you meant, but it exists. Be thankful for small mercies" (120). Atwood's dialectic exposes the mechanisms of a system in which everyone is caught – Offred did participate in her own subjugation, too. When women were gradually deprived of their independence and all constitutional rights in the pre-Gilead era, she adopted the dominant male perspective and remained a self-absorbed, passive woman. She is not innocent of her own condition. Although the society is monopolized by men, women are still part of the system and apply the same norms that objectify them. "Woman" participates in dystopia, at the same time that she is excluded.

The split between the self and the alienated *other* within Gilead's totalitarian system is obvious; Atwood's criticism, however, is more subtle and aims at the psychological oppressive determinism of gender roles and its expression in language. While it is easy to divide the world in black and white, these categories do not necessarily apply to the self. The dividing line between the self and the *other*, the fragmentation, does not merely exist outside of a person, but within.

Offred is an anti-heroine; her passivity and her attempts at making her life livable rather than effecting change has been extensively emphasized by critics. The point, however, is that through story-telling she establishes her fragmented voice against the male discourse, slowly taking on existence as a voice and therefore ensuring psychological survival. Through the telling Offred subversively decentres Gilead's perspective and recognizes the arbitrariness of its perpetuation. She allows for new possibilities to exist (Nick as love interest) and permits a new awareness of the limitations of herself (Ofglen; Moira). The text remains in a state of ambivalence though. Moira's and Ofglen's fates (prostitute at Jezebel's; driven to suicide) show that acting against Gilead fails. There are no heroical physical deeds – it all remains in the realm of language. To acquire, to scrutinize language and its forming power, to be heard, are the only ways of acting. She is a victim, but comes to rebel against that role through telling her story.

This split self becomes obvious in Offred's two voices. She speaks as a suffering and passive victim, mourning the loss of husband and child; and as a defiant survivor, reducing the oppressors with sarcasm. Just as the chapters alternate between day and night, night being the time when Offred relates her personal thoughts and memories, between clear rational, male Gilead and the associative female world, so does Offred vacillate between the pros and cons of collaborating with the system, unsure which guarantees survival. While Gilead condemns the feminine to absence, it is precisely this *otherness* that generates Offred's "discourse of survival."

Offred undergoes several stages: desperation, then hope for change within the system, and hope for romance, and finally the possibility of escape. During the first stage she is paralyzed and obedient; then she is stimulated into creativity, breaking her isolation; and at last she vacillates between suicidal petrification and again desperate hope.

Open to multiple interpretations through the attached "Historical Notes" and a dethroned narrator-author, the story continues to reappear in a new context, just as Offred repeatedly remarks, "Context is all" (136). The self without a centre is fragmentary, constantly shifting and dependent upon images of other equally fragmentary selves. Caught in the ongoing dialectic between the self and the *other*, the narrating "I" is constantly displaced. Offred "circles" around her perception, looking in vain for the centre she has been indoctrinated to believe in. Offred's voice does not speak from a centre, but rather from various positions around it. Memory is a tricky thing, thus Offred gives different versions, each time admitting the insufficiency and fictionality of each version and at the same time admitting her need for reconstruction. Language can only *approximate* events and emotions, and moreover Offred needs different versions, to have choice at all. She continually draws attention to the text as reconstruction, making it clear that reality is always mediated, intermingling fiction and reality.

Being indoctrinated with Gilead's and even with the pre-Gilead misogynist concepts of the self, Offred cannot possibly erase or destroy the governing ideas of the ruling system, but she can disrupt her internalized pattern of thought by telling how these have been constructed, how the female side has been relegated to the margins. Thus Offred decentres the official male position and places herself at the centre in the act of telling. Through imaginative creation Offred becomes the centre that counteracts the official male centre. Her task is then really to find the weaknesses in the privileged views of the ruling men and to create her (own) perspective. Offred is continually seeking an*other* perspective ("What I need is perspective," 153). The difficulty she encounters in her story-telling is that she is dependent upon the same structures of language and thought that she seeks to expose. Language equally enables and limits Offred.

Offred probes the construction of language through the etymologies of words, analyzing different meanings, comparing meanings from before and after the coup, exposing the multiple ironies of the English language. Offred notes that language is phallocentric, leaving out female realities, for instance, the Latin-rooted word "fraternize" has "no corresponding word that meant *to behave like a sister*" (11). Language reflects and determines a culture's perception of reality and in Gilead the Platonic concept of the logos, the word, as a key aspect of the Divine Logos is carried to its extreme. Offred's story is a struggle to be given access to this logos. If women establish their story and change language for their needs, then, the text suggests, they will have a chance to exist on equal terms with men. Although Offred becomes increasingly aware of the possibilities of the fluid realm of wordplay, association and *choice*, she is far from creating her own language. Nevertheless her "rebellious" *otherness*, her difference from the ruling male class and from the other handmaids, allows her (mental) liberation in the end. [10]

Atwood also addresses the topic of "writing the body" verbalized by the *écriture féminine*, especially Hélène Cixous and Luce Irigaray. Both theorists use metaphors linking the female body with a female poetics of orality. Susan Gubar has drawn attention to the pun on pen/penis, and the connection between writing and intercourse. Atwood consciously plays with this pun, stressing that literacy ought to be equally accessible and must not be withheld from women. Offred voices this explicitly: "The pen between my fingers is sensuous, alive almost, I can feel its power, the power of words it contains. *Pen is Envy*." (174, emphasis D.M.).

The handmaids' only means of personal communication is conspiratorial whispering, their form of verbal rebellion. Offred empowers herself by taking language back. She always stresses that she is *telling* her story. Atwood opposes "feminine speech" with "masculine writing," showing at the same time how "his-story" silences and belittles "her-story," how there is a gap between women's history and "official" (male) history. In *The Handmaid's Tale* women, reduced to silence, are living in the gaps of history. Professor Pieixoto, downplaying Gilead's sexist politics, refuses to pass judgment on Gilead: "Our job is not to censure but to understand" (284). Pieixoto trivializes Offred's story; condescendingly he apologizes for Offred's bad style and muddled mind. While he tries to establish *the text*, needing one reality, one history and a definite authorship (very much in accordance with traditional European monolithic principles of absolutes), he reduces Offred's life to an academic question.

On the personal level, Offred conjures an *other* just as she creates herself through language as a means of communication with an other: "I compose myself. My self is a thing I must now compose, as one composes a speech" (62). Story-telling enables her to exist, imagining an alter-ego, an opposite, in form of a reader or listener. Only if her story finds a reader or listener, will she then be remembered and raised above anonymity as an individual at last. Here, Atwood introduces another form of the mirroring self. With the incantation "I tell, therefore you are" Offred invokes the *other* self, the reader, or rather the reader*s*. To move beyond the subjective space at last is to survive; as Lorna Sage formulates it: "the important thing is to trade with the world outside" (1992, p. 168).

The reader supplies that part outside the text, while Moira represents the mirror inside the text. Women as the mirror to each other, doubling one another, is a recurring moment in Atwood's oeuvre:

> Atwood establishes a characteristic pattern of self-division. [...] her plots often supply the narrator/heroine with a best friend who's wild, irreverent, swaggering [...]. These characters are [...] narrative traces of the novelist's split. They raise questions about the relation between inside and outside views, 'I'and 'she', author and character (and reader). (Sage, 1992, p. 162)

Just as Cordelia is 'the evil other woman' in *Cat's Eye* (1988), or as Xenia functions in *The Robber Bride* (1993), Moira is 'the good other woman' in *The Handmaid's Tale*. The function of the rebellious woman is relegated to Moira. She was aware of the approaching oppression of women in the pre-Gilead era, and took action. Her *other*ness allows her to perceive the applied concept of reality differently, even in pre-Gilead times. But Moira, too, falls into the trap of assuming automatic equality between women, claming that "the balance of power was equal between women" (160). An all-female society is not the solution either, as Offred bitterly observes: "if Moira thought she could create Utopia by shutting herself up in a women-only enclave she was sadly mistaken. Men were not just going to go away" (161).

Twice Moira tries to escape from the training centre for handmaids, an audacity that turns her into a collective "fantasy" (125) of rebellion and *otherness* in a most positive sense. Offred has internalized Moira as a counterbalancing and judging authority, it is she who represents the role of the self-assertive woman. Moira's difference provides Offred (and female readers) with hope for her (their) own sex.

It is interesting to note that the rebellious role is relegated to Moira, one of the rare lesbian characters in future extrapolations.[11] Moira's double *otherness* – as a woman in a patriarchal totalitarian system *and* a lesbian in a "female community" enforced by men – makes her a double outsider (or insider, depending on the perspective), from male and female groups.[12] Her perspective is not blurred by sexual desires for the opposite sex. She vehemently refutes heterosexual inequality, the male/female binary oppositions. Even when her escape fails and she is sent to Jezebel's, she continues to resist the system. Remaining aloof, she subverts the purposes of Jezebel's and focuses on the women in the state-authorized brothel. Moira surrenders her body but not her mind at Jezebel's. On the contrary, forcefully abused and enslaved in this place of ultimate fulfillment of male sexual fantasies she dares to live it up. While Moira's physical escape fails, her spiritual or inner resistance remains unbroken, and although Offred's physical escape is not sure, her tapes survive, combining orality (female) and technology (male) to a kind of secondary orality. With that Offred offers, as the multiple pun of her name suggests, a different view of the otherwise official male history of Gilead: her story, fragmented as it is.

Notes

1 Marleen S. Barr has suggested the term "feminist fabulation" for feminist texts dealing with future and fantasy settings.

2 E.g., Ursula K. Le Guin's *The Left Hand of Darkness* (1969) and *The Dispossessed* (1974), Joanna Russ' *The Female Man* (1975), Suzy McKee Charnas's triology *Walk to the End of the World* (1974), *Motherlines* (1978) and *The Furies* (1994), to name just a few.

3 An example of a female dystopia concerned with racial issues is Octavia Butler's *The Parable of the Sower* (1993). Writing from an African-American feminist perspective, Butler creates a coloured female protagonist within a mixed races environment. Marge Piercy also makes an effort in *Woman on the Edge of Time* (1976) to address issues of race (and class). The female Mexican-American protagonist Connie even dis-

cusses racism with a a character from a future world. In Atwood's *The Handmaid's Tale* issues of racism are nonexistent.

4   Thomas More, for instance, shows women as subordinates to their husbands; Bellamy introduces only women who are content with their mother roles, fulfilling their "biological function"; Morris also sees women simply as servants doing the household chores. H. G. Wells even proposes in *A Modern Utopia* a class society in which men can experiment with women.

5   Here I draw on Shulamith Firestone's provocative *The Dialectic of Sex*, especially the conclusion, pp. 205ff.

6   In *Woman on the Edge of Time* Marge Piercy, for instance, changes the gender specific pronouns "he" and "she" to "per", derived from "person". Ursula K. Le Guin tries something similar in *The Left Hand of Darkness* (1969) by designing new gender-free words like "ammar".

7   E.g. Doris Lessing's *The Four Gated City* (1968) and *Memoirs of a Survivor* (1974), Angela Carter's *Heroes and Villains* (1969) and *The Passions of New Eve* (1977) or Zoe Fairbairns's *Benefits* (1979).

8   In the male hierarchy the Commanders hold the top position, followed by the Eyes (secret police), the Angels (military) and the Guardians (police). Within the male hierarchy there is a certain mobility. In order to be allowed to marry, Guardians need to be promoted to the status of Angels, if they acquire the rank of a Commander they might be "allotted a Handmaid of their own" (22).

9 The very act of reading, the tease of the Scrabble Game, but also the erotic display of women as objects for male desire at Jezebel's, reveal Gilead's foundation, which is the restriction of erotic desire to (selected) members of the male sex.

10   Here, Atwood refers to the liberating potential carried by Julia Kristeva's theory of the semiotic as a language which emerges from women's marginal position as *other*. For Kristeva, *otherness* is rather a celebration of women's difference than a sign of their limitations.

11   In general, the issue of differences among women has been neglected in women's utopian visions. Joanna Russ addresses lesbian love, the struggle of becoming a lesbian in *The Female Man*: "It's the crime of creating one's own Reality, of " 'preferring oneself '" (208). See Farley, 1984. Another science fiction novel addressing lesbianism is Nicola Griffith's *Ammonite* (1993)

12   Homosexuality is condemned in Gilead: "gender traitors" are executed with "purple placards" (41) around their necks. Lesbianism isn't even taken into consideration by the regime.

References

Atwood, Margaret, 1986, *The Handmaid's Tale*. Toronto: McClelland-Bantam.

Barr, Marleen S., 1992, Feminist Fabulations: *Space/Postmodern Fiction*. Iowa City, University of Iowa Press.

Baruch, Elaine Hoffmann, 1984a, "Introduction," in: Rohrlich, Ruby/ Baruch, Elaine Hoffman (eds.), *Women in search of utopia, mavericks and mythmakers.* New York: Schocken Books, 204-208.

Baruch, Elaine Hoffmann, 1984b, "Women in Men's Utopias," Rohrlich, Ruby/ Baruch, Elaine Hoffman (eds.), *Women in search of utopia, mavericks and mythmakers.* New York: Schocken Books, 209-218.

Farley, Tucker, 1984, "Realities and Fictions: Lesbian Visions of Utopia," in: Rohrlich, Ruby/ Baruch, Elaine Hoffman (eds.), *Women in search of utopia, mavericks and mythmakers.* New York: Schocken Books, 219-232.

Firestone, Shulamith, 1970, *The Dialectic of Sex. The Case for Feminist Revolution.* New York: Bantam Books.

Foucault, Michael, 1970, *The Order of Things.* New York: Pantheon Books.

Gearhart, Sally Miller, 1984, "Future Visions: Today's Politics: Feminist Utopias in Review," in: Rohrlich, Ruby/ Baruch, Elaine Hoffman (eds.), *Women in search of utopia, mavericks and mythmakers.* New York: Schocken Books, 296-309.

Ingersoll, Earl G., (ed.), 1990, *Margaret Atwood. Conversations.* Willowdale: A Firefly Book.

Lefanu, Sarah, 1989, *In the Chinks of the World Machine: Feminism and Science Fiction.* Bloomington: Indiana University Press.

Mihailescu, Calin Andrei, 1991, "Mind the Gap: Dystopia as Fiction," *Style,* 25:2, 211-222.

Pache, Walter, 1996, "Canadian Literature in English: A Retrospective and Retrogressive Survey," in: Schultze, Rainer-Olaf (ed.), *Aus der Werkstatt der Augsburger Kanadistik: Analysen – Berichte – Dokumentationen.* Bochum: Brockmeyer, 3-20.

Pfaelzer, Jean, 1983, "A State of One's Own: Feminism as Ideology in American Utopia," *Extrapolation,* 24:4, 311-328.

Roberts, Robin, 1990, "Post-Modernism and Feminist Science Fiction," *Science-Fiction Studies,* 17, 136-152.

Sage, Lorna, 1992, *Women in the House of Fiction. Post-War Women Novelists.* New York: Routledge.

Suvin, Darko, 1973, "Defining the Literary Genre of Utopia: Some Historical Semantics, Some Genealogy, A Proposal and A Plea." *Studies in the Literary Imagination,* 6, 112-140.

Bodyscape/s: Access, Colonization and Exclusion: An Emancipation of Literary Landscapes

Katja-Elisabeth Pfrommer / Tamara Pianos

> Could it be [...] that femininity is experienced as a space that often carries connotations of the depths of night [...] while masculinity is conceived of in terms of time?
> (Irigaray, 1987, p. 120)

Space has become a truly interdisciplinary matter of analysis and its examiners range from geographers and philosophers to historians, cultural theorists and literary critics. Within this wide field the persistent link between woman and space, the metaphoric transfer of the attributes of woman to space, has become an outstanding subject of feminist literary theorists and critics as well as writers (Best, 1995, p. 181). Mary Douglas notes: "The body is a model which can stand for any bounded system. Its boundaries can stand for any bounded system. Its boundaries can represent any boundaries which are threatened or precarious" (1991, p. 115). The body model is not only an indicator for demand or desire for a clear and visible limit but also an invocation of uncertainty of boundaries. "The female body delivers a conception of bounded mappable space, space which can still be understood as a totality even if it is internally fractured or carved up," Best states (1995, p. 184).

The idea of space as a container seems to underlie innumerable examples of bounded feminine space. The body matter of woman within this particular theory of space seems to have been inaugurated by Plato, who states in his later version of *chora*[1]: "We may indeed use the metaphor of birth and compare the receptacle to the mother, the model to the father, and what they produce between them to their offspring" (1965, p. 69). There also exists a more "active" version of Best's chora, but as the following examples will demonstrate it is the later, passive female space that has until now dominated our imagination.

The metaphors that were used to describe the man-landscape relationship, especially on the American continent, were those of man trying to conquer the virgin land. As Annette Kolodny has shown in *The Lay of the Land (1975)*, metaphors of seduction or rape are abundant. Henry Kreisel wrote on the same topic, surmising that: "The breaking of the land becomes a kind of rape, a passionate seduction. The earth is at once a willing and unwilling mistress, accepting and rejecting her seducer, the cause of his frustration and fulfillment, and either way the shaper and controller of his mind, exacting servitude" (Kreisel, 1971, p. 261).

One of the first major examples of the "woman as landscape"-metaphor in English-speaking literature is John Donne's "Elegy XIX: To his Mistress going to Bed" where we find "O my America! my new-found-land/ My kingdom, safliest when with one man mann'd/ My Mine of precious stones, My Empery/ How blest am I in this discovering thee! [...]" (Donne, 1993, p. 195). One rarely finds such obvious equations of the female body with land or landscape, but there are a number of examples of the general trend in several works of literature.

In literary texts, in myths and legends all over the world, there seems to be a striking similarity in the perception of the landscape as female. "Since classical times, at least, and in many cultures, the earth has been regarded as female, fertile if properly probitiated, but barren, like a wasteland, if incorrectly dealt with. Father sky provides semen in the form of rain [...]" (Porteous, 1990, p. 70). Gaia is the mother goddess of the earth who is inseminated by the skygod Uranos; Demeter is the "earth-mother," the goddess of fertility. The Maori have the male skygod Rangitane and the female earth goddess Papatuanuhu and there are probably countless other female goddesses who are associated with the earth. However, there are also a few examples of myths that tell of a male origin of the earth. The people of Northern Europe have created the myth of Ymir, a giant who was born out of melted water. When Ymir died his head became the sky and his flesh became the land. Although Ymir is male and the origin of the earth is male as well, we still have the upper division of head and spirit and the lower body or flesh. The unity that had existed in several myths in the beginnning was later separated into upper and lower sections, head and body, and usually male and female (Sheperd, 1994).

We assume, however, not that there is a universal truth and that there is an innate connection between women and land but that these connections are strongly dependent on current ideologies, philosophies and tastes and that examining literary texts will provide some information on how one particular author or sometimes the dominant society of a certain era saw or shaped the relationship between body and landscape; thus the respective image of women in general can be inferred. The status of women and the way "female landscapes" are represented in literary texts seem to develop in the same manner. When women were still viewed as emotional and intellectually inferior beings who lived their lives at the mercy of their fathers and husbands while those who led quite autonomous lives were viewed as witches, prostitutes or other dangerous and unworthy females, the "female" landscape was also represented in these categories. With the emancipation of women was the emancipation of the landscape was possible as well. A look at a few selected works in Canadian Literature shows us how widely the representations of body and landscape differ.

One early example is Morley Roberts' *The Western Avernus, or Toil and Travel in Further North America* (1887). In this autobiographical travel book Roberts describes the landscape of British Columbia. Phrases such as "the Bow River [...] born of the mountains," "the heart of the mountains," "the untouched virgin peaks of snow, [...] and the birthplace of rivers [...] are sacred" use more or less common metaphors to describe the landscape (Roberts, quoted from Deringer, 1996, p. 91). As Porteous has shown, the human body is a very rich *metafiér* and so "the heart of the mountain" is an easily comprehendable metaphor (Porteous, 1990, p. 73). Numerous authors have personified Nature in one way or other and so the mountain having a heart does not strike the average reader as anything unusual; the description of the landscape as obviously female – the virgin peaks giving birth to the rivers – is in line with countless other Mother Nature images. The construction of the railway involves the destruction of nature and is thus another example for "the lay of the land" whereby "the brute power of man's organized civilization had fought with nature and had for the time vanquished her" (Roberts, quoted from Deringer, 1996, p. 92). This image reflects the ongoing struggle about hierarchies and power.

The ocean as an important element of nature possesses several distinct female traits. In Robert's text the ocean is a mixture of the mother – the beginning of all things – and a dangerous *femme fatale* or Medusa figure who will eventually seduce and kill men.

> I looked still, and the mystic water grew alive, subtle, serpentine, and more mysterious, coiling and wonderful. She became eyed like the peacock's tail, with faint eddies of currents, and grew personal and feminine. This was the ocean from which the earth arose, this was the grave to which she descended to be renewed; and the eyes grew intense and vivid, prophetic and full of kindness unutterable, and of cruelty [...]. From her came the primeval slime of life [...] Ships sailed on her bosom [...] Her eyes were as those of one who knew all things, and her lips were touched with the melancholy of cruelty satiated, and yet her hands and fingers were eager for slaughter [...] in her dwell all things evil and good, and all knowledge and all power and all possibility of being. (Roberts, quoted from Deringer, 1996, p. 244f.)

This passage not only tells us that Roberts definitely saw both sea and landscape as female but the descriptions also suggest that there are three basic female character types: the virgin, the mother and the *femme fatale*.

In Frederick Philip Grove's texts the word "virgin" is abundantly used in his depictions of nature: strong men breaking up the virgin soil, or wishing to go further into virgin territory, or clearing virgin forests, can be found in almost all his Prairie texts. In *Over Prairie Trails* he describes the ugly landmarks of civilization as "scars on nature's naked body"[2] (Grove, 1970, p. 14). Grove's protagonists (strong men) are often portrayed working on their level fields thus being at right angles to the earth as Ricou has shown in *Vertical Man/Horizontal World* (1973) In Grove's and other prairie writers' texts one can find the distinct opposition between vertical man (male) and horizontal, flat landscape (often female). There seems to be no harmony; the only possible "relation" is penetration whereby the virgin soil is broken up to seed "the fruits of the earth." Often the same men who mercilessly break up more and more soil or tear down virgin forests "penetrate" their wives just as mercilessly to produce more "fruits of the womb," or just to demonstrate they always hold the top position (e.g., Grove 1992 and 1996).

The flat prairie is also often portrayed as being hostile towards human beings. It/she offers no shelter; one cannot hide from storm or rain or from the curious eyes of neighbours because the prairie in these descriptions offers no hiding places except for man-made huts. In this respect, nature is viewed as a *femme fatale* seducing men to follow her and then killing them by mercilessly exposing them to cruel weather conditions offering absolutely no shelter. Today, there are several writers who present the same prairie quite differently. Since the prairie itself has not changed and since the actual shape of the prairie was never as important as the politics and views of the person describing the prairie there are some further implications in this change of metaphor. The rejection of the old "flat female prairie" metaphor goes hand in hand with the questioning of several other metaphors which are indicators of power-relations. Seeing or presenting nature still as female but as an entity capable of thought and emotion, as a space that provides shelter, is in most cases not the production of a "back to nature"-generation but that of a counter-myth.

An interesting turning point in the human being – landscape relation came with Martha Ostenso's *Wild Geese*. The different characters in this novel all have extremely unique relationships with the landscape. While Fusi Aronson is the typical "giant figure of a man" (WG, 32) fitting into the vertical man – horizontal world image, Caleb Gare is somebody who, though not a giant figure and though not at right angles with the earth, still penetrates the soil in order to produce more and more wealth and who is ultimately killed "by nature" (Atwood, 1972, p. 47) in a fire on his fields. In his

"Afterword" to *Wild Geese* (*WG*), David Arnason likens the landscape in its relationship with Caleb Gare to a "demonic lover" (*WG*, 308). Arnason quotes from passages describing Caleb's fight with the fire in his flax-field to prove his point and indeed he deems the vocabulary that Ostenso chose to describe this last struggle "is a grotesque parody of sexual fulfilment," as this passage shows:

> Now the silky reeds were beginning to tangle themselves about Caleb's legs [...]. But the strength in the earth was irresistible. [...] the insidious force in the earth drew him deeper [...] the twisting and heaving of his body [...] ah, the over-strong embrace of the earth [...] The earth was closing ice-cold, tight, tight, about his body [...] (*WG*, 298f.)

Here we have the typical "nature-monster" or "nature as femme fatale" image[3] and yet Ostenso uses it in a very distinguished way. For Caleb the earth's turning out to be a "femme fatale" thus is the logical consequence of his relation to the earth. He loves his fields and treats them far better than the human beings around him. "He would creep between the wires and run his hand across the flowering, gentle tops of the growth. A stealthy caress – more intimate than any he had ever given to woman" (*WG*, 147). He loves the earth and what it/she produces but only because this increases his wealth. Caleb's tragic death in the field is foreshadowed by the way he is always drawn towards the earth. He is never the vertical man in a horizontal world: "Caleb walked in the approaching dusk like a thing that belonged infinitely to the earth, his broad, squat body leaning low over it" (*WG*, 156). Judith glimpses Caleb walking in the bush, his top-heavy body forming an arc toward the earth" (*WG*, 224) and the author later describes "his squat body leaning forward toward the earth" (*WG*, 276). Caleb is drawn towards his demonic lover as he is drawn toward death, finally united with the earth.

In extreme contrast to Caleb, his daughter Judith establishes an intimate relationship with the earth. For her, the earth is not a demonic lover but some kind of erotic entity that she gets in touch with lying naked on the soil in a sheltered place where she usually meets her lover. Ostenso writes:

> Judith took off all her clothing and lay flat on the damp ground with the waxy feeling of new, sunless vegetation under her [...] Oh how knowing the bare earth was, as if it might have a heart and a mind hidden here in the woods. The fields that Caleb had tilled had no tenderness, she knew. But here was something forbiddenly beautiful, secret as one's own body. (*WG*, 61)

Judith and her body establish an erotic relationship with the landscape that is based on direct touch and connection. Judith lies flat and naked on the ground so as to form no clearcut border between her body and the landscape. The earth is "bare" and the touch is not intercepted. However, the earth is also "knowing" and "might have a heart and a mind" and is thus not only seen as body but also as soul; there is some kind of spiritual connection between the two entities. While both Caleb and Judith get in touch with the landscape, Caleb's relation is one of exploitation that ultimately leads to destruction whereas Judith's relation is characterized by connection and a blurring of ego-boundaries. When Caleb dies, his ego-boundaries are violently split open as he becomes part of the landscape. Judith also dissolves into landscape but there is no violence involved; the blurring of boundaries is part of the erotic connection. Nature, or landscape, is personified, having a body and possibly "a heart and a mind," since after Caleb is killed "there (comes) a change in the mood of the earth" (*WG*, 301).

Another example of the closeness of women and Nature is Maggie Kyle in Hodgins' *The Invention of the World* (*IW*, 1977). As Deringer puts it, "Maggie verkörpert damit insgesamt nicht nur die naturhafte Ur-Identität Vancouver Islands, sondern als Demeter-Gestalt die 'Mutter Erde' selbst und die Erdhaftigkeit des Menschen schlechthin" (Deringer, 1996, p. 214). Maggie is a "chthonische Frauenfigur, die sich gleichsam in die Erde selbst verwandeln kann [...]" (Deringer, 1996, p. 216). Maggie is in some respects the typical sensuous woman who has the ability to become one with nature: "sometimes she could dissolve right into one of the offensive lines and go rushing off to disappear in unmarked regions of green" (*IW*, 44). On the other hand, Hodgins' picture is not so simple after all. Although Maggie is often represented as a person who seems to be in close contact with the natural world she is not presented as a typical "natural female" who possesses all the prototypical female character traits. She is not bestowed with a natural mother instinct. "She had never in her life met anyone else who'd been quite so much a flop as a mother" (*IW*, 20).

In *Eiriksdottir* (*E*) Joan Clark has created a female character whose body also merges seemingly completely with the surrounding landscape. Clark describes Freydis Eiriksdottir early on in the book:

> She felt her body enter the land: her lap became a smooth hollow, her knees and elbows rounded stones, her fingers alder twigs. The longer she sat above Gardar [...] the more Freydis felt herself transformed, becoming as silent and undemanding as stone [...] (she) blended with the landscape in a way that made woman and fells appear one. (*E*, 39)

Freydis literally assumes the characteristics of the landscape around her, she and "the other" becoming one. This woman explicitly *enters* the landscape. Aritha van Herk once blamed the male creations in Prairie literature for being unable to really enter the prairie and for always needing a vantage point to look at landscape but never to become part of the landscape (van Herk, 1992, p. 141). Another passage from *Eiriksdottir* can be read as an ironic remark about the entry and penetration of landscape. When Hofgrim, an old blacksmith, asks Freydis, "'Where is an old man [...] to put his risen penis after his wife has passed on?',″ Freydis replies, "'Why don't you stick it between the rocks? [...] There are enough small holes and cracks hereabouts'" (*E*, 10).

There seems to be a limited number of images of possible relationships between either men and nature or women and nature that have been used in literary texts abundantly. For men, nature is usually "the other" in the sense of a different being or a different entity. Men can be nature's antagonists and struggle with "her" in an effort to break the soil or clear the woods or traverse the mountains, or they can declare their love for nature and see themselves as outdoor creatures and nature's men who know how to survive with the help of nature. If they feel any unity with nature it is usually in a spiritual, metaphysical and not in a physical sense.

For women, nature frequently is represented as "the other" in the sense of another being with shared characteristics. The ego-boundaries are blurred and women are often presented as feeling an archaic physical unity with nature. One exception in these different representations is death. Only in death do men have the possibility to join the earth and lose their ego-boundaries while their bodies and the soil merge, as the case of Caleb Gare shows. And, as van Herk has pointed out in her essay "Mapping as Metaphor: The Cartographer's Revision," Rudy Wiebe's male protagonist Big Bear also becomes part of the landscape when he dies: "He finally becomes one with the land; [...] not straight lines but smooth curves – the mound of his body becoming part of the horizon, earth, rock" (van Herk, 1992, 62). There is a blurring of ego-boundaries when Big Bear and the landscape become one.

Including this possible connection in this examination of body-landscape-relation one has to be aware that this particular image can prove to be very tricky. This image can be seen as one of the few examples of a male character peacefully becoming one with the female or genderless landscape. Apart from the fact that this merging is usually only possible in death one cannot ignore that in this case it is a Native person becoming one with the landscape. This could imply the assumption that Native people, analogous to women, are closer to nature while at the same time being usually less intelligent and less civilized. This would suggest a biologically or genetically determined affinity of Natives and women to nature[4].

Recently some authors have started to create counter-myths and counter-metaphors that directly or indirectly question the old assumptions of the simple equation of female body to landscape versus male intellect to spirit.

Arachne Manteia, the protagonist of van Herk's *No Fixed Address* (*NFA*), who at the end of the book disappears into the Northern geography, has an erotic relationship with the landscape. She and Josef, her 90 year-old lover, climb a hill in the prairie, the "nipple of land on the breast of the world," to find Wild Woman, a "stone-shaped" woman who lies in one of the hill's folds. Van Herk descibes:

> Arachne stands between her legs [...] She stretches out inside the woman, lies within the stones on her back beneath that wheeling sky, arms outflung like the woman's, her head cushioned on a circle of breast [...] Arachne will never get tired of looking at the sky from within the woman's arm [...] (*NFA*, 232f.)

Arachne merges with the stone-woman who is in turn merged with the hill which is part of the landscape and looks at the sky from the "landscape's point of view." Woman and landscape again are one but they do not form a unity due to simple biological similarities but rather "mutual" attraction. Arachne and the stone woman unite in an erotic act that makes Josef obviously feel superfluous since "he stumps away" (NFA, 233). The human woman harmoniously lying within the stone woman is a counter myth to all the rape and seduction images of vertical men breaking virgin land.

The erotic counter-myth is elaborated in van Herk's *Places Far From Ellesmere* (*PFFE*). This erotic tension between place and person has nothing in common with traditional heterosexual relationships as no hierarchies are involved and a temporary fusion of two beings seems possible. The landscape of Ellesmere, the human body of the author/narrator, and the body of the intertextual protagonist Anna Karenina sometimes merge into one being. While in direct contact with a river the author/narrator experiences truly ecstatic feelings and wants to submerge into the liquid element. The author/narrator always keeps in direct touch with the landscape; there is no case or shell intercepting the touch. This freedom is in direct opposition to a tradition where women travelled in all kinds of compartments while men went on expeditions by foot or on horseback.[5] While Tolstoy's Anna Karenina is always travelling in train compartments or carriages, the author/narrator and her companion Anna are free to walk on Ellesmere Island and come into direct contact with the rivers or plants and the bare soil. Ellesmere and Anna Karenina also merge into one being due to physical similarites: "her [Anna's] flesh has appetite. And Ellesmere is a fat island" (*PFFE*, 96). Both Anna and Ellesmere are sensuous beings with an erotic aura and thus Ellesmere has nothing in common with the usual virgin territory that needs to be conquered and although it is an arctic desert it is in no way presented as barren or infertile. Ellesmere is not only explicitly female but is also bestowed with some kind of intelligence, being a "female desert island" with "its secret reasons and desires [...]" (*PFFE*,130). While former personifications of landscape often presented the virgin or the "femme fatale," Ellesmere is an autonomous and independent being as she is "no one's mistress" (PFFE,139).

In *A Likely Story* (*ALS*) Robert Kroetsch describes the narrator's/author's first erotic encounter with an erratic bolder. He remembers the bolder as "a composition of pure and erotic curves" (*ALS*, 49). About the actual sexual encounter he writes: "I became quite literally aroused at the sight of that rock [...]. Not I – we – touched. We knew a rough and blind joining; we knew the bereavement of separation. We found our lover's talk and found, the limits of all words" (*ALS*, 50). Throughout the short text this particular bolder is attributed with several explicitly female features. In Kroetsch's representation the rock as part of the landscape has just as much free will as he/the narrator himself. If we are to believe the narrator/author, the bolder reacted to the touch and also desired to touch, so that this sexual encounter of man and landscape is a meeting of equal partners and not the traditional version of man raping a landscape that cannot escape the rape.

Van Herk's and Kroetsch's landscapes are erotic entities in their own right. Although these two authors pull their visions of landscape over the "indifferent"[6] landscapes like all the others before them, their visions include a self-reliant and autonomous landscape that decides for itself/herself whom it/she will touch.

As our examples demonstrate, there seems to be a movement through the decades away from the one-way comparison of the terms *space* and *woman* through the transference of metaphoric use towards a concept of space not simply illustrated but produced by the metaphor of woman (Spivak, 1987, p. 169). The "reduction of the transferred term" (Hegel, 1975, p. 404) in literary language is shown in the writings of Roberts and Grove, where landscape is virgin, mother or femme fatale; here the only relationship exists through penetration. The concept changes with the appearance of either the female writer or the female (main) character's relation with nature: nature as erotic entity (Ostenso), unity with nature (Hodgins), explicit entering and becoming part of nature (Clark) are typical examples of linking the female body with space. Until now the attitude of man / male characters towards nature has frequently been antagonistic (redemption or unity is possible through death only; Wiebe), while women / female characters live the unity, see nature as a being with shared characteristics, as van Herk shows in her almost counter-metaphoric use of human and stone woman images (exceptional here is Kroetsch's encounter with the rock). As soon as there are more narrative levels beside the character-landscape relationship,[7] the linear transference or production of a concept will dissolve into the almost playful

> interacting system, whereby landscape is seen as body but, also, body is regarded as landscape, that the body in question, in male-dominant cultures, is very often the female body, [...]; and that, although no longer part of a dominant world-view, the metaphor has continued in use, at least in imaginative literature, well into the machine-age twentieth century. (Porteous, 1990, p. 69 f.)

Notes

1   Transl. Lee, 1965. Note: female ending of chora (= space).
2   Although Grove does not explicitly say in this passage that it is a female body he goes on to liken the body to a dead bird; and the equation of women and birds in literature is well-documented. See e.g. Moers, 1977.
3   Compare also Atwood, 1972, pp. 49ff. The image of the "world" as femme fatale can be traced back into the middle-ages as Barbara Becker-Cantario (cited in Poag, 1986, 61–73) has shown.
4   We do not want to imply that this was Wiebe's intention. We merely want to mention that images of male bodies (especially western white male bodies) with the earth are extremely rare and point out some dangers.
5   See Pelz, 1993, p. 6 and p. 69.
    Compare also Schenkel, 1993, p. 117, ..."indem sie [feministische Schriftstellerinnen] sich mit männlichen Mythen über weibliche Räume auseinandersetzen und ihnen eine Perspektive entgegenhalten, die aus der eigenen Erfahrung von Körper und Räumlichkeit entstanden ist."
6   Van Herk has argued that landscape as such is indifferent to the representations that writers create.
7   Van Herk constructs levels of author-intertext-protagonist-landscape connexions.

References

Arnason, David, 1994, "Afterword" in Ostenso, Martha, *Wild Geese*. Toronto: McClelland and Stewart, 303-309.

Atwood, Margaret, 1972, *Survival*. Toronto: McClelland and Stewart.

Becker-Cantario, Barbara, 1983, "'Frau Welt' und 'Femme fatale': Die Geburt eines Frauenbildes aus dem Geiste des Mittelalters," in: Poag, James W. and Gerhild Scholz-

Williams (eds.), *Das Weiterleben des Mittelalters in der deutschen Literatur.* Königsstein/Taunus, 61-73.

Best, Sue, 1995, "Sexualizing Space" in: Grosz, Elisabeth and Probyn, Elspeth (eds.), *Sexy Bodies: The Strange Carnalities of Feminism.* New York: Routledge.

Clark, Joan, 1995, *Eiriksdottir.* Toronto: Penguin.

Deringer, Ludwig, 1996, *Das Bild des Pazifischen Nordwestens.* Tübingen: Stauffenburg Verlag.

Donne, John, 1993, "Elegy XIX: To his Mistress going to Bed," in: *The Oxford Library of English Poetry.* Vol. I, London: Oxford University Press, 195f.

Grove, Frederick Philip, 1992, *Fruits of the Earth.* Toronto: McClelland and Stewart.

——, 1970, *Over Prairie Trails.* Toronto: McClelland and Stewart.

——, 1966, *Settlers of the Marsh.* Toronto: McClelland and Stewart.

Hegel, Georg W. F., 1975, *Aesthetics: Lectures on Fine Art.* transl. by G. C. Gill, Ithaca: Cornell University Press.

Hodgins, Jack, 1977, *The Invention of the World,* Toronto: Macmillan of Canada.

Irigaray, Luce, 1987, "Sexual Difference," in: Moi, Toril (ed.), *French Feminist Thought: A Reader,* Oxford: Blackwell.

Kolodny, Annette, 1975, *The Lay of the Land.* Charlotte: University of North Carolina Press.

Kreisel, Henry, 1971, "The Prairie: A State of Mind," in: Mandel, Eli (ed.), *Contexts of Canadian Criticism.* Toronto.

Kroetsch, Robert, 1995, *A Likely Story.* Red Deer: Red Deer College Press.

Moers, Ellen, 1977, *Literary Women.* Garden City.

Ostenso, Martha, 1994, *Wild Geese.* Toronto: McClelland and Stewart.

Pelz, Annegret, 1993, *Reisen durch die eigene Fremde.* Köln.

Platon, *Timaeus and Critias.* Trans. by D. Lee, Harmondsworth: Penguin.

Porteous, J.W., 1990, *Landscapes of the Mind.* Toronto: University of Toronto Press.

Ricou, Laurie, 1973, *Vertical Man/Horizontal World.* Vancouver:

Roberts, Morley, 1887, *The Western Avernus, or Toil and Travel in Further North America.* Westminster.

Schenkel, Elmar, 1993, *Sense of Place: Regionalität und Raumbewußtsein in der neueren britischen Lyrik.* Tübingen: Max Niemeyer Verlag.

Sheperd, Sandy, 1994, *Myths and Legends from Around the World.* London: Marshall Editions.

Spivak, Gayatri C., 1987, "Displacement and the Discourse of Woman" in: Krupnick, M. (ed.), *Displacement: Derrida and After.* Bloomington: Indiana University Press.

Tolstoi, Leo N., 1993, *Anna Karenina.* München: Deutscher Taschenbuch Verlag.

Van Herk, Aritha, 1992, *A Frozen Tongue.* Sydney: Dangaroo Press.

——, 1986, *No Fixed Address.* Toronto: McClelland and Stewart.

——, 1990, *Places Far From Ellesmere.* Red Deer: Red Deer College Press.

Wiebe, Rudy, 1973, *The Temptation of Big Bear.* Toronto: McClelland and Stewart.

Re-membering Self and (M)other in Daphne Marlatt's *Ana Historic*

Caroline Rosenthal

"Who's There? She was whispering. knock knock. In the dark."[1] This opening sentence of Daphne Marlatt's *Ana Historic* epitomizes the novel's central theme of searching, of searching for the other in yourself and yourself in the other. The reader is included in this search from the start: We neither know the speaker of the first sentence nor the addressee. As readers, we participate in *making* sense of words as well as of the three life-stories presented to us in the novel.[2]

In Marlatt's novel, Annie is the research assistant of her husband, Richard, a renowned history professor who dedicates his books "[...] to my wife without whose patient assistence this book would never have been completed" (79). During her research, Annie stumbles upon the name of a Mrs. Richards in the Vancouver city archives. The historical record only mentions Mrs. Richards with three sentences and ends her story when she is married to a Mr. Ben Springer. Annie is left alone with her curiosity and – for lack of facts – starts *imagining* Mrs. Richard's life.

Searching for Mrs. Richards' story, using the gaps as spaces for imagination, propels the story as well as Annie's development. Based on the few extant facts and on Mrs. Richard's diary which Annie excavates in the library, she decides to write a historical novel about her. Annie gives Mrs. Richards, whose first name is unknown, a time-spanning identity by naming her Ana: "Ana/that's her name:/back, backward, reversed/again, anew" (43). The anacyclical name is Janus-faced, looking into the past as well as the future, and encourages Annie to go back into history and rewrite it.[3] Ana's story, however, increasingly develops its own dynamics, because Annie's thoughts are frequently interrupted by the voice of another woman. The reader gradually comes to understand that this voice belongs to Annie's mother, Ina, who recently died. As a British immigrant Ina felt alienated and lost in Canada and consequently tried even harder to fit into society's rigid gender roles. She suppressed her own desires and tried to live up to her "lot" as a woman, thinking she had no other choice. Ina tried to stay on the linear track that society had assigned her, not knowing that "the 'right track' is full of holes, pot-holes of absence"(17) and finally went "off the deep end" (93). In hospital, her hysteria was treated with electroshock "therapy;" her thoughts were erased, not understood or *re-membered*. Annie decides to give Ana – in contrast to Ina – a choice in life. She thus invents different outcomes for Ana's story: either she really married or she met another woman, and together they stepped outside of oppressive gender roles by starting their own business. Creating the different versions of Ana's story leads Annie to discovering her own desires. Gradually she realizes that she has an alternative to being her husband's dedicated research assistant and devoted wife. The novel ends with the lovemaking of Annie and Zoe, a woman she met in the archives. The story thus moves from A(nnie) to Z(oe),[4] but not in a linear fashion.

Linearity as manifestation of reason is one of the pillars of Western thought rejected in *Ana Historic*. Marlatt draws on theorists like Derrida and Foucault in rejecting binary oppositions for establishing monolithic meaning, and in speculating that since truth is a discursively constructed effect it can be deconstructed. Truth is a palimpsest in *Ana Historic*; it has many different faces and voices that are superimposed to arrive at a multi-voiced story.

History, a man-made discourse, is called into question in *Ana Historic* by dissolving the "groundwork of fact" (134). As Hayden White has argued, facts are merely the "narrativization of real events."[5] The events really took place, but which events are 'fact-worthy' enough to be included in the book of history depends on subjective choice and hierarchical structures. Annie starts questioning her role as assistant, collecting facts, when she realizes that her diligent research only provides her with one version of the story, and that "there are missing persons in all this rubble" (134). The notion of margin versus center is challenged in *Ana Historic* by criticizing history from various perspectives, sometimes from within, by Annie, sometimes from the outside, by Ina, the "ex-centric."[6] The novel also plays with the similarity of history and narrative; both narrate events and claim authority and authenticity for their story. Annie's version of Ana's story is constantly examined and criticized by Ina's matter-of-fact voice undermining Annie's credibility.

Ana Historic falls within the genre of historiographic metafiction. The text is highly self-reflexive; it deconstructs its own narrative subject, and constantly thematizes the writing process. The continuity of the narrative is interrupted by inserted intertexts. These devices make the reader aware that this novel, after all, is just another human construct. *Ana Historic* demonstrates what Hutcheon terms "the presence of the past" (Hutcheon, 1988a, p. 4) in historiographic metafiction. History is an essential part of the novel, the past is omnipresent, but at the same time historical truth is challenged. Historiographic metafiction does not question whether or not something happened, but is critical of how we achieve historical knowledge and of how and who attributes meaning to an event. Thus, it frequently undercuts the authenticity of a historical/narrative version by fragmenting it, by dis-

and remembering the story. In a critical reworking of Ina's and Ana's lives, Annie recognizes her own desires. In *Ana Historic*, historical representations of gender roles are shown to dictate 'gendered' identities for the present.[7]

Marlatt's awareness of the strong connection between words and identity is most palpable in her use of personal names charged with meaning. At the beginning, Annie notes that the historic persona, Mrs. Richards, a widow, is only recorded with a dead man's name. She is 'dressed' in somebody else's identity. Mrs. Richards' fate is a warning to Annie who increasingly becomes Richard's Annie. Marlatt's anagrammatic word-plays manifest the interrelation between language and history. *Ana*grams not only reconfigure letters but seem to question de Saussure's notion of the synchronic sign by evoking past meaning, or at least by acting as reminders of a theme. Annie is an anaphonic version of the anacyclical name Ana as well as a palindrome of the name Ina.[8] The fate of Ana and Ina is separated by one letter only. This otherness and yet similarity gives Annie a vantage point from which she can look into the past. Marlatt deconstructs but also constructs identities. In the end, Annie constructs her own identity by baptizing herself Annie Torrent.

Role models for female identity in *Ana Historic* are often presented as society's 'strait-jackets' for women. Therefore, Marlatt employs the metaphor of words as ill-fitting clothes throughout the novel. She speculates that words are the 'containers' for a conglomeration of attitudes, and that certain words prescribe rather than denote attitudes and ideas.

The earlier quoted opening sentence of the novel leads the reader back to Annie's childhood where she searches the house for a threatening, ubiquitous, yet elusive presence. Annie tries to fight the lingering fear in the house "[...] stealing at night into the basement with the carving knife toward those wardrobes at the bottom of the staircase. wardrobes. wordrobes. warding off what?" (9). Marlatt plays with the notion that words dress ideas and attitudes, and that the resulting wordrobes ward something off, they protect somebody's interest or property. Marlatt pursues the metaphor of words as (word)robes in the different strands of the narrative. The image not only vividly evokes the socially conditioned masking function of words but also connects the life-stories of Ina, Ana and Annie. The "wardrobes [...] big enough to hide Frankenstein [...]" (10) that Annie opens with a pounding heart as a child are always empty, yet the fear remains. Words also contain unspoken but real fears: "skid row was a name we learned. rape was a word that was hidden from us. 'but what would he do?' 'bad things you wouldn't like'" (19). Rape turns out to be a word(robe) big enough to hide a monster.[9]

Later in the text it becomes clear to Annie as well as the reader that the silent fear in the house emanated from Ina, who – at a loss for words – loses herself in the monstrous wordrobes of 'wife' and 'mother'. The more Ina shrinks beneath the robe, the more firmly she holds on to society's standards of femininity. Day after day she hides behind "the perfect, implacable Garbo face" (58). In retrospect, while coping with her own roles as wife, mother, assistant, Annie says, "my fear began when I realized you never saw, as you turned away with a sudden frown or laugh, the you that was you, invisible in the mirror, look out at last" (58). Brought up to only recognize herself in opposition to the other, man, and in fulfilling a certain role/identity, Ina is incapable of perceiving her own reflection.

As Shoshana Felman points out in "Women and Madness": "From her initial family upbringing throughout her subsequent development, the social role assigned to the woman is that of *serving* an image, authoritative and central, of man: a woman is first and foremost a daughter/a mother/a wife."[10] Ina has been objectified, and, deprived of a subject position, she is unable to actively deny the distorted image imposed on her. Ina "died of reason" (17), not because she really was mad but because reason was the standard she was measured against, a standard she could not meet because reason excluded large parts of what she felt and experienced. Ina did not have a place/space to form an identity. She was the other, condemned to being the outsider who could not communicate her reality because: "How can one speak from the place of the Other? How can the woman be thought about outside of the Masculine/Feminine framework, other than as opposed to man, without being subordinated to a primordial masculine model? How can madness, in a similar way, be conceived outside of the dichotomous opposition to sanity, without being subjugated to reason?" (Felman, 1975, p. 4).

In the end, Ina commits suicide because she is rendered invisible and literally disappears under her wordrobes. Annie comes to see that Ina's fear stemmed from "what lay below names" (13). In re-membering Ina's fragmented life-story, Annie attempts to discover "where the real began, under the words that pretended something else" (77). She is struggling to get behind Ina's "implacable Garbo face" and starts by taking apart the word-mask that obscures Ina:

> *im-* not / *plak-* to be flat. layer, coating, floe(ice). flatfish, flake.
> to be calm (not). to please (not). placebo, placid, pleasant. none of
> these. a raging fire underneath, a tumult, sharp tongue, an
> inability to coat with sugar, please (dissemble), to fit in, no matter
> how you tried. (58)

By dissecting 'implacable', Annie can at least partly get behind the mask and grasp Ina's fate. Words communicate experience, and Ina experienced life as a disrupted minefield behind her masked Garbo face. By dismembering the word implacable Annie re-members her mother's story, and makes the reader *feel* what life was like on the other side of the mask. She reaches "[...] – that certain space where words turn from abstraction [...] in the world you read or listen in on, and then in a flash wing in to the core of your being and you recognize all that they stand for and that you have a stake in them, a share as speaker/writer/reader/listener, all of you there in that active complex" (Marlatt, 1990a, p. 188). Getting into the word – according to Marlatt – means getting into the world of Ina which Annie felt fearfully excluded from as a child. Not only Annie, but the reader also has a stake in the wor(l)ds evoked in *Ana Historic*. Marlatt deliberately defamiliarizes words that we use every day to make us aware of their conventional nature. De-contextualising words also challenges the reader to participate in making sense, a new sense of the wor(l)d. Taking words apart enables the narrator to reach into the gap of what Ina experienced and what she could utter in a language that seemed as alien to her as the new country.

Ana, who was also a woman immigrant to British Columbia, shared Ina's position as her diary entry shows: "words, that shifting territory. never one's own. full of deadfalls and hidden claims to a reality others have made" (32).[11]

In an interview nine years prior to *Ana Historic*, Marlatt uses the term 'divining', in the sense of looking for a source, for her use of language (Bowering, 1979, p. 49). I find the term appropriate for describing language in *Ana Historic* as well. Marlatt breaks the surface structure of language and 'divines' her way to the other meaning of words by following their sounds. Words gain their own rhythm in *Ana Historic*; they "bounce off the flat surface of patriarchal ways-of-speaking towards a deeper place" (Scott, 1989, p.73).

When Annie, while creating Ana's life, complains that women's stories are always omitted from history, Ina's voice interferes saying "[...] that's woman's lot. it's what you learn to accept like bleeding and hysterectomies, like intuition and dizzy spells – all the ways we don't fit into a man's world" (79). Ina accepted her position as 'woman' in contrast to man and increasingly became irrational and hysterical. But as Felman asks: "Is it by chance that hysteria (significantly derived, as is well known, from the Greek word for 'uterus') was originally conceived as an exclusively female complaint, as the *lot* and prerogative of women?" (Felman, 1975, p. 2, emphasis C.R.). Significantly, Ina mixes up biological features like bleeding and hysterectomies and features that are by no means biological but were conventionally attributed to women because they were "the other," the opposite of reason: intuition. Annie's worst fear is evoked by Ina's statement: the lack of choice for women, their pre-determination, the route of no escape. And as she tried earlier to break through her fear and through Ina's mask by taking the threatening word apart, she does the same with:

> woman's lot, lot. An object used in making a determination or choice by chance (x and y, xx or xy and all that follows from the chance determination); a number of people or things ('fed up with the lot of you'); a piece of land (a lot too small for dogs and one mad Englishwoman); one's fortune in life; fate (predictable as the five potatoes to peel every day at five o'clock). (79)

Evoking the various meanings of 'lot' that seem irrelevant to the expression 'women's lot', makes it possible to take a new look at the word and at the presumed reality beneath it. Lot is a "choice by chance (x and y, xx or xy and all that follows from the chance determination)": Looking the arbitrariness of an accidental combination of chromosomes in the face probably helps Annie to reject that this is going to irrevocably determine her fate and deprive her of choice. Annie unravels robe after robe and realizes that there is no certain lot allotted to women's lot.

At first Ina could not fill the role/robe of a 'perfect mother' and 'proper lady' because she could not live up to the prescribed identity hidden in the words. After her nervous breakdown and the consecutive treatment, she entirely disappears under the robe. When her husband, Howard, brings her back from the hospital:

> [...] he brought home a new fear (who's there?) that no one was there at all.
> Mum: mum. [...] under the role or robe was no one. [...] the you that was curled up like a small animal inside. lost in the harm [...] they erased whole parts of you, shocked them out, overloaded circuits so you couldn't bear to remember. re-member. (148)

Annie is calling "mum," trying to invoke the familiar role/identity Ina had tried to fill. But the word has become as empty as the identified person behind it. It is up to Annie now to re-member the different parts of her mother's story and to overcome Ina's fate. Ina was turned into an object, which by definition is passive, and consequently was predestined to become a victim: "[...] madness is the impasse confronting those whom cultural conditioning has deprived of the very means of protest or self-affirmation."[12] Madwomen do not threaten society's conventions, they become ex-centrics instead.

Femininity is another construct that is challenged in the novel. Whereas earlier feminist theories have brought forth the crucial distinction of gender as the (arbitrary) socio-cultural construct and sex as the (given) biological category, more recent theories have pointed out that this distinction does not hold because both categories are discursively constructed. In *Gender Trouble*, Judith Butler furthermore claims that 'gender' is not merely the opposition to 'sex' buth that 'gender' is ther very apparatus which produces and naturalizes the category of sex.[13] However, the distinction of sex and gender is imperative for the understanding of 'femininity' as a construct which is by no means natural. Marlatt She disentangles the conflation of sex and gender and reveals the oppressive forces this conflation enacts on the lives of women by interrogating the hidden messages in words prescribing feminine behaviour. Ina, Ana and Annie are, e.g., disowned by words that demand feminine behaviour: "lady, for instance. a word that has claimed so much from women trying to maintain it" (32). Marlatt looks at the word "lady" from different angles throughout the book. Ana fears that she is "not a Proper Lady perhaps" (32) and that "She should have been born a man, she wanted too much" (104). As soon as Ana feels or wants something the brand-name feminine does not include, she feels unworthy of her sex.

Reflecting upon the wordrobe "Proper Lady," Annie observes: "[...] and it is barely sounded the relationship between proper and property" (32). In looking at the phrase 'proper lady', Annie's initial question "wardrobes. wordrobes. warding off what?" seems to be answered. The content, the 'monster' hidden in the word 'lady' is a conglomeration of (male) projections that disown women from their bodies and desires. Marlatt repeatedly names the monster Frankenstein: another man-made, human construct that does not serve but haunt humanity.[14] She also realizes that Ina died because she could not lower the stakes of what 'lady' demanded from her: "i didn't realize the only alternative to lady you knew, was tramp [...]" (34). Ina did not know how to break up rigid oppositions and subscribed to an extreme she could not really live up to. She became "I-na, I-no-longer" (11), erased from the world. Ana's story seems to lead into the same fate that killed Ina, a fact that increasingly upsets Annie and prompts her into imagining a different outcome for Ana's story. She wants Ana to be able to deconstruct the identity prescribed for her. Annie therefore imagines that Ana can rise above the construct femininity which relegates her to the passive victim position of the other.

Ana attends a tea party before the first white baby is born at Hastings Mill. The women of the community are "having tea as if manner maketh woman, into lady – the lady – [...] figurehead, and having nothing" (116). Ana clearly sees at the party that the women strive to keep up their femininity by all means; they are shell-shocked when she suggests holding a dance. She is reminded by the women that, as a lady, you neither run, nor dance, nor roam the woods by yourself. Yet, Ana loves the wilderness where she is free of convention, and finds an empty space to imagine herself. She knows that the real danger is not among the trees in the bush but in the city where men lie in ambush, she being a woman without (male) protection, after all.[15]

The tea party scene is juxtaposed to the birth of Jeannie Alexander's child that – without a doctor being available – unites the women in labour. Marlatt dismantles the cliché of lady, which by definition excludes physical work, by contrasting the birth scene at Hastings Mill with an intertext about longshoremen unloading ships: "a pride of muscle [...] a body armature that can be counted on, a body that doesn't secretly transform (from month to month...)" (118). This intertext is challenged when during the birth, Ana grows to admire the strength of the female body: "the sheer work of giant muscle moving under the sheet" (124). Marlatt de-mystifies men's muscle power and makes apparent what the wordrobe 'proper lady' leaves out: the hard work of women.

Triggered by two contradictory accounts of Ana's place of residence which Annie finds in the historical records, she envisions an alternative life story for Ana. In this other version, Ana meets Birdie, who has a parlour in Gastown, gives piano lessons, and is anything but a lady. She is – nomen est omen – free as a bird from society's claims. Ana moves in with her, the two become lovers, and they support themselves by giving piano lessons. Birdie is purely Annie's invention. Nonetheless, she applies the forces 'fate' and 'choice' to her as well which is apparent in the word-play with her name: "B*ri*die or B*ir*die with the wandering 'r'?" (*Ana Historic*, 108, italics C.R.). The pun implies the 'approved' fate of women in the nineteenth century to become a wife or the choice to be an independent woman. For Annie, sanity and madness increasingly seem to depend on whether or not a woman can cast off the gender role society imposes on her.

How identity, language and history are connected is clarified by the historical plaque that Annie later finds attached to Hastings Mill. Although the event of the first birth – without any medical assistance – was remarkable, it is not 'fact-worthy' enough to be included in the historical inscription, which only mentions the deeds of the male inhabitants of the house.

Writing Ana's story inevitably leads Annie to questioning her own position in life. Although she witnessed and rejected her mother's fate, she herself gave up studying to marry her history professor who is admired by all his (female) students: "'he's such a wonderful prof, you must feel so lucky Mrs. Anderson'" (59), a student says at a party. Although their marriage has become meaningless, Annie keeps up the facade of "the lie. the defensive lie our lying together is" (59). Reflecting on her adolescence Annie realizes what led her into this role: wanting to be part of the center, seeking approval from male eyes. She remembers her growing into a woman: "now she was walking her body as if it were different from her, her body with its new look. (o the luck to be looked at. o the lack, if you weren't. o the look. looking as if it all depended on it)" (50). The interplay between look, luck and lack shows how closely not only the sounds but – in this social context – the meanings of the words are connected. Ina and Annie grow up believing that part of being feminine is to look good. A good looking woman is lucky to be looked at, and it is 'tough luck' if she lacks the good looks. This is not merely a poetic wordplay but palpably conveys the pressure that the adolescent girl felt from constantly being evaluated by others, by the gaze of men who appropriated a certain value to her. At the same time she realizes that language does not provide her with the tools to express the changes of her body:

> but the words for our bodies betrayed us in the very language we learned at school: 'cunt,' 'slit,' 'boob' [...] 'got the curse,' 'falling of the roof'. catastrophic phrases we used that equally betrayed us. handed down from friend to friend, sister to sister, mother to daughter. *hand me downs*, too small for what I really felt. (62, italics C.R.)

Not only is the image of words as clothes evoked again here but the fact stressed that women (involuntarily) participate in the oppressive force of language by passing words and attitudes on to their daughters. Annie thus wants to break this vicious circle by revealing gender identity to be simply a role. Remembering how she pretended to be a mother as a child, Annie says: "trying. a trying child. trying it on for size. the role. all that she had been told would make her a woman. (knock, knock)" (49). Annie 'sounds out' the depth of words to find out what is hidden in them just like she searched the wardrobes in the basement for monsters.

In the beginning, Annie is only looking for Ina and Ana but then she extends her search to all the "missing persons" (138): "who's there? (knock, knock) who else *is* there" (46). Annie dreams of "making fresh tracks my own way," she doesn't want "history, the already-made" (98). Annie knows that leaving the track of history encompasses a tremendous danger and is punished by the academic community as well as by her husband. The sentence, "faculty wife fails as research assistant fails as wife" (79) reappears in her head. The factual style reminiscent of a newspaper heading makes her action sound like a criminal offense that will draw consequences, which it does. When her husband finally takes her "scribbling," as he devalued her writing earlier, seriously, he decides to find a new research assistant to give her more time. Annie is torn and is "dying to offer [her] time again, so as not to be left out of the book, the marriage, history" (147). Annie has a choice but it means choosing between having a voice on the margin or being muted in the center. By imagining Ana's story, she is moving into unknown territory, a territory without somebody else's standards or expectations, a territory she will have to map out on her own – a task which is both invigorating and threatening. History's reprimanding voice keeps crossing her mind:

> come back, history calls, to the solid
> ground of fact. You don't want to fall
> off the edge of the world –
> (111)

This 'poem' appears in *Ana Historic* on an otherwise blank page. The edge of the world is made palpable by the dash that leads the reader into the empty page ahead. Staying with the facts omits people but is safe; leaving the path of linear facts is threatening and was fatal for Ina who "[went] right for the edge. Over it and off the deep end" (93). However, Ina did not know the alternative to fate/facts: imagination. Ana's story strays further and further away from historical data as Annie discards her role as research assistant, and moves from the position of dependent wife to that of an independent woman.

The novel ends with Annie and Zoe making love. But before Annie can enter a new relationship she has to come to terms with her various (word) robes and reconcile herself with Ina's life. She addresses Ina a last time saying "no you're not just a role, a robe I put on, one of your long evening gowns with the coffee-coloured beads [...] you're not the empty dress of some character hanging on the line. you go on living in me, catching me out. my fear, my critic [...]" (141). Annie acknowledges Ina's otherness as part of herself and draws strength from it. What Ina passes on to her no longer is a "hand me down too small to express reality" but the ability to rise above certain restrictive roles. In the end the fictional characters collapse; they all become part of Annie who leaves her old role and enters a new one:

> [...] Annie Richards. the sound of a door closing. i want to knock: can you hear? i want to answer her who's there? not Ana or Ina, those transparent covers. Ana Richards Richard's Anna. fooling myself on the other side of history as if it were a line dividing the real from the unreal. Annie / Ana – arose by another name, whole wardrobes of naming guarding the limitations – we rise above them. Annie isn't Richard's or even Springer's. Annie Torrent, i said. (152)

As Strauss in *Mirrors and Masks: The Search for Identity* has pointed out, "[t]he changing of names marks a rite of passage" (1969, p. 16). Annie rejects being anybody's property by renaming herself Annie Torrent. She not only abandons her husband's last name but also identifies herself with the torrent of speech that Ina had kept damned up inside for so long.

The relationship with Zoe offers an alternative to the restrictions Annie's life with Richard involved. Yet, the novel ends before we can find out whether life with Zoe produces new restrictive roles and hierarchies, and before we find out whether a community consisting solely of women would avoid marginalizing whatever represents the other.

The ending is consistent with Marlatt's approach of undermining conventions. In traditional novels, the whole plot strives for and culminates in the heterosexual partnership (marriage) of the protagonist. Each and every moral message in conventional novels or even more so in the popular Harlequin Romances is verified in the end when the efforts and personal development of the protagonist are rewarded by the perfect match. Conventional novels also end before disillusionment sets in, before everyday life shows the limitations of the relationship. In *Ana Historic*, Annie's development culminates in a lesbian relationship because this enables her to reject her position as object in the male-female economy twice. She frees herself from being Richard's 'devoted wife' by becoming Zoe's lover, thus rejecting the 'official' heterosexual matrix of desire,[16] and from being his "patient assistant" by creating Ana's story. The novel uses a traditional quest-for-identity plot structure but subversively parodies it in re-writing the ending.

A crucial point in *Ana Historic* is Marlatt's attempt to connect women's creativity to the female body.[17] She excavates the Other in words or in historical discourse by following cyclical rhythms reminiscent of women's menstrual cycle. Following such critics as Cixous[18] and Irigaray, Marlatt wonders in an essay: "how can the standard sentence structure of English with its linear authority subject through verb through object convey the wisdoms of endlessly repeating and not exactly repeated cycles her body knows?" (Marlatt, 1984, p. 55). In the novel she plays with the three dimensions of the word period as menstruation, epoch and point:

> there is still even now the innate pleasure of seeing on a fresh
> white pad the first marks of red, bright red when the bleeding's at
> its peak. innate because of a childish astonishment, *i made that*! the
> mark of myself, my inscription in blood. i'm here. scribbling again.
> writing the period that arrives at no full stop. not the hand
> manipulating the pen. not the language of definition, of epoch
> and document, language explaining and justifying, but the words
> that flow out from within, running too quick to catch sometimes,

> at other times just an agonizingly slow trickle. the words of an interior history doesn't include.... that erupts like a spring, like a wellspring of being, well-being inside... (90)

This quotation makes tangible how Marlatt changes the function of punctuation: The period no longer marks the conventional end of a sentence but – similar to the pauses in a musical score – sets an individual rhythm. Capital letters are abandoned when Annie speaks in the novel because she is trying to break through hierarchical structures.[19] Another means to undermine history's authority is evoked in the quote by picturing menstruation as a trace, a trace which differs from word-symbols but that nonetheless signifies presence and achievement.

Marlatt's attempt to overcome the phallogocentrism of Western discourse by connecting power to the female body could be perceived as. Thus Grisé has pointed out that the search for a foremother in *Ana Historic* "might be considered a return to an essentialized prelinguistic maternal economy" (Grisé, 1993, p. 90). She convincingly reaches the conclusion, however, that Marlatt tries to "Resist Amnesia of the Maternal," that she wants to re-claim which has been lost to women.

Moreover, I think that sentences like "*i made that!*" (90) have an ironic overtone. Historical intertexts in the novel (which like the quoted sentence are always printed in italics!) prove how meticulously even the smallest achievements of men have been recorded whereas women's deeds, e.g. giving birth, have passed unnoticed. Marlatt repeatedly mentions the innumerable photographs of men posing on cut down trees as if saying: 'I made that'.

In the end, Marlatt's novel becomes *An a-Historic* novel, it turns into the other body of the story re-membered. "Which is not the end. the story is only a story insofar it ends. in life we go on" (150).

Notes

1. Marlatt, 1988, p. 9. All further reference to *Ana Historic* will appear behind the quotes in the body of the essay.
2. The following essay seeks to elucidate how Marlatt traces the other meanings of words and how she (re)constructs alternative life stories for women.
3. The Roman God Janus is the animistic spirit of doorways. As is well known, his symbol is a double-faced head but he is also regarded as the god of all beginnings (compare entry in the *Encyclopedia Britannica*) by some scholars. Ana marks a radically new beginning for Annie.
4. See Banting, 1991a, "Translation A:Z: Notes on Daphne Marlatt's *Ana Historic*."

5   See White, 1981, p. 793, who also points out that turning events into historical stories gives them a moral impact, because historical representation is based on common sense which is no more than a "set of commonplaces comprised of beliefs about the meaning or ultimate nature of reality, shared by the average members of any given culture [...]," p. 797.

6   Hutcheon, 1988a, p. 12. Hutcheon assumes that through the realization that our culture does not consist of monolithic, homogeneous values, the marginalized, "the ex-centric" will gain more significance and that the "concept of alienated otherness [...] gives way to that of differences." The "ex-centric" is "the off-center: ineluctably identified with the center it desires but is denied," p. 60. See also Hutcheon, 1988b, which provides an interesting elaboration on the term "ex-centric." Hutcheon sees the postmodern writer as ex-centric because s/he challenges cultural universals. She moreover describes Canada's position in international relations as ex-centric. The latter aspect is explored in depth by Bennett, 1986, who points out the correlation of feminist issues and Canada's search for identity as a nation; and Bennett, 1987, where she examines Canada's political and literary marginalization.

7   I am alluding to the fact that historical representations of the past usually help to enforce gender constructions in the present. Marlatt turns that very process around by rewriting Ana's story. For a more detailed study of the interaction of history and gender see Wallach-Scott, 1988.

8   In *Wörter unter Wörtern*, 1980, Starobinski defines an anaphon as an incomplete anagram in so far as it only imitates certain syllables of a word but does not aim at reproducing the whole word, Starobinski, 1980, p. 20. He also claims that anagrams function as a reminder, a memorization of a theme, and that they connect the surface and deep structure of language, p. 48. Greber defines palindrome as a subcategory of an anagramm when the letters are exactly reversed. Anacyclical anagramms can be read the same forward and backward, Greber, 1993, p. 40.

9   Offred, the protagonist of Margaret Atwood's dystopia *The Handmaid's Tale*, also muses about the expression 'date rape': "date rape [...] It sounds like some kind of desert. *Date Rapé*" (Atwood, 1985, p. 35). For Offred, language conceals the violence of rape by turning it into a word-dessert.

10 Felman, 1975, p. 2. Quoting Phyllis Chesler (*Women and Madness*, New York: Avon Books, 1973), Felman continues: "'What we consider 'madness' whether it appears in women or in men, is either the acting out of the devalued female role or the total or partial rejection of one's sex-role stereotype.' [p. 56]", Felman, 1975, p. 2. Chesler's quote supports my hypothesis that gender identities often turn into strait-jackets.

11 See Davey, 1993, pp. 195f., who examines the correlation of language and place in *Ana Historic*. Ina and Ana at first perceived Canada as the new country that would liberate them and only later realize that they are governed by "the law of the father" there as well.

12 Felman, 1975, p. 2. Hysteria has a long history as a carefully constructed and even 'staged' medical phenomenon. When the neurologist Jean Martin Charcot began to investigate hysteria in 1870, he asked his female patients to demonstrate the symptoms of hysteria to an audience. See Mentzos, 1980, and Bronfen, 1998.

13 See, e.g., Judith Butler, *Gender Trouble* and *Bodies That Matter*. For an overview of Women's and Gender Studies compare Rippl, 1995, and Hof, 1996.

14 Towards the end of the novel Annie points out: "[A]ctually Frankenstein was the man who created him. [...] and now we call the monster by his name. a man's name for man's fear of the wild, the uncontrolled" (142). Once again Marlatt emphasizes how misleading wordrobes can be.

15 See Klooß, 1994, who claims that an archeological understanding of history where you excavate the lost stories promotes a diachronic rather than a synchronic quality of place. This new understanding of place gives the ex-centrics a voice. Klooß also illustrates that some Canadian historiographic metafictions use nature and wilderness to show the protagonists' consciousness, an observation that is applicable to *Ana Historic*. Ana loves the wilderness because she is aware of the gender restrictions society imposes on her. In *Ana Historic* women are frequently compared to trees because they both suffer from the dominance of men. Intertexts about the function of certain woods, e.g., the use of the red cedar as "*a wood for shingles* (20)" [all factual accounts in the novel are in italics] are inserted into the novel. Marlatt implies that trees are conquered, cut down and labeled just like women have to fulfill roles prescribed by men. She also portrays both as powerless: "the silence of trees/the silence of women/ if they could speak an unconditional language/what would they say?"(75).

16 Various critics have correctly pointed out that 'the monster' in the closet also stands for lesbian desire denied women by the heterosexual matrix which society enforces. See Goldman, for instance: "Of course, the image of wardrobe and the anxiety associated with it also play on the fears surrounding 'coming out of the closet' as a lesbian" (Goldman, 1997, p. 127).

17 For approaches fostering a poetic procedure that would give women a voice outside hierarchical, linear discourse but reject the existence of a 'feminine' writing style, compare: Kristeva, 1974, *Die Revolution der poetischen Sprache*. Kristeva opposes the semiotic chora, a pre-symbolic, prelinguistic category to the symbolic order of linear language. The semiotic can only surface after the symbolic order has been installed, but the semiotic breaks through this symbolic order as a subversive subtext. The semiotic as a poetic procedure can be used by both sexes, yet, Kristeva illustrates it with male authors only because you need a subject position in the symbolic order first to enact the semiotic. Compare also Weigel, 1983, "Das Weibliche als Metapher des Metonymischen," and Lachmann, 1983, "Thesen zu einer weiblichen Ästhetik."

18 Compare, e.g., Cixous, 1976, p. 886: "Women must write through their bodies, they must invent the impregnable language that will wreck partitions, classes and rhetoric, regulations and codes, they must submerge, cut through, get beyond the ultimate reserve-discourse." See also, Irigaray, 1979.

19 When Annie looks through the archives and only finds the story "the city fathers tell of the only important events in the world [...] (where are the city mothers)," she says "[...] – all these capital letters to convince themselves of its [history's], of their [men's] significance." (28)

References

Atwood, Margaret, 1985, *The Handmaid's Tale*. Toronto: Mc Clelland-Bantam.

———, 1972, *Survival: A Thematic Guide to Canadian Literature*. Toronto: Anansi.

Banting, Pamela, 1989a, "Translation A:Z: Notes on Daphne Marlatt's *Ana Historic*," in: Douglas Barbour (ed.), *Beyond Tish*. Edmonton: NeWest, 123-29.

———, 1989b, "S(m)other Tongue?: Feminism, Academic Discourse, Translation," *Tessera*, 6 (Spring), 81-91.

Bennett, Donna, 1986, "Naming the Way Home," in: Shirley Neuman/Smaro Kamboureli (eds.), *A Mazing Spaze: Writing Canadian Women Writing*. Edmonton: Longspoon, 228-45.

———, 1987, "On the Margin: Looking for Literary Identity," *Canadian Forum*, 768 (April), 17-21.

Bowering, George, 1979, "Given This Body: An Interview With Daphne Marlatt," *Open Letter*, 4:3, 32-88.

———, 1989, "On *Ana Historic*: An Interview with Daphne Marlatt," *Line*, 13, 96-105.

Brand, Di, 1989, "The Absence at the Center," in: *Canadian Forum*, 779 (March), 38-40.

Bronfen, Elisabeth, 1998. "Die Vorführung der Hysterie," in: Aleida Assmann/Heidrun Friese (eds.), *Identitätskonstruktionen/Constructing Identities*, to appear.

Butler, Judith, 1990, *Gender Trouble: Feminism and the Subversion of Identity*. New York: Routledge.

———, 1993, *Bodies That Matter: On the Discursive Limits of Sex*. New York: Routledge.

Cixous, Hélène, 1976, "The Laugh of the Medusa," *Signs*, 1:4, 875-93.

Cooley, Dennis, 1989, "Recursion, Excursions and Incursions: Daphne Marlatt Wrestles with the Angle Language," *Line*, 13, 66-79.

Davey, Frank, 1993, *Post-National Arguments: The Politics of the Anglophone-Canadian Novel since 1967*. Toronto: University of Toronto Press.

———, 1988, *Reading Canadian Reading*. Winnipeg: Turnstone.

Felman, Shoshana, 1975, "Women and Madness: The Critical Phallacy," *Diacritics*, 5:4, 2-10.

Goldman, Marlene, 1997, "Daphne Marlatt's Ana Historic: A Genealogy for Lost Women," in: Marlene Goldman (ed.), *Paths of Desire: Images of Exploration and Mapping in Canadian Women's Writing*. Toronto/Buffalo/London: University of Toronto Press, 1997, 101-132.

Greber, Erika, 1993, "Anagrammatisches und Anazyklisches: oder klebe dir Irrgraphen," *Emile*, 16, 39-45.

Grisé, Annette C., 1993, "'A Bedtime Story for you, Ina': Resisting Amnesia of the Maternal in Daphne Marlatt's *Ana Historic*," *Tessera*, 15 (Winter), 90-98.

Hof, Renate, 1995, "Die Entwicklung der Gender Studies," in: Renate Hof/Hadumod Bußman (eds.), *Genus: Zur Geschlechterdifferenz in den Kulturwissenschaften*. Stuttgart: Kröner, 2-33.

Hutcheon, Linda, 1988a, *A Poetics of Postmodernism*. New York/London: Routledge.

—, 1988b, *The Canadian Postmodern: A Study of Contemporary English-Canadian Fiction.* Toronto/New York/Oxford: Oxford University Press.

—, 1989, "Incredulity towards Metanarrative: Negotiating Postmodernism and Feminism," *Tessera*, 7 (Summer), 39-43.

Irigaray, Luce, 1979, *Das Geschlecht, das nicht eins ist.* Berlin: Merve.

Klooß, Wolfgang, 1994, "From Colonial Madness to Postcolonial Ex-centricity: A Story about Stories of Identity Construction in Canadian Literature," in: Bernd Engler/ Kurt Müller (eds.) *Historiographic Metafiction in Modern American and Canadian Literature.* Schöningh: Zürich, 53-79.

Kristeva, Julia, 1978, *Die Revolution der poetischen Sprache.* Frankfurt a.M.: Suhrkamp.

Lachmann, Renate, 1983, "Thesen zu einer weiblichen Ästhetik," in: Claudia Opitz (ed.), *Weiblichkeit oder Feminismus?: Beiträge zur interdisziplinären Frauentagung in Konstanz 1983.* Weingarten: Drumlin, 1984, 181-194.

Marlatt, Daphne, 1984, "Musing With Mother Tongue," *Room of One's Own: A Feminist Journal of Literature and Criticism*, 8:4, 53-56.

—, 1988, *Ana Historic.* Toronto: Coach House Press.

—, 1990a, "Difference (em)bracing," in: Libby Scheier/Sarah Sheard/Eleanor Wachtel (eds.), *Language in Her Eye: Views on Writing and Gender by Canadian Women Writing in English.* Toronto: Coach House Press, 188-193.

—, 1990b, "Lesbera," *Tessera*, 9 (Fall), 123-25.

Mentzos, Stavros, 1980, *Hysterie: Zur Psychodynamik unbewußter Inszenierungen.* München: Kindler.

Pache, Walter, 1985, "'The Fiction Makes Us Real': Aspects of Postmodernism in Canada," in: Reingard M. Nischik/Robert Kroetsch (eds.), *Gaining Ground: European Critics on Canadian Literature.* Edmonton: NeWest, 64-78.

Rippl, Gabriele, 1995, "Feministische Literaturwissenschaft," in: Miltos Pechlivanos et al. (ed.), *Einführung in die Literaturwissenschaft.* Stuttgart: Metzler, 230-40.

Scott, Gail, 1989, *Spaces Like Stairs.* Toronto: The Women's Press.

Starobinsky, Jean, 1980, *Wörter unter Wörtern.* Wien: Ullstein.

Strauss, Anselm L., 1969, *Mirrors and Masks: The Search for Identity.* Mill Valley: Sociology Press.

Tostevin, Lola Lemire, 1989, "Daphne Marlatt: Writing in the Space that Is Her Mother's Face," *Line*, 13, 32-39.

Wallach-Scott, Joan, 1988, *Gender and the Politics of History.* New York: Columbia University Press.

Weigel, Sigrid, 1983, "Das Weibliche als Metapher des Metonymischen," in: Inge Stephan (ed.), *Frauensprache – Frauenliteratur.* Tübingen: Niemeyer, 108-118.

Williamson, Janice, 1989a, "Sounding a Difference: An Interview with Daphne Marlatt," *Line*, 13, 47-56.

—, 1989b, *Sounding Differences: Conversations with Seventeen Canadian Women Writers.* Toronto: University of Toronto Press.

Women Writers as Historical (Re)Source: Leading a Double Existence

Colleen M. Ross

This paper addresses four major veins of theory in contemporary literary studies: historicism, narratology, translation, and the feminist theories that weave them together. It also aims to introduce the reader to recent controversies about the bordered nature of historical writing and its connection to narrative discourse and, above all, its relationship with an/other feminist discourse. Male and female versions of history not only tell different tales but they are also told in quite different ways; until recently, however, the patriarchal version of narrative has unquestionably been the accepted norm. Historian Hans Kellner argues that feminists "are concerned with the dilemmas of entering a discourse [including historical discourse], which, by its very structure as rational, sequential thought, they assert, excludes a certain notion of *woman,* as body, freedom, Other" (Kellner, 1987, p. 17). Through my research I have sought a connection between the two sides of the equation: the "real" (history) and the "imaginary" (the translation of this history through the translator's imagination). To translate a male-centered history into a discourse that celebrates, or at least recognizes, female experiences, women must make sounds, hear their own voices. Women writers, more so than men, have felt the need to push the borders/boundaries of narrative, creating a space in which they can re-write themselves by articulating their thoughts and emotions. Canadian authors Daphne Marlatt (*Ana Historic*) and Lola Lemire Tostevin (*Frog Moon*) seek to break out of the closed patrilineal circuit which has expressly denied female story a significant presence in its exclusive monologue on past events.

Feminist authors such as these two do not desire to create an essentialist, binary opposition between male and female writers by diverging from the "official" man-made history to write their own historical narratives, so much as to instill a mode of writing in which women can enforce their *selves,* their individuality. This paper focuses on what narrative innovations women have adopted to establish their presence in the masculine canon and re-present themselves by voicing their hitherto untold stories, for, as feminist critic Luce Irigaray suggests, to find a voice (*voix*) is to find a way (*voie*). The way in which women can encourage an appreciation and valuing of their experiences is not by fixating on *the* sexual difference between Woman and Man, but by contemplating the diversity between and within women. Sally Robinson makes an important distinction between Woman and women, observing that Woman "identifies a difference," whereas women "as a plural and heterogeneous category fractures that singularity" (Robinson, 1991, p. 3) and brings in all women in under that sign. Citing Women's (with a capital "W") body as the overarching difference between the genders risks enclosing women writers in a theory of difference marked by specificity and locality, whereas viewing women's multiplicitous gender distinctions within culture opens up a more generalized, systemic theory of women's writing.

"Gender difference is a difference in language" affirms Robinson, "but it is also a difference in experience, widely conceived as a subject's relation to discourse and social systems" (1991, p. 27). While women write about their experiences as female in a patriarchal culture, using its limited language, they adapt it to more effectively express their thoughts and emotions and to alot a space for themselves in the narrative network. In keeping with post-structuralist theory, feminists realize the importance of language as a site of social reality, the place where they construct their subjectivity to enable them to think, speak, and give meaning to the world around them. Identifying themselves as subject, women feel in control and are thus in a position to give meaning to their lived reality, hitherto bypassed by a history which claims to speak for everyone in an allegedly ungendered humanism.

A feminist post-structuralist view sees that experience has no essential meaning but is given value through discourse, within a patriarchal language. Women authors (Marlatt and Tostevin, for my purposes) effectively transcribe their own autobiographical fictions by using narrative innovations to differentiate them from history as we know it. While working to disseminate the liberal-humanist subject (which, though positing to be "ungendered," masks structures of male privilege and domination), theorists and writers simultaneously construct a subject which can speak of/for/about events in women's lives. The two writers referred to in this paper disassemble structures inherent in a fixed economy of expression, reformulating a new method of writing that allows them to translate their thoughts into text. We will ultimately see how Marlatt and Tostevin use translative techniques to decode historical writing and re-code it in order to tell their own stories.

First, let us deal with the question: what is history? One common dictionary describes it as "that form of pure representative discourse the subject of which is some fact or event, single or continuous" whereas "[i]f the event or fact is imaginary, it is fiction" (*Funk & Wagnall's*, 1937, p. 1163). This split definition raises two essential questions: if history is composed of facts, what then constitutes a "fact," and how can history (composed of these facts about past events) be *other* than an imaginative reconstruction of the past, since no historian can possibly accurately and fully re-create past lives or events in all their facticity.

Historical evidence, more obviously than evidence in some other disciplines, is not scientifically created but rather interpreted by human understanding of human experience. Since history reflects the culture in which it is written, its "human" experience has been male-tainted, and its liberal-humanist subject has concealed structures of male privilege and control. We must ask ourselves what type of histories women are able to construct for themselves if they are empty-handed of concrete evidence (though they have handfuls of ideas) about their past.

Controversy has thus arisen over what kind of histories female writers can create, using their imagination. We return to the second part of the definition of "history" to further the argument: "if the event or fact is imaginary, it is fiction." Defined as "something invented by the imagination" or "an invented story" (*Webster's Dictionary*, 1990, p. 460), fiction, it appears, bears close but not whole resemblance to history. To imagine is merely to form a mental image of something not present which is what a historian does each time s/he re-scribes the past. Because "historical events are never present for examination, the 'facts' must always be inferred rather than directly apprehended" (Stanford, 1986, p. 23); thus, historian-philosopher Michael Stanford asserts that a past can only be known imaginatively and that the most reliable explorer of the past is one best able to integrate facts into a living imagined reality. Marlatt and Tostevin do just that, writing their own historical fictions by weaving together the past lives of women with their own present lives to produce a "made-up" account, for these women have only scant historical details – facts – to use as a basis for the imagined story – a fact/ion (characterized as "self-seeking").

Feminist, together with new historicist and post-structuralist, writers argue that a work which incorporates imaginary events and persona should not be overlooked as an untruthful record of the past simply because it does not resemble the acknowledged narrative, which, laden with historical dates, events and personages, claims to be *the* truthful account of what happened at a specific time and/or place. Post-structuralists would argue that the subjectivity and meaning of a narrative (history, in this case) are never absolute but rather are precarious structures that change, depending on their discursive context, and thus should always be open to challenge and re-definition.

While agreeing that fictional discourse does bear uncanny resemblance to historical discourse in format, I posit that the events appropriate to being recounted within the narrative alter, depending on who is writing the story. The teller of the narrative/story/tale determines both *what* is told and *how* it is told. The way of telling a history, too, differs from one person to another and from one gender to the other. By focusing on methods of narration (how the story is told), and distinguishing between narrative as it has been conventionally written, and as it may be conceived in a female-characterized narrative, I will discuss the female history or "herstory" (a "translation" of the accepted discourse that focuses on women's bodies, desires and experiences) that is created when writers deviate from the usual methods of narration.

To translate, or to "right" (write) a text which has been negligent with regard to women, is to both "invent, create, and often to betray – the source" (Mezei, 1989, p. 9) and "to remake or remodel out of old material" (*Funk &Wagnall's*, 1937, p. 2550). Marlatt and Tostevin work on the original to de-center and displace it, creating what translator Barbara Godard terms a "woman-handled" text. Recent theories posit that translation is transformation and creation whereas more dated rationales have perceived translation as equivalence or transparence. Proponents of the latter position argue that, rather than giving her own interpretation, a translator should be faithful to the original (the source text) in order to ensure an identity between the two texts: Mounin states: "La traduction consiste à produire dans la langue d'arrivée *l'équivalent naturel* le plus proche du message de la langue du départ, d'abord quant à la signification, puis quant au style" (cited in Godard, 1989, p. 47). Godard proposes that a "co-textual" view of interpretation, according to which two undifferentiated texts exist side by side, must be modified into a "con-textual" view within which the two works are interrelated and given equal stature (Godard, 1989, p. 47 f.). Because in such a reckoning language is not transparent – words do not act as windows that offer a single, crystalline meaning but as mirrors which reflect a myriad of different meanings – translation provides equivalence not between the contents/words of two texts, but between the coding and decoding of two text systems (content *and* form).

This linguistic concept of translation can be further extended to a "gendered" transference of meaning as we perceive that when women (re)read and (re)write standard discourses, they are converting the words on the page into their "own" language: inscribing the values of a developing women's culture into the words in order to give them a meaning with which they can identify. Interpretation of a written work then becomes more a cultural than a trans-coding act; a word in one language cannot always be merely replaced by a word that carries a similar meaning in another language for there is often an underlying, unwritten meaning attached to the word that cannot be transferred without difficulty into a different culture. Because words carry both linguistic and cultural baggage, we cannot sufficiently determine the sense of a word without placing it within the entire textual system, or larger culture. Mary Snell-Hornby contends that the person who has any hope of adequately interpreting a literary work must not merely be bilingual, but *bicultural:* "[i]f language is an integral part of culture, the translator needs not only proficiency in two languages, he must also be at home in two cultures" (Snell-Hornby, 1988, p. 42). Female authors, like many other groups marginalized on the basis of nationality, colour or class, find themselves in a comparable position as translator, living and working between a patriarchal, and a struggling culture in which they are wholly integrated as active participants. While these authors write about female interactions and desires, women still remain to a large extent tied to standard forms and language in order to effectively communicate their realities.

Translation, when paired with feminism, invokes the doubleness of women's reading/writing the exclusive discourse for women commonly not only move from this language to another but also immerse themselves in two languages at once. Translator Dore Michelût, whose maternal tongue is Furlan (a regionalized Italian dialect) but who speaks predominantly in English, remarks that her two languages together constitute the whole bracket that is the extent of her experience (cf. Michelût, 1989, p. 67). Lola Lemire Tostevin, a Franco-Ontarian author, would agree for she finds that for her a wholeness of self is to be found in a space between (both inside and outside) her two languages, French and English – a mi/lieu in which she can more completely utter herself than if she were communicating in one language or the other. A similar sentiment is shared by many writers who see themselves living the life of a double agent, working in (bonded to) the dominant discourse, but interpreting, communicating and inventing a "feminist" dis-course that lies somewhere within/beside/around the established one. A writer from Canada's West Coast, Daphne Marlatt describes translation as "what writing itself is about: sensing one's way through the sentence, through (by means of) a medium (language) that has currents of meaning, its own drift" (Marlatt, 1989, p. 27 f.).

A feminist story about the past d/rifts from the established historical canon through its variations in both form (its use of narrative innovations) and content (its concentration on female experiences). Because both post-structuralists and new historicists experiment with narrative form, feminist writers cannot claim sole jurisdiction in this area; it is the combination of both discursive deviations *and* a female-centered story line that create the difference in a history told by a woman. In such a way, the works of Marlatt and Tostevin open a re-writing, or a *translation,* of the privileged discourse.

Marlatt and Tostevin modify a traditional story of the past by firstly resisting and subverting the unfavourable image of the body presented (or excluded) in historical, economic, medical, and theological discourses, and secondly, by offering their own image of the body as emerging through a female-inclusive discourse. Their translation can be named as both a structural process (how the story is told) and a referential process (what is told in the story) or how the fiction refers to the world in progress. For the moment, we will focus on the structural to determine how Marlatt and Tostevin employ narrative techniques to disconnect the power line of an insular historical discourse.

In *Ana Historic*, Daphne Marlatt aggrandizes the life of a woman mentioned briefly in the Vancouver Archives by piecing together meager scraps of information about her activities to re-create for her a whole life (a patchwork). In Marlatt's writing, the purported heterosexual piano teacher "Mrs. Richards" of the archives becomes the self-confessed lesbian writer "Ana," a woman who has re-possessed her body which had been over-written in the archives. As the narrator writes Ana's "coming out" so too does she gain the courage to admit her own homosexuality to her friend, who "asks me to present myself, to take the leap, as the blood rushes into my face and i can speak: you. i want you. *and* me. Together" (Marlatt, 1988, p. 152).

Tostevin also brings insight into her own life as she threads together her personalized – what Barbara Godard terms "woman-handled" story. She is conscious of working between a pre-conceived idea of history, and her own (con)version of this history/*histoire* (meaning both "history" and "story" in French). She leads a double existence, not only as a woman, writing against the patriarchal discourse in order to invent a feminist discourse, but also as a Franco-Ontarian whose mother tongue is French and who has been conditioned to write, speak and live in English. Throughout *Frog Moon*, the narrator, Laura, wrestles with this doubleness as she fluctuates between her present life as anglophone mother and wife and her past life as a young francophone girl in a convent, attempting to reach a unified self who will encompass her vast array of experiences, languages and traditions. Tostevin posits that we reproduce ourselves as we participate in a cyclical process (like the internal cyclical female rhythm) that causes us to return to our past and our roots, and relate/supplant those experiences as we return to new contexts in the present. So, like a frog, we are always shifting, moving, changing contexts, shedding our skin – metamorphosing.

Present and past become inseparable as the narrators realize that they need to temporally re-order other events in their lives to give them a coherence they may not have had in "real" life. The past emerges through the telling of the narrative, which shows how the past relates to the present. The female protagonist cannot take steps into her future without glancing back to her past to determine where she has come from and how she has changed; any new story told about the narrator is interrupted by old stories so that she finds herself moving forward and backward, backward and forward in time. The narrators seek to reconcile their memories--what they desire to retain or reject from the past--with their longings--what they want from the future--in order to be content with their present life.

Luce Irigaray and Hélène Cixous among other feminist theorists, believe women's writing is particularly influenced by this fluctuation, this cyclical movement in which women are pulled by diverse longings. Irigaray, especially, sees this multiplicity of female desire by which women circle to/around/back from their objects of desire as representing a new economy, "one that upsets the linearity of a project, undermines the goal-object of desire, diffuses the polarization toward a single pleasure, disconcerts fidelity to a single discourse" (Irigaray, 1991, p. 354). Opposing the linearity of a hierarchical language by transcribing the cycle that simulates the female orgasm, female authors, Irigaray says, express their sexual difference in writing. In taking on the rhythm of the female body, the text opposes the narrative code of a beginning, middle and ending by becoming a coda--its ending enfolds back into the story to create an unceasing narrative flow which defies the boundaries of chronological time. Nicole Brossard surmises that "female stories become dérivées, de-rived, or off the main stream, beaching on the banks, the margins" (cited in Wildeman, 1989, p. 36). Women writers of historical fiction shatter the hourglass, rebelling against a linear concept of time, and the female figure which has been molded to fit this construct. The archaic hourglass is tipped over to produce a more female-oriented writing which receives and diffuses diverse material and which in its beginnings and conclusions will "tend to be expressed more as gradations than as abrupt cut-off points" (Bennett, 1986, p. 241). Writing a story told in the present about the past, these women authors oscillate between the two tenses, combining them to emphasize their co-dependency. Although the gap between present and past cannot be filled, women seek to go where the "Magic Boat goes through that gap in the horizon" (Thomas, 1979, p. 30): the space between water and sky which symbolizes the meeting of past, present and future.

A second way in which writers have sought to create a more personal and less authoritative account of history points to narrative innovations. The use of diverse types of narrators and narrations gives a new twist to monologic accounts which are typically recited in omniscient third-person. Assuming the role of the narrator, the authoritative author writes in third-person, telling the reader about events from a distant or removed position. Contrastingly, the second type of narrator is more focused, writing in limited third person or first person, assuming a character's role to show the story from a personal perspective. It is this type of narrator that has been more frequently employed by historical fiction writers in order to personify and individualize a hitherto public and generalized history.

Because the author may tend to revert to her own life to provide information for her story, her composition often resembles an autobiography, narrated in the first person. Susan Lanser cites the fundamental difference between the authority inherent in a personal narrative and that in an authorial work: "authorial narrative is understood as fictive and yet its voice is accorded a superior reliability, while personal narrative may pass for autobiography but the authority of its voice is always qualified" (Lanser, 1992, p. 20). She further states that "an authorial narrator claims broad powers of knowledge and judgment, while a personal narrator claims only the validity of one person's right to interpret her experience" (Lanser, 1992, p. 19). A personal account permits a female author to forefront herself, a self that is finally expressed, "ex-pressed," which "presses outward, outered, uttered" (Cooley, 1989, p. 71).

By transcribing a story using (splitting themselves between) both "I" and "she," the authors create a dual, non-authoritative voice. Marlatt and Tostevin write in the first person to personalize their story, but also employ a third person narrator: Marlatt to recount the life of an archival woman, and Tostevin to narrate her own past. For Tostevin, it is the *combination* of these voices--the "she" of her younger, inexperienced self re-born when she is the presence of her parents, and the "I" of her more experienced adult self, re-established when she is among her husband, son and daughter--that makes up who she is. As *Ana Historic*'s subjective narrator, Annie does not claim full authority over the characters of her story for she refrains from penetrating the mind of her principal character, Ana, and thus appropriating her thoughts and feelings. By refusing to take "control" of Ana by objectifying her in the third-person, Annie allows for Ana's eventual conversion from object in Annie's story to subject in the imagined journal entries of Ana.

As techniques like narratorial shifting and time manipulation allow Marlatt and Tostevin to deviate from the standard narrative, opening up the text for further translation, so do the particular discursive innovations that Marlatt and Tostevin adopt in their novels. Marlatt writes in her own quirky syntactical style and, like Tostevin, plays extensively with words themselves, breaking them down into their original sense (or non-sense): "words. words, that shifting territory. never one's own. full of deadfalls and hidden claims to a reality that others have made" (Marlatt, 1988, p. 32). Marlatt attempts to get past the external covering of words ("wardrobes. wordrobes" [p. 9]) to compare their original meanings to the meanings they have acquired through social usage: words like "lady" and "hysterical." Tostevin, also using discursive innovations, transcribes her story in a hybrid, English/French language, shunning the accepted practice of writing in a single language. Her narrator, Laura, goes even so far as to ask: "Should language account for everything? It almost never [says] what you [want] to anyway" (Tostevin,

1994, p. 146). Only by working between two languages can Laura feel like she is being loyal to her two selves.

Furthermore, both of the authors resist "closure" of their novels, encouraging instead the reader to creep into the tale and open it up by relating her own life to those of the narrators. In this manner the reader adds her/his voice to the diverse voices narrating the story and thus becomes part of a community or culture of writers and readers bound through their shared experiences.

Thus, we arrive at the referential process of translation, or how the fiction refers to the society and culture from which it is born--what experiences are related in the female-authored story. Both Marlatt and Tostevin represent versions of (hi)stories that differ from the canonical version not only through their narrative innovations, but also in their transcription of female bodies, desires and perspectives. Is is through the *process* of converting a male-biased history (source text) into a female-inclusive one (target text) that these writers re-create their identity, showing that they are not persons unto themselves, but rather an amalgamation of many other voices, lives and traditions.

Marlatt's and Tostevin's stories, reflecting their multi-faceted lives, are flexible and able to incorporate new information and diverse perspectives offered by an amalgam of sources. *Ana Historic* and *Frog Moon* are built on a collectivity of voices which creates a dialogue both within the text and between the text and reader, interweaving many points of view rather than projecting a single perspective. Mikhail Bakhtin, theorist of the polyvocal, argues that the dialogue produced by the internal dialogic character of the word allows for the writer to create a chorus of voices:

> Those individual voices – or points of view, or individual languages – make up a pluralistic world in which a continual dialogue goes on, while the word itself becomes a shared property of the author, reader, and all those who in any way participated in the creation of its history. (cited in Tabakowska, 1990, p. 71)

While multi-voiced dialogues are common practice in a plethora of poststructuralist writings, such voices speak particularly, seem especially central, in a female-inclusive writing in which women are able to move beyond their position as separate (and isolated) individual entities into a communal space in which women become both writers and readers of their shared histories. Novels so inspired partake in dialogic communication with the dominant discourse, working within it to persuade, subvert and transform it, converting a form of subordination into an affirmation that would challenge an order resting on sexual indifference. The political force of interpretation lies in its ability to redress through different discourses the imbalance between dominant and dominated cultures: men and women, English and French Canadians (which Tostevin addresses), and heterosexuals and homosexuals (which Marlatt touches on). The discourse in *Ana Historic* and *Frog Moon* infers a certain running back and forth, speaking at length, running in different directions--it is not a unilateral, but a mutual translation that is inherent in these histories.

References

Allen, Thomas & Son Ltd. (ed.), 1990, *Webster's Ninth New Collegiate Dictionary*. Markham, Ontario: Merriam-Webster Inc.

Bennett, Donna, 1986, "Naming the way home," in: Shirley Newman and Smaro Kamboureli (eds.), *Amazing Space: Writing Canadian Women Writing*. Edmonton, Longspoon Press, 228-45.

Cooley, Dennis, 1989, "Recursions Excursions and Incursions: Daphne Marlatt Wrestles with the Angel Language," *Line* 13 (Spring), 67-79.

Funk & Wagnall's (ed.), 1937, *Funk & Wagnall's New Standard Dictionary of the English Language*. New York: Funk & Wagnall's Co.

Godard, Barbara, 1989, "Theorizing Feminist Discourse/Translation," *Tessera* 6 (Spring), 42-53.

Irigaray, Luce, 1991, "This Sex Which is Not One," in: Robyn R. Warhol und Diane Price Herndl (eds), *Feminisms: An Anthology of Literary Theory and Criticism*. New Brunswick, NJ: Rutgers University Press, 350-356.

Kellner, Hans, 1987, "Narrativity in History: Post-structuralism and since," in: *The Representation of Historical Events*, Supplement 26, Wesleyan University.

Lanser, Susan Sniader, 1992, *Fictions of Authority: Women Writers and Narrative Voice*. Ithaca and London: Cornell University Press.

Marlatt, Daphne, 1988, *Ana Historic*. Toronto: Coach House Press.

——, 1989, "Translating MAUVE: Reading Writing," *Tessera* 6 (Spring), 27-30.

Mezei, Kathy, 1989, "Traverse," *Tessera* 6 (Spring), 9-10.

Michelût, Dore, 1989, "Coming to Terms with the Mother Tongue," *Tessera* 6 (Spring), 63-71.

Robinson, Sally, 1991, *Engendering the Subject*. Albany: State University of New York Press.

Snell-Hornby, Mary, 1988, *Translation Studies: An Integrated Approach*. Amsterdam and Philadelphia: John Benjamins.

Stanford, Michael, 1986, *The Nature of Historical Knowledge*. Oxford and New York: Basil Blackwell.

Tabakowska, Elzbieta, 1990, "Linguistic Polyphony as a Problem in Translation," in: Susan Bassnett und Andre Lefevore (eds.), *Translation, History and Culture*. London und New York: Pinter Publishers, 71-8.

Thomas, Audrey, 1979, *Latakia*. Vancouver: Talonbooks.

Tostevin, Lola Lemire, 1994, *Frog Moon*. Dunvegan, Ontario: Cormorant Books.

Wildeman, Marlene, 1989, "Daring Deeds:Translation as Lesbian Feminist Language Act," *Tessera* 6 (Spring), 31-40.

The Ethics of Difference in Jane Rule's Work

Christina Strobel

> We differ. We always have.
> We always will, but there is
> no alienation that I can see in this. Tension
> sometimes, yes, but tension is, for me,
> one of the vital facts of living.
> (Jane Rule in letter to E.K.,
> Dec 28, 1957; 19-3)[1]

Difference: binary opposition or relational tension?

Identity is a category that cannnot stand alone. To distinguish a self requires a consideration and conceptualization of the other, and of the relation between self and other. Ethics is a code of norms which regulates this relation. Ethics can also be understood as the field of the negotiation of sameness and difference between individuals and groups. As the epigraph of this article announces, difference is a vital consideration for Rule. What difference means for her, and how she proposes to deal with identity and alterity will be explored in the following.

There are several ways to understand difference. The regime of differentiating by binary oppositions – I/not-I, man/woman, and other analogous binaries in the history of Western thought – will be called dichotomy or distinction here.[2] Such pairs of opposed terms carry with them systems of domination in that these dichotomies are inherently non-reversible and non-reciprocal hierarchies. Difference "as different-from Man," notes Rosi Braidotti, "is a mark of inferiority" (1991, p. 158). Read in analogy: "different from white," "different from heterosexual." This is what defines a stigma: the difference from a norm.[3]

Oppositional and hierarchical distinctions imply normative codes and moral judgements. This is especially evident in the area of sexuality. Experts in the field of sex research have criticized Western societies' attitude towards sexual difference and the advancement of a moral monopoly. Kinsey and his coworkers remark (speaking about the US):

> The publicly pretended code of morals, our social organization, our marriage customs, our sex laws, and our educational and religious systems are based upon an assumption that individuals are much alike sexually and that it is an equally simple matter for all of them to confine their behavior to the single pattern which the mores dictate. (1948, p. 197)

Carole Vance has addressed the question of difference with an emphasis on how society deals with power differentials. She has analyzed our "discomfort with difference" around questions of sexual variation as one that is grounded in "a cultural system that organizes sexual differences in a hierarchy in which some acts and partners are privileged and others are punished" (Vance, 1884, p. 19). Vance argues that while sexual orientation is certainly not the only, and may not be the most significant sexual difference among women, our ability to think about sexual difference is severely limited by a system which establishes and enforces a power differential.

Jane Rule shares a conceptualization of difference in which two (or more) terms have an autonomous existence: "Each term exists in its own right" (Grosz, 1989, p. xvii).[4] As in Saussurian linguistics, each (term/sign) can only be understood in terms of what it is not. Brought to the relations of the sexes, this concept allows to define both without privileging one, or regarding them as oppositions. Applied to other areas, it equally generates a wider and non-hierarchical angle.[5]

This "diversifying" and "democratic" aspect is the essential quality of the ethics of difference on which Rule has based her thinking from early on. She has adopted a view of difference which regards it as integral to her life. In her correspondence with her close friend Ellen K., she repeatedly makes that point. The 26-year old Rule writes:

> I think, you see, that I don't at all believe in marriage as the Church conceives it, nor in generosity, nor in salvation, nor even in communion. For me communion is not the brotherhood of those of the same faith, but the brotherhood of mankind, crying out a dozen faiths, irreconciled but for love, but for the absolute perceiving and accepting of otherness. Do I sound like a Russian-peaceful co-exitance [sic]?
> (Letter to E.K., Nov 25, 1957; 19-3)

> There is no alienation for me in your decison to join the church. It is not my way. I cannot see that it will ever be a choice for me to contemplate. It is a brilliant, powerful vison of the nature of the world, and I listen to and see it with deep respect, but I am more, by philisophical [sic] inclination, something like a Moslem. I can no more embrace one vision of the nature of the world than I can one political view. *I am much more interested in living in terms of the tension of many visions, many views. I can really live no other way.* The kind of book I want to write, the life I want to live requires involvement and distance, and my only deep conviction is that I must somehow accept and understand all that is given. I know I am limited, by the general nature of my inheritance, by the particular nature of myself, and *I know that it is out of that limitation that what strength and insight I have must come, but I must, for myself, always remember that the strength and insight are limitations, vital limitations not virtues.* But, if I chose to let your decision to accept a particular faith alienate you from me or me from you, I would then be alienated from everyone I know and love, for no one I know holds the view I hold, and I don't claim that anyone should. It is in its own way as limited as any other.
> [...]
> We differ. We always have. We always will, but there is no alienation that I can see in this. Tension sometimes, yes, but tension is, for me, one of the vital facts of living.
> (Letter to E.K., Dec 28, 1957; 19-3, emphasis C.S.)

This "absolute perceiving and accepting of otherness" resonates in the often quoted words of Audre Lorde, who argued that merely to take difference into account or to tolerate it was "a total denial of the creative function of difference in our lives." Lorde, like Rule, emphasizes the creative aspect of tensions:

> Difference must be [...] seen as a fund of necessary polarities between which our creativity can spark like a dialectic. Only then does the necessity for interdependency become unthreatening. Only within that interdependency of different strengths, acknowledged and equal, can the power to seek new ways of being in the world generate, as well as the courage and sustenance to act where there are no charters." (Lorde, 1984, p. 111)

A society of outsiders and a community of outlanders

In feminist theory, the stigma of being female or lesbian has often been theorized in terms of outsiderness. Rule's approach to sameness and difference places different emphases from those of other feminists. This can be shown clearly in a reading of some of her literary texts.

In her last novel, *After the Fire* (1989), Jane Rule is concerned with the building of a community which, in its main focus on five women, offers the portrait of a society of outsiders, or of a community of 'outlanders'. These outlander women balance independence and mutual interdependence, validating both. They support each other in their struggle to resist hegemonic power relations and how these have shaped their bodies. They emphasize rituals in their community building in one of their endeavours to order and reformulate their world.

The society of outsiders, as Virginia Woolf has described it, is a way – and a necessity – of survival for women.[6] In *Three Guineas*, Woolf proposes to her correspondent an "Outsiders' Society," founded by the daughters of educated men. She has in mind a society without any formal self-organization. The name, Woolf suggests, "has the advantage that it squares with facts – the facts of history, of law, of biography" (1938, p. 106), which tell us how women, of all classes and races, have not been equal members of Western societies for centuries, but how they legally, economically, politically, socially, and culturally have been kept at the fringes. Woolf cites examples to prove the Society is already in existence; its members are actively and passively resisting structures which oppose their goals of justice, equality and liberty for all men and women. To describe women as outsiders has become a familiar approach to an understanding of their position in society. Whether as "muted group" (Showalter, 1981; referring to Ardener/Ardener), or as "oppossums" who survive "by ones and twos in the chinks of your world-machine" (Tiptree, Jr. 1973, p. 154), whether as "stigmatized group" (Goffman) or as Sister Outsider (Lorde), women as a group have been conceived of as excluded by the system or as kept at its margins.

After the Fire explores the creation of a community of outsiders through the lives of five women of different ages and backgrounds. They have all been hurt by the patriarchal, capitalist, and racist society they live in. They all begin to come to terms with the various wounds inflicted on their minds and bodies.

The oldest of the five, Miss James, is a retired school teacher waiting to die. When she was young, she "defied her daddy" and ran from the South. Resisting her patriarchal society's conventions for women, she tried an independent life outside marriage. She lived and taught in a wide variety of places, moving frequently.

Red, the youngest of the five women, has just turned 18. About four years ago, she came to the island alone, escaping her mother who was on trial for killing a man. Red's mother worked as a whore, joking Red's last name "should be Heinz for fifty-seven varieties" (*AF*, p. 166). Her background has made Red an outsider who values separateness.

Henrietta and Hart Hawkins started out as summer people, and later retired on the island. "Hen" is, as her nickname indicates, the epitome of selfless, supportive, competent and caring womanhood.[7] In Milly's view, she loses "interest in people without needs" (p. 72). As Mrs. Hart Hawkins, her husband is her "social legitimacy" (p. 114).

Karen Tasuki, 28, is of mixed descent. Her father is an acculturated Japanese Canadian; her mother a white Canadian, in a chosen exile of traveling. The young woman is an outsider by even more respects than most of the women on the island; her jobs and her silence about a failed lesbian relationship set her even further apart.

Class-conscious Milly Forbes, 45, needs to put down others mainly to convince herself that she is still superior – i.e., white, and not a pervert -, even though she has been left by her ex-husband for a younger woman. Milly acts as a model of patriarchal femininity, believing sexual attractiveness her only currency.

These five women share more than the fact of their sex/gender as a basis for their outsider status. For none of them a man is at the center of their lives (even before Hart's death, his existence was more an enabling foundation than the center of Hen's life). Even within the range of women's positions in patriarchal society, they live on the fringes – away from heterosexual marriage plus motherhood. For Henrietta it is old age and being a widow, for Karen her sexual orientation, for Miss James being a spinster, for Milly her divorce, and for Red choosing to be an unwed mother that removes them from what a patriarchal model considers (the fulfilment of) a woman's life. Rule does not make heterosexual partnership and erotic love or motherhood her targets,[8] but focusses her attention on the large number of women who live outside those models, whether by choice or not. She also reminds us that to define women by marriage and having children is at most appropriate for certain stages of some women's lives.

The position of the five women, as well as the pain a sexist, racist and homophobic society has inflicted upon them, and the processes through which they deal with the damages, cannot fully be explained in terms of their status as outsiders. To be an outsider, to return to Woolf's formulation, is a) a fact, and b) a position of conscious resistance. In her story "Outlander," Jane Rule uses a concept of the outsider which in some ways differs from Woolf's. Where feminists such as Virginia Woolf and Adrienne Rich have warned women of giving up their outsider status, Jane Rule risks integration. Both Woolf and Rich have good reasons for their caution. Woolf, speaking of how to prevent war, refuses to join even a man's society which is fighting for her own aims of liberty, equality, and peace, because by joining "we should merge our identity in yours, follow and repeat and score still deeper the old ruts in which society, like a gramophone whose needle has stuck, is grinding out with intolerable unanimity 'Three hundred millions spent upon arms'" (1938, p. 105). Women's own views and experiences must be analyzed and put forward, she insists, and these differ profoundly from men's. Rich names a related danger of integration: tokenism. Masculine society, Rich argues, will offer power to a few female tokens, on the condition that they use it to maintain the status quo (1986, p. 5). "Tokenism essentially demands," Rich asserts,

> that the token deny her identification with women as a group, especially with women less privileged than she: if she is a lesbian, that she deny her relationships with individual women; that she perpetuate rules and structures and criteria and methodologies which have functioned to exclude women; that she renounce or leave undeveloped the critical perspective of her female consciousness. Women unlike herself – poor women, women of color, waitresses, secretaries, housewives in the supermarket, prostitutes, old women – become invisible to her; they may represent too acutely what she has escaped or wished to flee. (1986, p. 6)

To argue that Rule's concept of 'outlander' proposes a possibility of integration, does not mean to suggest that Rule either rejects women's status as outsiders nor that she courts the very real dangers of integration. The concept's characteristic difference is that it allows us a glimpse of a – both very real and at the same utopian – possibility of cooperation within a mixed community, and of mutual support between very different individuals, or between the sexes. At the same time, however, outlander women remain each other's primary concern.

The concept of the outlander is best explained in an analysis of the story it is taken from. "Outlander" (in the collection *Outlander*, 1981) tells us about two women who decide to make a life in the country in New Hampshire. Ann Bacon, at 50, sees this as her only chance to survive, and Fran O'Connell, her younger friend, stays on with her in a house that was meant to be lived in only during the summer.

In the country, Ann Bacon is considered an outlander in terms of her sex/gender, her age, and as a city person, all of which is summed up in the comment that it "wasn't likely that anyone would call on a woman in her fifties to help with a barnraising" (p. 41).

The women finally make a place for themselves that will do in any season, also of their own lives. They also make a place within the larger community. Gradually they become accepted in the rural neighborhood, and this happens, interestingly, largely because of their own strengths. Ann even gains respect for her way with a level and plane; for the country people it still may not be a women's job she is doing, and they may still consider it strange that she sings and talks to the wood as she works it, but she is finally judged by the quality of her work. Rule grants the country people she describes a trust in what they recognize as real: "If there was a lot of narrow prejudice in those farming people, still they would believe what they could see" (p. 41), and what they see is work well done.

Relationships within the rural community are based on a mutual giving and taking. Or, as we read in the story, "you couldn't really be neighborly with anyone until they owed you something" (p. 38). It is one of the rather extraordinary circumstances which favor the women's integration that the rural society functions not as a money economy, but is based on trading (of goods, labor, favors), on "mutual owing." In this system, the two women have "useful" (as opposed to singing and painting) skills and vital goods which can be offered in exchange for help. A second favorable circumstance is that when the US enters World War II, sex/gender boundaries cannot be observed as strictly as before anymore. Finally, the farmers do not only accept what they see, but are capable of showing insight into the nature of strangeness. They notice outlandishness in others, but are also aware of some of their own. The luxury of the women's second bathroom for a daughter-in-law and her son is shrugged off with the thought that "everybody had peculiarities. You didn't have to look far past your own family to know that. Some had a hard time not knowing it under their own roofs" (p. 42). Thus, 'outlander' does not need to remain an absolute category, but becomes one of degrees, and one into which the self is included. This enables sharing the position of the outlander, if at different intersections, and thus to leave difference intact. It also enables a mutual rapprochement.

That being an outlander is a matter of degree, and of context, is also shown by the arrival of a Polish couple who escaped from the war in Europe. For the farmers, they are enemies and spies; not being able to communicate with them reinforces suspicions. The couple represents more foreignness than the community can be reconciled with; they also do not stay long enough for the process to start.[9] The Polish couple is one of the devices by which Rule keeps reminding her readers that other categories than sex/gender are being used to construct hierarchized difference, whether in interdependence with sex/gender or not.

Finally, an important characteristic of being an 'outlander' is her complicity with her oppression. One of the aims of the members of Woolf's Society of Outsiders is "to maintain an attitude of complete indifference" to that which Woolf describes as the male values of patriotism, chivalry, and the manly qualities of fighting and glory. Such an indifference would help prevent war, Woolf argues (p. 109). Ann Bacon, however, shares the emotions of patriotism, "and the dangerous heroism appealed to her" ("Outlander," p. 40). She resents not having the privileges of a man but does not seem concerned with achieving equality as a woman. Unlike Woolf's conclusion that as a woman she has no country, Ann remains supportively involved with the very structures which oppress her. Where Woolf and Rich describe a real beginning, and remind us of the necessity and viability of political action, Rule shows the reality of most women's lives: All women participate in patriarchal society, and most actively help perpetuate it.

While reflecting on a lesbian position of resistance, Elizabeth Meese notes the difficulty of being both within and outside a structure, and argues that only by inhabiting it, we can take accurate aim to destroy it. At the same time, subversion from within provides only a limited range of tools to dismantle the master's house. Meese writes:

> I would like to think that lesbianism, like feminism, could position itself "outside." There's a comfort in the tidiness offered by the absence of complicity and the certainty of an absolute difference. But lesbianism, as an attack on hetero-relations, takes (its) place within the structure of the institution of heterosexuality. The lesbian is born of/in it. We know the condition(ing) is not fatal, just as we mark its torturous limits. It might even afford a strategic value to be "there," if Derrida is right that attacks occur from within [...]. But, as Derrida continues, danger lurks in this structural relation [...]. The illusionary and visionary project (it must be both of these) of lesbianism is to be writing the "beyond" of heterosexual phallologocentrism, even though this is also what is always recuperating us, claiming to (re)produce us as one of its effects. (1990, p. 82)

The embeddedness which Meese describes for lesbianism, structurally works the same for other marginalized groups attempting to reshape society. Rule's variously positioned outlander is marked by this involvement and complicity which also permits her resistance. The outlander women share the real and visionary project of building a community which offers glimpses of a "beyond" of present oppressive hierarchies.

To summarize, 'outsider' and 'outlander' share a firm grounding in the factual reality of women's lives. Yet the evaluation of this reality and the conclusions drawn differ. 'Outsider' is a more oppositional and more exclusive concept of difference than 'outlander' is. 'Outsider' as defined here emphasizes and demands difference as separateness, while 'outlander' invites and allows a coming together in change. Both concepts value the specific insight a position from outside can provide. A second major shift of emphasis in the concept of 'outlander' is in terms of women's lived reality not as it should be, or as an origin for a different point of view, but on women's complicity with systems which oppress them, while envisioning something beyond and taking steps towards it. Given present economic, political, and social structures, the outlander is best at home far from any centre, in some ways separate from its demands.

In *After the Fire*, the five main characters are outlanders in this sense. There are also extraordinary circumstances that allow an outsider's society to develop. One is the island situation with its small, interdependent population, a situation which allows for very different and disagreeing individuals to co-exist, recalling Rule's description of Galiano society in her essay "Stumps" (in *Outlander*). The other circumstance is a symbolic event of violent destruction. The novel begins with a fire in which the father's house, literally and metaphorically, goes up in smoke. We never meet this young man – given the unmisunderstandable first and last names "Dickie John" – whom Red has deliberately chosen to father her child. Red does not love him, or expect him to be a father to the child when it will be born; she chose him for suitable genetic potential. Dickie is described as a misogynist; he brags about his "collection of 'pussy'" (p. 8). He does not live to find he was not a great seducer, but rather put to use.[10]

Science fiction writers such as Joanna Russ and Suzy McKee Charnas have commented on the fact that they have not been able to imagine a truly egalitarian society inhabited by two sexes (see Keinhorst, 1985, p. 147). Single-sexed societies provide an opportunity to escape the dilemma of both writer and reader to portray and perceive through a gendered lens. Peter Fitting's argument holds for readers of both sexes when he says that "in the patterns of social interaction and behavior of these societies without men, the male reader can glimpse a society in which present-day gender roles and the sexual division of labor have finally disappeared" (1985, p. 160). Since individuals are both enabled and limited by the discourses and practices of their respective societies (as, for example, Meese has pointed out), they will be enabled (and limited) differently in a society in which the male sex, presently structurally dominant, has been eliminated or repositioned as marginal. Jane Rule, in a move to liberate her outlander women from patriarchal constraints, dispenses with the father/patriarch in the opening paragraphs of the book. She begins with the apocalyptic fire which, incidentally, must have been started through carelessness of the father in his house.[11]

The firefighters are not very organized in their attempts to extinguish the fire, but even if they had been – and we can read this as Rule's optimistic prediction for the future of patriarchy -, "there had never been a chance of saving the house or anyone or anything in it" (p. 2). Of Homer, one of the fire fighters, it is said that "he's been around forever,'" and that he "'should have learned *something*'" (p. 5), but he only knows how to drive the fire truck. Figures from classical mythology cannot offer a way to put this symbolic fire out. The fire brings about a "post-patriarchal" society in which the community of outlander women can be established. As the pine cone on the front book cover of the Naiad edition signals, some seeds, such as Sequoia seeds, only flower after they have been through a fire. The "beauty" of the fire which "blooms" into the winter night both destroys and makes room for new life.

The symbolic father/patriarch who is removed to enable a vision of a post-patriarchal society is at the same time a young man who finds a tragic death. Dickie represents a product of patriarchal society, but as an individual he is also freed from stereotype. His friends have "genuinely liked" (p. 40) him as a buddy, and he is spoken of, here in Henrietta's words, as a boy "'still figuring out how to live'" (p. 25). He is also a young man who has chosen life on this island, away from the centres of power, and thus shares some outlander ways. The outlander is a figure that emphasizes that stigma is a relative and a relational concept.

Men in this island community are no longer women's opposites, or enemies, or even their main concern. The first sex is either absent, or, in the final consequence, irrelevant; men are "reduced" to ordinary individuals, some more likeable than others, and certainly none of them the focus of the story. This provides the space for a single-sexed society which at the same time reaches out into the larger community, helping to shape it on women's terms. The women move away from male and patriarchal definition, conferring recognition and value on each other.

The essence of the outlander

Both in her theoretical and her fictional representations of identity, Rule assumes the givenness and validity of female/lesbian experience of body and sexuality as (the result of) a social fact. Rule takes a difference of "women" and "men" for granted, but never investigates to find some deeper, ingrained meaning for that fact. As in her essays, Rule's fictional representations of identity tend to deflect attention from a dualism of women and men and of homosexuality and heterosexuality as they de-emphasize sexual identity and foreground individual and relational difference.

In conclusion to this article, Rule's short story "The Killer Dyke and the Lady" (in *Outlander*) provides an example from her work which both affirms lesbian existence and lesbian sexuality/bodies/desire, and which resists its essentializing.

Difference appears here not as the sexual difference of man/woman, or of heterosexuality/homosexuality, concepts which suggest an exclusionary opposition of the terms at the same time that they confer normalizing sameness within these terms. This essential sameness of the categories of "woman," or, in analogy, of "lesbian," has persistently been questioned by Rule.

In the story, two white lesbians from diverse backgrounds meet as resource persons at a social workers' conference. Fay McBride, called Mac, is the narrator whose perceptions filter the reader's view; Dr. Ellen Compton is accessible to the reader through her actions and in dialogue (as narrated by Mac). The jeans-and-leather dyke Mac has to restrain her aggression towards elegant Dr. Ellen Compton, a model of well-bred civility, "an aristocrat with impeccable professional credentials" (p. 81), with whom she shares nothing but her age – and sexual orientation.

For Mac, there is no natural solidarity between them merely because of that last fact; rather it requires work, i.e., the awareness of a political position: "If you're a killer dyke into leather, into aggressive visibility, it takes a lot of consciousness-raising along with a basic social conscience to call one of those expensively pant-suited, family-jeweled, narrow-nosed women 'sister,'" the story begins. Seven pages later, with their sexual encounter on the last page, the story ends unromantically affirming that the two women still inhabit different time zones.

To make love after a day of social work for them is a way of affirming a commonality of lesbian experience, of setting a lesbian "we" against "them," those well-meaning liberal heterosexists who have nurtured mixed feelings of anger, aggression and pain in them. It is as much an act of political solidarity as it is one of communication – with words and movements – as it is an expression of desire.

The lesbian must have been a difficult concept to grasp for the polite social workers, for Ellen is full of cynicism when they undress:

> "And now, ladies and gentlemen, exhibit A and exhibit B are going to show you what lesbians actually do in bed," she says, pulling my belt off. "First, however, they have to remove their armor. It comes in two styles," she explains, as she removes the rings from her

finger, "killer dyke and lady. But take a good look, ladies and gentlemen, because in a moment you may not be able to tell one from the other." (p. 87)

The truth about the lesbian is unveiled in her naked body. But the "naked" body is part of human sign systems and as such is part of of the "masquerade" or the fashioning of meanings. The masquerade of exhibits A and B does not end at the skin. The naked body still allows us to tell one from the other; each incorpates its history of backgrounds such as class and age – and individuality. The bodies are not described at the moment of undressing; the reader does not know about their sameness or difference. One small remark, however, about Ellen's body looking younger than her face, refers us back to the beginning and to Mac's reflections on how differently age has marked their faces – "she looks older than I do, the skin at her throat, along her fine jaw, loose with the flesh that has melted away [...] I won't look any different at sixty, 'applecheeked,' 'sunny.' Only my guts age" (p. 81).

The naked lesbian body as constituted by Mac's look is one that is vulnerable, inscribed with having come out to the heterosexual world all day. It is neither presented as the ultimate lesbian sign, nor does the story indulge in a postmodern play with identities. Neither of the two protagonists could slip into the other's protective armor and enjoy drag for its artificial character. Both have a firm investment in their specific lesbian identity, which is not shed with their clothes. The body of the other appears even more fragile and vulnerable to Mac than her appealing face, and the naked lesbian bodies stand "before each other like creatures ready for the gas chamber" (p. 87). The truth of recognition in the face of nakedness is that of the ultimate societal sanctions against deviation; the lesbian body faces the danger of violent extinction. Female masquerade – a continuing topic in interpretations of gender difference – here is neither mere performance without any essential basis nor does it express a criticism of the repression of the essential female. Rule in her story resignifies the lesbian body from an essential truth about lesbian difference (and sameness) to the social facts of power and how difference has historically been dealt with. She affirms lesbian identity as a specific desire and as a political necessity.

The outlander, as this story suggests, may need to affirm her difference for political reasons, as a survival strategy. "Strategic essentialism" functioned as a powerful slogan of feminist theory from the mid 1980s to the early 1990s. In 1995, Bonnie Zimmerman stated somewhat belatedly, "essentialism has become part of a political strategy" (1995, p. 2). At the end of the 1980s, Diana Fuss suggested that "more than any other notion in the vocabulary of recent feminist poststructuralist theory, 'essentialism' has come to represent both our greatest fear and our greatest temptation [...] Essentialism is the issue which simply refuses to die" (1989, p. 62).

The question of strategy emerged from heated debates about the respective values of essentialism vs. constructivism. Ann Snitow in her essay "A Gender Diary" lists other names for the opposing sides: minimizers and maximizers; radical feminists and cultural feminists; essentialists and social constructionists; cultural feminists and poststructuralists (1990, p. 14ff.). The differences between these positions, Snitow argues, arise from "a common divide [which] keeps forming in both feminist thought and action" (p. 9). The divide forms "between the need to build the identity 'woman' and give it solid political meaning and the need to tear down the very category 'woman' and dismantle its all-too-solid history" (Snitow, 1990, p. 9). Linda Alcoff developed the notion of "woman as positionality" in order to transcend the paradox by a third course: "woman is a position from which a feminist politics can emerge rather than a set of attributes that are 'objectively identifiable'" (1988, p. 434f.). Alcoff suggested:

> If we combine the concept of identity politics with a conception of the subject as positionality, we can conceive of the subject as nonessentialized and emergent from a historical experience and retain our political ability to take gender as an important point of departure. Thus we can say at one and the same time that gender is not natural, biological, universal, ahistorical, or essential and yet still claim that gender is relevant because we are taking gender as a position from which to act politically. (p. 433)

Snitow did not think this viable since the "urgent contradiction women constantly experience between the pressure to be a woman and the pressure not to be one will change only through a historical process; it cannot be dissolved through thought alone" (1990, p. 19). Still, notions of a politics of location, of position, and a number of other suggestions dressed in geographic metaphors prevailed and even flourished. For many, lesbianism ceased "to be an identity with predictable contents," while it remained "a position from which to speak, to organize, to act politically" (Martin, 1988, p. 103).

The body, "as essentialism's great text" (Spivak/Rooney, 1989, p. 125), became the ground of reflection and research, began to "be seen as a socially inscribed, historically marked, psychically and interpersonally significant product," requiring a thoroughgoing analysis of its interaction with discursive systems (Gross, 1986, p. 140). Vicki Kirby asked: how does essence "congeal into an embodied reality?" (1991, p. 9).

Gayatri Chakravorty Spivak, who, at about the same time as Stephen Heath, spoke about the strategic use of essentialism and inadvertently initiated the ensuing debate, called for caution on several accounts later: A strategy might easily freeze into a position; and it is important who it is that uses it (Spivak/Rooney, 1989, p. 127). In her review of Diana Fuss' book *Essentially Speaking* (1989), bell hooks addresses the issue that a totalizing critique of subjectivity, essence, identity "can seem very threatening to marginalized groups, for whom it has been an active gesture of political resistance to name one's identity as part of a struggle to challenge domination" (hooks, 1991, p. 172f.).

Spivak reconsidered her concept of "the strategic use of a positivist essentialism in a scrupulously visible political interest" (1987, p. 205) after observing developments in North America:

> I would say that one of the reasons why the strategic use of essentialism has caught on within a personalist culture is that it gives a certain alibi to essentialism. The emphasis falls on being able to speak from one's own ground, rather than on what the word strategy implies, so I've reconsidered it. I think it's too risky a slogan in a personalist, academic culture, within which it has been picked up and celebrated. (Spivak/Rooney, 1989, p. 128).

Teresa de Lauretis suggests that what motivates the common fear to really deal with essentialism is the further risk essentialism entails, namely "the risk of challenging directly the social-symbolic institution of heterosexuality." She notes an "unwillingness to confront and come to terms with the stakes, indeed the investments that feminism may have in the heterosexual institution" (de Lauretis, 1989, p. 32).[12]

What all of the contributions to the debate share is, as Snitow has argued, that there is no way out: Any repudiation of universalizing, naturalizing, or essentialist assumptions already participates in them. "There can be no feminist position that is not in some way or other involved in patriarchal power relations [...] Feminists are not faced with pure and impure options," Elizabeth Grosz reminds us (1995, p. 56). The important thing is not some (impossible) theoretical purity of never speaking in essentialising or universalising terms, but to recognize how these terms and practices function "as unavoidable and therefore possibly strategically useful" ones, to be vigilant, and use them as "tools and weapons of struggle," as Grosz cites Spivak (1995, p. 56f.). Elsewhere, Spivak says about deconstruction that it offers us "the critique of something that is extremely useful, something without which we cannot do anything. That should be the approach to how we are essentialists" (Spivak/Rooney, 1989, p. 129).

Some years before this debate in feminist circles began to flourish, Jane Rule proposed the strategic deployment of identity in the struggle for political change in her essay "Hindsight," published in the collection *A Hot-Eyed Moderate* in 1985. She writes:

> We don't yet have the political freedom to be able to be homosexuals only when we are making love with members of our own sex, but it is that freedom I know I'm working for. I may have to go on calling myself a lesbian into great old age, not because it is any longer true but because it takes such a long time to make the simple point that I have the right to be. (*Hot-Eyed Moderate*, p. 73)

Rule's use of 'lesbian' suggests that someone could occupy the position while not or no longer being able to lay claim to 'essence', thus distinguishing between an identity which may lead to a political position, and a political position which may lend itself to be grounded in a particular identity. What Rule cares about is a certain goal; what she proposes is a strategy to approach it. She is well aware that she "falsifies" and contradicts herself in the process, creating an essence of herself after the fact, designed for public appearance: Enter the figure of a senior-citizen-in/authentic-public-lesbian. Rule plays with the notion of authenticity by suggesting this creature may turn (yet again) into the original; she may not remember or feel like making "a political speech rather than a sexual overture" (Rule, 1985, p. 73). She also plays on cultural prejudice; even great old age, we note with hope not horror, remains no safeguard against perverse desire. Rule's concern once again is to gain more room for individuals and their interactions by subverting rigid categorizations.

Rule regards sexual identity as an epistemological tool rather than as an unalterable fact which is grounded in the body, "essentialism's great text" (Spivak/Rooney, 1989, p. 125). By conceiving of identity as a fiction, Rule can utilitze it as a means to find out facts about the social reality she lives in. Fictions are for finding things out, Jeffrey Weeks argues, relying on Frank Kermode's distinction between myth and fiction: fictions change as the needs of sense-making change.[13] The outlander is a fictional figure which permits to tell stories of creative tensions – whether within or between individuals, or of contradictory concepts of identity.

The ethics of difference

Thus the outlander mobilizes her energies to work for change. While setting her own identity against that of the other for political purposes, in her definition she relies and depends on that other, and on the creative tension which is vital to both self and other. There are two concepts of the relationship between self and other which describe Rule's ethics of difference. They are not compatible in the sense that they cannot be supported at the same time, but both can be found in Rule's writing.

The first is what Jessica Benjamin has called "the intersubjective view." Intersubjective theory, Benjamin says, explores "the representation of self and other as distinct but interrelated beings" (1988, p. 20). A self meeting another self, or a subject another subject, that is "different and yet alike." Benjamin describes the ideal relationship between self and other as one that upholds the "necessary tension between self-assertion and mutual recognition that allows self and other to meet as sovereign equals" (1988, p. 12). Assertion and recognition, says Benjamin, are poles of a delicate balance; they are integral to 'differentiation', i.e., the individual's development as a self that is aware of its distinctness from others. The human need for recognition gives rise to a paradox:

> Recognition is that response from the other which makes
> meaningful the feelings, intentions, and actions of the self. It allows
> the self to realize its agency and authorship in a tangible way. But
> such recognition can only come from an other whom we, in turn,
> recognize as a person in his or her own right. (Benjamin, 1988,
> p. 12)

It only works if recognition is mutual. Benjamin proposes an intersubjective view in which subjects meet as distinct but interrelated beings and in which the requirement is not separation or a growing out of relationships, but to become more active and sovereign within them. Mutuality must be sustained as a constant tension in this concept; not be "resolved" as in the Hegelian drama of master and slave.

In Benjamin's concept, "sameness and difference exist simultaneously in mutual recognition" (p. 47). Jane Rule makes this point in different words when she demands:

> We have got to be peers, respecting each other's strengths without
> dependent envy, sympathetic with each other's weaknesses
> without cherishing or encouraging them, interdependent by
> choice, not by terrified necessity. (1981, p. 185)

Another example of the mutual relation of self and other which Rule imagines is that between lovers: neither domination nor clinging dependency; nor the idea of "a *real* marriage, not only of the flesh but of the imagination" (1981, p. 184); nor the "infantile in romantic love" (1981,

p. 185) strike her as models to be encouraged. Rule wants to "get past the pattern of dominance and submission, of possessive greed" and to live as peers, to "set us free to be loving equals" (1981, p. 185). "Loving equals" is far removed from romantic love for Rule, a state which usually "is finally degrading to both people, patterned as it is on the relationship between a mother and a dependent child" (1981, p. 185). Only those who stand alone, who speak for themselves, will find themselves in "remarkably good and large company" (1981, p. 178).

The second concept does not focus on the mutuality of self and other but emphasizes the alterity of the other: The other must not be understood as a variation of the sameness of self. The most influential proponent of the concept is the Judaic scholar Emmanuel Lévinas; Luce Irigaray has used it in her work.

The other, in this concept, "is irreducibly other, different, independent;" it is "outside the binary opposition between self and other, [...] outside of, unpredictable by and ontologically prior to the subject" (Grosz, 1989, pp. 141; xiv).

This radical alterity is characterized by the subject's dependence on the other – the other is a condition of subjectivity – and by responsibility to the other. The other chooses the subject, which is passively positioned in relation to it; it is *made* responsible and is not an active moral agent. Elizabeth Grosz summarizes these central points of Lévinas' conception of alterity:

> Otherness is thus not conceived on the Hegelian model of mutual recognition of two equal self-conscious subjects; rather, the other is the irreversible and non-reciprocal material support of the subject. It is prior to the subject. Ethics is the domain of the response to the other's needs; it is a responsibility for the other's actions – even if those actions are inflicted on the subject. (1989, p. 142f.)

While Rule shares the concept of "mutual recognition of two equal self-conscious subjects" (minus the Hegelian resolution in domination and subordination, but upholding the continuing tension), she also brings forward views that set the other as prior, as given. Her ethics derives from and evolves out of the need to negotiate between existences without a regulating code of norms. Resisting abstract fixed regulations, Rule's ethics responds to the needs of the other who is given to the subject to be responded to.

This does not mean to suggest that in Rule one can find Lévinas model of alterity in all its dimensions; rather, it means to point to an unusual affinity: Rule affirms not choice or love as criteria that make her care for an other, but the givenness. It does not matter whether I like my students, she has said; it matters that they happen to be there for me to require my attention. Having chosen to live in a small community where people must depend on each other to a certain extent, she knows she can expect the same of others. She takes on a responsibility for others who happen to be there, expecting to disagree with them or not even like them (cf. "Stumps" in *Hot-Eyed Moderate*, 1985).

Responsibility is a term that serves as a useful synonym for power. Rule formulates her understanding of how we should responsibly deal with the power differentials in human relations. Rule's ethics of difference requires the shifting of hierarchies to a more equal balance and an understanding of difference as a potential source of social enrichment. Among moral actions count the curtailment of their power by the privileged themselves, or the acceptance of the responsibility which the (sometimes morally required) use of power entails.

Rule never rejects power. She clearly states: "It is not power but its abuse which should concern people" (1985, p. 146). In relationships, so Rule argues, unequal power may mean that different strengths and gifts are responsibly used: "For strengths and gifts are there to be of service in any loving circumstance" (1985, p. 146). Or: "To acknowledge difference, otherness, is the beginning of real love in which each can be depending and dependable according to her own gifts and needs" (1985, p. 147). She considers only "people unafraid of power, willing to risk being vulnerable to it and to take responsibility for it" to be "real candidates for serious relationship" (1985, p. 147). To accept power does not mean sovereignty for Rule, but to claim the authority to act and create meaning with responsibility (cf. Jones, 1991).

Mutual recognition; the appreciation of difference; the givenness of the other; the necessary and inevitable implication of the self within power and hence its responsibility; difference within the self and sameness of self and other; and moral pluralism mark Rule's ethics of difference. This ethics is finally distinguished by a characteristic which here is called an "erotics of difference:" Rule's specific combination of respect of and love for an other by which she establishes the relationship between self and other as an erotic one. In the context of writing about her dis/agreements with Kate Millett, Robin Morgan, and Jill Johnston, Rule speaks of this bond between herself and others whom she respects in terms which capture all of the above concepts:

> I do, however, respect the right of each of those women to choose what she chooses; and given the privilege of arguing with any one of them, I would contend as I do with a lover, to know and be

known, without will to discredit, without will to win or lose, in a contest designed to strengthen both people. (1981, p. 178)

Notes

1. References to materials from the "Jane Rule Papers" housed at the Archives of the University of British Columbia follow the inventory's practice, giving first the box number, then the number of the folder, e.g., (12–5).
2. In my definition of these terms, I rely on the glossary in Grosz (1989, pp. xivff.).
3. Sociologist Erving Goffman defined 'stigma' as "an attribute that is deeply discrediting" in a certain social context. The attribute is "neither creditable nor discreditable as a thing in itself" (1963, p. 3); in the language of social interactionism the term refers to the relation of these attributes to the stereotypical ideas which "normal" individuals produce of those who are marked by these attributes. In other words, female identity, as well as lesbian identity, or the identity of any stigmatized group, is always relationally bound to "normal" (i.e., male, heterosexual, etc.) identity. The stigmatized individual is told that she is a human being like everyone else, Goffman suggests, but at the same time different and belonging to a certain group of "differents." This implies that the identity of a stigmatized individual is never authentic, but always identity politics (1963, p. 124): To claim an identity as a stigmatized person means to find a point of balance between various suggestions and pressures for one's own identity from both "normals" and spokespeople of "one's own" group. The self which the individual will have accepted for herself/himself is, "as it necessarily must be, a resident alien, a voice of the group that speaks for and through him [sic]" (Goffman, 1963, p. 123).
4. "Autonomous existence" means a relation not of presence and absence, or affirmation and denial, as Grosz points out. It emphasizes the connectedness to other terms/signs, since any one term/sign can only be understood through others.
5. A unique document about difference from the early 1970s is Jill Johnston's reflection on how difference is multiple, interrelated, and changing over time:

    first or second off i'm into thinking weird all in these difference places in fact in as many places as we are women and so i ask myself where i meet this one or that one i ask where is them politically sexually & where is one in relation to this one or me or where am i now sexually politically since i'm not the me i was yesterday or last year and where are we going or am i already ahead of myself or behind and is somebody else slightly behind or ahead of that and if not then what or what anything i mean how should we behave and where should we think [...]. (Johnston, 1973, p. 89)

6. The following reflections took off from Keith Louise Fulton's paper on *After the Fire*, presented at the October '92 conference "Female Friendship in Canadian Writing" at Malaspina College, Nanaimo. Keith Fulton argues that the novel presents an outsider's or separatist society.
7. The name is a reference to a nursery rhyme. See also Atwood's parody "The Little Red Hen Tells All" (1992).

8 Neither in this nor in other novels. Consider also the Anna and Harry stories in which Rule writes lovingly and humorously about a heterosexual couple and their two children.

9 While she observes the limits in human generosity and understanding, Rule never condemns them. Rather, her weapons are to describe them openly, and also to submit them to a gentle, teasing humor, as when she has her narrator say: "The minister's wife was about to acquire an alien spy for the vicarage, a European cousin who was an artist and could not find a job until his English had improved" (51).

10 The (symbolically speaking) post-patriarchal society in *After the Fire*, and its community of outlander women is one of Rule's referential representations of a marginal reality. As such, it suggests one vision of how this process might continue, and of how women might change reality. This duplicity in the text – the realistic representation which in its portrayal of a functioning women's community points beyond itself to a utopian possibility of the marginal as repositioned in the center – creates the book's underlying vision.

11 Marianne Hirsch has noted that in women's texts of the 1970s in order to allow women access to plot "the elimination of fathers has become either a precondition or an important preoccupation" (1989, p. 129). From both feminist fiction and feminist theorizing, "the father, the brother, the husband, the male lover" were killed or eliminated. In what Hirsch calls "the feminist family romance," "the retreat to the pre-oedipal as basis for adult personality, the concentration on mother-daughter bonding and struggle, and the celebration of female relationships of mutual nurturance leave only a secondary role to men" (p. 133). However, Rule does not focus on the woman as daughter, at the expense of *othering* the woman as mother, which is how Hirsch describes the feminist family romance of the 70s (p. 136).

12 There is serious disagreement with feminism coming from a number of lesbians. E.g., Cheshire Calhoun provocatively asks if it is "possible that the feminist frame itself operates in various ways to closet lesbians" (1995, p. 8). Gayle Rubin, about ten years earlier, challenged "the assumption that feminism is or should be the privileged site of a theory of sexuality" (1984, p. 307), a challenge taken up by lesbian and gay resp. queer studies.

13 Weeks posits that gay and lesbian identities are "the necessary ways we mobilize our energies in order to change things" (1989: 210).

References

Rule, Jane, 1981. *Outlander: Short Stories and Essays*. Tallahassee, FL: Naiad Press, 1982.

——, 1985. *A Hot–Eyed Moderate*. Tallahassee, FL: Naiad Press.

——, 1989. *After the Fire*. Tallahassee, FL: Naiad Press.

Atwood, Margaret, 1992, "The Little Red Hen Tells All," *Zeitschrift für Kanada–Studien* 12:1, 7–12.

Benjamin, Jessica, 1988, *The Bonds of Love: Psychoanalysis, Feminism, and the Problem of Domination*. New York: Pantheon Books.

Braidotti, Rosi, 1991, "The Subject in Feminism," *Hypatia* 6:2 (Summer), 155–172.

Calhoun, Cheshire, 1995, "The Gender Closet: Lesbian Disappearance Under the Sign 'Women'," *Feminist Studies* 21:1 (Spring), 7–34.

De Lauretis, Teresa, 1989, "The Essence of the Triangle or, Taking the Risk of Essentialism Seriously: Feminist Theory in Italy, the U.S., and Britain," *differences: A Journal of Feminist Cultural Studies* 1:2 (Summer), 3–37.

Fitting, Peter, 1985, "'So We All Became Mothers:' New Roles for Men in Recent Utopian Fiction," *Science Fiction Studies* 12:2 (July), 156–183.

Goffman, Erving, 1963, *Stigma: Notes on the Management of Spoiled Identity*. Englewood Cliffs, NJ: Prentice Hall.

Grosz, Elizabeth, 1995, *Space, Time, and Perversion: Essays on the Politics of Bodies*. New York, London: Routledge.

Hirsch, Marianne, 1989, *The Mother/Daughter Plot: Narrative, Psychoanalysis, Feminism*. Bloomington, IN: Indiana University Press.

Hooks, bell, 1991. "Essentialism and Experience," *American Literary History* 3:1 (Spring), 172–183.

Johnston, Jill, 1973, "The Comingest Womanifesto," in: Phyllis Birkby, Bertha Harris, Jill Johnston, Esther Newton and Jane O'Wyatt (eds.), *Amazon Expedition: A Lesbian Feminist Anthology*. Washington, N.J.: Times Change Press, 89–92.

Jones, Kathleen B., 1991, "The Trouble With Authority," *differences: A Journal of Feminist Cultural Studies* 3:1, (Spring), 104–127.

Keinhorst, Annette, 1985, *Utopien von Frauen in der zeitgenössischen Literatur der USA*. Frankfurt/Main: Peter Lang.

Kinsey, Alfred C., Wardell B. Pomeroy, and Clyde E. Martin, 1948, *Sexual Behavior in the Human Male*. Philadelphia: W.B. Saunders.

Kirby, Vicki, 1991, "Corporeal Habits: Addressing Essentialism Differently," *Hypatia* 6:3 (Fall), 4–24.

Lorde, Audre, 1984, *Sister Outsider: Essays and Speeches*. Trumansburg, NY: The Crossing Press.

Martin, Biddy, 1988, "Lesbian Identity and Autobiographical Difference(s)," in: Bella Brodski and Celeste Schenck (eds.), *Life/Lines*. Ithaca: Cornell University Press, 77–103.

Meese, Elizabeth A., 1990, "Theorizing Lesbian: Writing – A Love Letter," in: Karla Jay and Joanne Glasgow (eds.), *Lesbian Texts and Contexts: Radical Revisions*. New York: New York University Press, 70–87.

Rubin, Gayle, 1984, "Thinking Sex: Notes for a Radical Theory of the Politics of Sexuality," in: Carole S. Vance (ed.), *Pleasure and Danger: Exploring Female Sexuality*. London: HarperCollins/Pandora, 1992, 267–319.

Showalter, Elaine, 1981, "Feminist Criticism in the Wilderness," *Critical Inquiry* 8:2 (Winter), 179-205.

Snitow, Ann, 1990, "A Gender Diary," in: Marianne Hirsch and Evelyn Fox Keller (eds.), *Conflicts in Feminism*. New York and London: Routledge, 9–43.

Spivak, Gayatri Chakravorty, with Ellen Rooney, 1989, "In a Word," (Interview), *differences: A Journal of Feminist Cultural Studies* 1:2 (Summer), 124–156.

Tiptree, James Jr., 1973, "The Women Men Don't See," in: *Warm Worlds and Otherwise.* New York: Ballantine Books, 1975, 131–164.

Vance, Carole S., 1984, "Pleasure and Danger: Towards a Politics of Sexuality," in: Carole S. Vance (ed.), *Pleasure and Danger: Exploring Female Sexuality.* London: HarperCollins/Pandora, 1992, 1–27.

Weeks, Jeffrey, 1989, "Against Nature," in: Dennis Altman, Carole Vance, Martha Vicinus, Jeffrey Weeks et al., (eds.), *"Homosexuality, Which Homosexuality?" International Conference on Gay and Lesbian Studies.* Amsterdam: Uitgeverij An Dekker/Schorer; London: GMP Publishers, 199–213.

Woolf, Virginia, 1938, *Three Guineas.* San Diego, New York, London: Harvest/HBJ, 1966.

Zimmerman, Bonnie, 1995,"Introduction." *NWSA Journal* 7:1, 1–7.

Angaben zu den Autorinnen

Andrea B. Braidt schloß ihr Diplom der Amerikanistik und Medienkunde im Februar 1997 ab, erhielt daraufhin ein Postgraduiertenstipendium des Bundesministeriums für ein Studium in Film Studies an der University of Newcastle, GB (MLitt) und arbeitet an einem Dissertationsprojekt. Forschungsschwerpunkte sind Filmtheorie, Genretheorie und Queer Theory, vor allem die Beschäftigung mit dem Dokumentarfilm und dem Horrorfilm. Lehrtätigkeit an der Universität Innsbruck zu feministischer Filmtheorie.

Hélène Destrempes unterrichtet Kanadastudien an der Universität Trier und frankophone Literatur an der Universität des Saarlandes, wo sie als Mitarbeiterin am Lehrstuhl für Interkulturelle Kommunikation und Romanistische Kulturwissenschaft tätig ist. Zur Zeit arbeitet sie an einer Doktorarbeit über die Darstellung von Ureinwohnern in frankokanadischer Literatur.

Pamela Z. Dube studierte in Siegen Anglistik und Medienwissenschaft und promovierte 1996 mit einer Arbeit zu "Contemporary English Performance Poetry in Canada and South Africa: A Comparative Study of the Main Motives and Poetic Techniques". Im Anschluß lehrte sie englische Literatur an der University of Natal, Pietermaritzburg in Südafrika. Ihre wissenschaftlichen Interessen sind vor allem Frauenstudien, New English Literatures, und performance poetry. Zur Zeit arbeitet sie als Wissenschaftliche Mitarbeiterin an der Universität Siegen und konzipiert interdisziplinäre Projekte im Multimediabereich.

Doris Eibl studierte Französisch, Anglistik und Amerikanistik an der Universität Innsbruck, wo sie seit 1991 als Assistentin am Institut für Romanistik lehrt und forscht. Veröffentlichungen liegen zum zeitgenössischen Frauenroman in Frankreich und Quebec vor. Ihre Forschungsschwerpunkte sind der zeitgenössische Frauenroman in Frankreich und Quebec, Dada und Surrealismus sowie Maurice Maeterlinck.

Christiane Harzig promovierte 1990 an der TU Berlin in (Frauen-) Geschichte und lehrt nordamerikanische Sozialgeschichte an der Universität Bremen. Sie hat vor allem im Bereich der Frauen- und Migrationsgeschichte veröffentlicht, u. a. Harzig, ed., *Peasant Maids – City Women. From the European Countryside to Urban America* (Ithaca, NY: Cornell University Press, 1997). Zur Zeit arbeitet sie an einer vergleichenden Studie zur Einwanderungspolitik und konnte dafür im Studienjahr 1996 am Centre for Refugee Studies an der York University forschen.

Ulrike C. Lange studierte Romanistik, Germanistik, (Anglistik) in Freiburg, Nantes, Montreal und Bochum und legte 1993 eine Staatsarbeit über "Antonine Maillet: Femme au volant - Antonine Maillets nautische Heroinen" vor. Anschließend arbeitete sie zwei Jahre als Lehrerin in Bochum. Seit 1996 promoviert sie in Bochum und Montreal zum Thema "Subjectivité et identité culturelle dans le récit au féminin au Québec de 1980 à 1995. Sie hat in Quebec, Canada und USA zu Quebecker Autorinnen (Maillet, Francine Noêl, Monique LaRue, Monique Proulx) vorgetragen und veröffentlicht.

Birgit Mertz-Baumgartner ist Assistentin am Institut für Romanistik der Universität Innsbruck und unterrichtet französische, frankophone und spanische Literaturwissenschaft. Ihre Promotionsarbeit *'Monologues quebecois' oder Geschichten eines 'Monsieur qui parle tout seul': Standortbestimmung einer Gattung am Rande* erschien 1997 im Dr. Wißner Verlag, Augsburg. Forschungsschwerpunkte: französisches Chanson, der "monologue" in Quebec, Rolle und Entwicklung des Theaters in Frankreich und Quebec, Migrationsliteratur(en) in Frankreich.

Dunja M. Mohr hat Anglistik, Amerikanistik und Germanistik in Marburg, London und Montreal studiert, arbeitete anschliessend als Redakteurin und freie Journalistin und unterrichtet seit 1997 als Lehrbeauftragte an der Universität Trier. Ihre Dissertation trägt den Arbeitstitel "Zeitgenössische weibliche Utopien und Dystopien in der englischsprachigen Literatur" und beschäftigt sich mit Texten von Suzette Haden Elgin, Suzy McKee Charnas und Margaret Atwood. Zu ihren Interessen zählt Science Fiction ebenso wie zeitgenössische englische Literatur, postmoderne und feministische Theorien, kanadische Schriftstellerinnen, der Kriminalroman und Native (American) Literature.

Tamara Pianos studierte an der Christian-Albrechts-Universität zu Kiel Geographie und Anglistik für das Lehramt. Ihre Staatsexamensarbeit befaßte sich mit Aritha van Herk's *Places Far From Ellesmere*. Nach dem 1.Staatsexamen trat sie im Oktober 1995 eine Stellung als wissenschaftliche Assistentin im Bereich Kanadistik an. Seitdem hat sie u. a. Seminare zu "Canadian Women Writers", "North American Native Writers", und "Margaret Laurence" unterrichtet.

Katja-Elisabeth Pfrommer arbeitet zur Zeit an einem Magistra Artium Abschluß in den Fächern Allgemeine und Vergleichende Literaturwissenschaft (AVL) und Philosophie an der Universität Stuttgart (Studienaufenthalte in Winnipeg und Calgary). Ihre Arbeitsgebiete sind innerhalb der AVL Kanadistik mit Schwerpunkt Women Poets/ Prairie Writers, innerhalb der Philosophie Hermeneutik mit dem Schwerpunkt 20. Jahrhundert. Ihre Magisterarbeit trägt den Titel "Metafiktion und Genre-Blurring in Aritha van Herks *Places Far From Ellesmere* und *InVisible Ink*".

Caroline Rosenthal unterrichtet seit 1995 kanadische und amerikanische Literatur an der Universität Konstanz. Neben literaturtheoretischen Seminaren liegt ihr Forschungsschwerpunkt hauptsächlich auf nordamerikanischer Literatur des 19. und 20. Jahrhunderts. Ihre Promotion trägt den Arbeitstitel "Factional Identities: Gender Renarrated" und beschäftigt sich mit der (De)Konstruktion von Geschlechteridentitäten in Romanen von Daphne Marlatt, Audrey Thomas, Maxine Hong Kingston und Louise Erdrich.

Colleen M. Ross unterrichtet Lehrveranstaltungen zu kanadischer Literatur und Kultur sowie Creative Writing an der Universität Greifswald. Zu ihren wissenschaftlichen Interessen gehören kanadische "pop culture" (insbesondere die kanadische Pop Musik Szene), postmoderne historische Literatur in Kanada, dabei vor allem die Texte von Autorinnen.

Marion Schomakers studierte das Literaturübersetzen an der Heinrich-Heine-Universität Düsseldorf. Ihre Diplomarbeit befaßte sich mit "Analysen zur frankokanadischen Erzählliteratur in deutschen Übersetzungen von 1945-1992". Nach dem Abschluß des Studiums (1994) war sie für verschiedene Verlage in Deutschland als Übersetzerin und freie Mitarbeiterin tätig. Zur Zeit lebt sie als freie Übersetzerin und Mutter in Detroit.

Christina Strobel erwarb 1981 ihren M.A. mit einer Arbeit über Margaret Atwood und schloß 1998 ihre Promotion (mit einer Dissertation über Jane Rule) ab. Zu ihrer Berufserfahrung zählt die Lehre in der Amerikanistik an der Universität Erlangen-Nürnberg, die Leitung des Büros der Frauenbeauftragten derselben Universität, Unterricht in der Erwachsenenbildung sowie F&E-Marketing für Sicherheit in der Informations- und Kommunikationstechnik in der Zentralabteilung Technik der Siemens AG. Neben den genannten Autorinnen befassen sich ihre wissenschaftlichen Vorträge und Veröffentlichungen mit Themen wie dem Kriminalroman oder Radclyffe Hall.